STUDIES IN SELF-INTEREST

FROM DESCARTES TO LA BRUYÈRE

STUDIES IN SELF-INTEREST

FROM DESCARTES TO LA BRUYÈRE

BY

A. J. KRAILSHEIMER

CLARENDON PRESS · OXFORD
1962

Oxford University Press, Amen House, London E.C.4

GLASGOW NEW YORK TORONTO MELBOURNE WELLINGTON
BOMBAY CALCUTTA MADRAS KARACHI LAHORE DACCA
CAPE TOWN SALISBURY NAIROBI IBADAN ACCRA
KUALA LUMPUR HONG KONG

PRINTED IN GREAT BRITAIN AT THE VILLAFIELD PRESS
BISHOPBRIGGS, GLASGOW

ACKNOWLEDGEMENTS

This book originally took shape as a result of my teaching at the University of Glasgow. My thanks go first therefore to the many friends and colleagues at Glasgow who helped me by reading and discussing draft chapters. A brief but stimulating visit to the University of Reading as guest lecturer enabled me to complete a whole chapter there, and there too I was lucky enough to find friends whose help I am glad to acknowledge. Finally at Oxford, where the book was completed, I have greatly benefited from the advice of several colleagues. I owe a special debt of gratitude to Dr. R. A. Sayce, who quite voluntarily devoted much time and trouble to reading the entire MS and giving me detailed comments, which proved invaluable at a critical stage of revision.

My use of the word 'lifemanship', for which I have been quite unable to find a substitute, calls for an acknowledgement, and perhaps an apology, to Mr. Stephen Potter. As the word is essential to the argument of this book, I offer my own definition: 'the art of playing life as a game to be won according to arbitrary rules laid down by the players themselves.'

A.J.K.

Oxford
May, 1962

CONTENTS

BIBLIOGRAPHICAL NOTE

There is no shortage of seventeenth-century bibliographies, and almost no limit to the number of works which could be cited as being of value and interest for the questions under discussion here. Three, however, must be considered essential reading for anyone seriously interested in the subject:

Antoine Adam, *Histoire de la Littérature française au* XVIIe *Siècle,* 5 vols., Paris, 1956.

Paul Bénichou, *Morales du Grand Siècle,* Paris, 1948.

Paul Hazard, *La Crise de la Conscience Européenne*, 1680–1715, 3 vols., Paris, 1935.

As regards the texts themselves, it was not easy to decide which editions to follow. In the end, for the sake of consistency, the editions of the *Bibliothèque de la Pléiade* have in every case been used. Even here some volumes have now been edited more than once, and there seems to be no system of reference both simple and fool-proof. In every case where this can be done, references have been identified by some means other than actual pagination. In fact it is only for Retz and Bossuet that page references have proved essential, and they are the two authors most likely to be consulted in the *Pléiade* edition. The classification of Pascal's *Pensées* poses a special problem, and if the *Pléiade* system has been adopted here, it is because it is one of the most accessible, not because it is thought to be the best. (It is, incidentally, that used in the Penguin translation of the *Pensées*). In the hope of minimizing inconvenience the Brunschvicg classification has been added throughout.

CHRONOLOGICAL TABLE

It is so important to be clear as to what present, past, and future mean in relation to the authors discussed that it has seemed desirable to summarize the main events, historical and literary, in the following table.

1494	Rabelais born
1509	Calvin born
1517	Luther's Ninety-five Theses
1532	*Pantagruel*
1533	Montaigne born
1534	*Gargantua*; Affair of the Placards
1536	Erasmus dies; Calvin, *Institutio*
1545	Council of Trent opens
1546	*Le Tiers Livre*; Luther dies
1547	François I succeeded by Henri II
1548	*Le Quart Livre* (partial)
1552	*Le Quart Livre*
1553	Rabelais dies
1559	Henri II succeeded by François II
1560	François II succeeded by Charles IX, with Catherine de Medicis as Regent
1562	*Le Cinquiesme Livre* (partial); Wars of Religion begin
1564	*Le Cinquiesme Livre*; Calvin dies
1572	Massacre of St. Bartholomew
1574	Charles IX succeeded by Henri III
1580	Montaigne, *Essais*
1588	Much enlarged edition of *Essais*
1589	Henri III murdered; Succession of Henri IV as first of Bourbon line contested by the League, led by Guise family
1592	Montaigne dies
1593	Henri IV converted to Catholicism
1595	Civil strife finally dies down; definitive edition of Montaigne's *Essais*
1596	Descartes born

1598	Edict of Nantes
1606	Corneille born
1610	Henri IV murdered; succeeded by Louis XIII, with Marie de Medicis as Regent
1613	Retz and La Rochefoucauld born; Bérulle found French Oratory
1619	(10 November) Descartes's dream in the 'poêle'
1622	Molière born
1623	Pascal born
1624	Richelieu assumes power
1625	Charles I becomes King of England and marries Louis's sister, Henriette-Marie
1626	Mme de Sévigné and Rancé born
1627	Bossuet born
1628	Descartes, *Règles* (unfinished); settles in Holland
1629	Corneilles's first play, *Mélite*
1633	Galileo condemned; Descartes holds up work on similar lines
1634	Vincent de Paul founds *Filles de la Charité*
1635	*Médée*, Corneille's first tragedy
1636	*Le Cid*; Boileau born
1637	*Discours de la méthode*
1638	Louis XIV born; Père Joseph and Jansenius die
1639	Racine born
1640	*Horace, Cinna, Polyeucte*; Jansenius, *Augustinus*
1641	Descartes, *Méditations*
1642	Richelieu and Galileo die; Newton born; *Augustinus* condemned
1643	Louis XIII succeeded by Louis XIV; Anne of Austria, as Regent, puts Mazarin in power; Battle of Rocroi makes fame of future Grand Condé; Retz named Archbishop-Coadjutor to his uncle, decides to take orders
1644	Corneille, *Rodogune*; Descartes, *Principes*; Henriette-Marie has to flee to France
1645	La Bruyère born
1647	Charles I imprisoned; Descartes meets Pascal in Paris and discusses vacuum
1648	Pascal organizes experiment on Puy-de-Dôme, leading to *Traité du Vide*; Treaty of Westphalia ends Thirty Years War; arrest of Broussel and other *Parlementaires* precipitates first Fronde, in which Retz at once takes a hand

1649 *Traité des Passions*; Five Propositions before Sorbonne; Charles I executed; agreement at Rueil reconciles Court and Parlement; Retz busy intriguing in Paris

1650 Descartes dies in Sweden; arrest of Condé, then Conti and Longueville, begins *Fronde des Princes*

1651 Fénelon born; Mazarin goes into exile while Princes and *Parlement* momentarily agree; La Rochefoucauld nearly kills Retz trapped in the door; Condé makes alliance with Spain; Mazarin returns

1652 Corneille leaves theatre after comparative failure of *Pertharite*; La Rochefoucauld seriously wounded at Faubourg Saint Antoine, la Grande Mademoiselle has Bastille guns fire on royal troops; Mazarin exiled again; King returns to Paris; Retz named cardinal, at once imprisoned at Vincennes; Bossuet ordained priest, begins career as Canon of Metz

1653 Mazarin returns; Frondeurs submit; Innocent X condemns Five Propositions

1654 (23 November) Pascal's *nuit de feu*; Retz forced to renounce succession to see of Paris on death of his uncle; moved to prison at Nantes, escapes, withdraws resignation, and after many adventures makes his way to Rome

1656 *Provinciales* begin; miracle of Holy Thorn

1657 (March) *Provinciales* end; Rancé reforms La Trappe

1658 Cromwell dies

1659 Corneille returns to theatre with *Œdipe*; *Précieuses Ridicules*

1660 Corneille, *Discours*; Vincent de Paul dies; Condé returns as part of peace with Spain; Restoration of Charles II

1661 Mazarin dies; Louis henceforth his own chief minister

1662 Pascal dies; *L'École des Femmes*; Bossuet's first sermon at Louvre; pirated edition of *Mémoires* of La Rochefoucauld; after travelling all over Europe, seeking support (even in England), and being accused of Jansenism and treachery, Retz at last agrees to resign the see he could never occupy, and is allowed back to his country seat at Commercy

1664 First version of *Tartuffe*, at once banned

1665 *Dom Juan*; *Maximes* of La Rochefoucauld

1666 *Le Misanthrope*

1667 *Andromaque*

1668 *L'Avare*; cession of present Nord department

1669 *Tartuffe* allowed; Henriette-Marie dies, *Oraison Funèbre* by

Bossuet; Jansenists submit (*paix de l'Église*); Bossuet named Bishop of Condom

1670 Corneille, *Tite et Bérénice*; Racine, *Bérénice*; *Bourgeois Gentilhomme*; Port Royal edition of *Pensées*; Bossuet becomes Preceptor of Dauphin; *OF* of Henriette-Anne

1673 *Le Malade Imaginaire*; Molière dies

1674 *Surèna*; Boileau, *Art Poétique*; Conquest of Franche-Comté

1675 Retz tries, unsuccessfully, to resign his cardinalate and become a monk, but succeeds in winning reputation for piety

1677 *Phèdre*

1679 Retz dies

1680 La Rochefoucauld dies

1681 Gallican controversy flares up; Bossuet translated to Meaux on completion of Dauphin's education

1682 Bossuet's drafting of Gallican articles rejected by Pope

1684 On death of Marie-Thérèse, Louis marries Mme de Maintenon; Corneille dies

1685 Revocation of Edict of Nantes; James II succeeds Charles II

1686 *OF* of Le Tellier; Condé dies

1687 Bossuet's last court sermon, *OF* of Condé; La Bruyère, *Caractères*; Newton, *Principia*

1688 English Revolution; James II flees to France

1689 William and Mary accede to English throne

1691 *Athalie*; Bossuet writes *Discours sur la Vie cachée en Dieu*

1694 *Traité de la Concupiscence, Maximes sur la Comédie*; Quietist quarrel between Bossuet and Fénelon begins

1696 La Bruyère dies, just before nineth and almost triply expanded, edition of *Caractères*; Mme de Sévigné dies

1699 Racine dies

1700 Rancé dies

1704 Bossuet dies

1711 Boileau dies

1715 Louis XIV and Fénelon die

1717 Retz, *Mémoires*

INTRODUCTION

'Il n'y a que le premier pas qui coûte.' By the time one can state a problem clearly enough for an introduction it is virtually solved and the long presentation of argument and evidence filling the space between introduction and conclusion should perhaps be regarded as a monstrously swollen footnote. So much was written in the seventeenth century, and so much has been written about it ever since, that it would be plainest folly to offer a master key to *le grand siècle*. All the same, some doors, and not the least, do not open as easily as they should, and one of the reasons may be that some of the keys provided have been too massive.

As one reads the great authors of the century one constantly comes up against the same set of problems, treated in a variety of ways, and with familiarity the vocabulary of the century becomes revealing in itself. Most people unfortunately do not start at the beginning and work straight through, and hardly any are lucky enough to read about the sixteenth century before they ever come on to the seventeenth. One result of this is that fertile islands of knowledge break the surface of the historical ocean in such random fashion that the contours of the submerged continent are hardly suspected. Chronology is not the same as causation, but it is a particularly useful guide to causation. Until certain events have taken place, no one can be quite sure of the consequences of a given act or idea. Much of the mentality of the seventeenth century will remain impenetrable unless one considers what events were most freshly and insistently in the minds of people then, and with what causes they associated them. Similarly, if one applies criteria of personal familiarity and works backwards through history, there is a real danger that moments of innovation will be missed simply because modern problems are taken for granted and their existence assumed for ages when they have not yet been invented. There are all sorts of reasons, apart from mere dating, why seventeenth-century writers seem nearer to us than sixteenth-century ones, and no doubt the welcome familiarity of language is an obvious one for readers who find the prose of Rabelais or Montaigne too hard. On the psychological level, too, the most casual reader can hardly fail to notice a change between the outlook of the two centuries, and it is the purpose of this study to indicate the reasons for this change, its nature and consequences. The very word 'psychology' may seem to beg a question, for it could plausibly be argued that what passes for it in the sixteenth century is a mixture of physiology, theology and ethics, but within its limits the word may be accepted as serviceable. If instead of labels, paraphrases are preferred, it may be said that what follows is concerned first with the questions men asked about themselves, then with the answers they gave.

The judgement of posterity and the traditions of examining boards offer only a rough and ready guide to the history of ideas, but they will do, and have the merit of being simple and concrete. Instead of anonymous slabs of time called centuries, it is useful to consider the men whose life-span corresponds to such periods. Thus for 'sixteenth century' one may substitute the period from the birth of Rabelais in 1494 to the death of Montaigne in 1592, and thanks to a symmetrical providence the seventeenth century can be represented as running from the birth of Descartes in 1596 to the death of La Bruyère in 1696. The authors who fall within these respective periods are not all equally typical or informative, but one must start somewhere, and if the best known authors cannot be made to yield an answer (or a question) there is little incentive to pursue the inquiry. At the same time, economy of effort demands selection, and there is no point in interrogating all famous men regardless of genre. Poetry is therefore a regretted omission, letter-writing another, the one because it is not the most suitable vehicle for ideas, the other because it is informative but not usually influential. On other grounds, the most notable omission from these pages is Racine. He seemed to add nothing to what emerges more clearly from other authors, and he is too great to be called in for a mere *acte de présence*. It goes without saying that a detailed study of Racine could not fail to be profitable in itself, but for reasons of balance and relevance it has found no place here.

In treating such a subject it is natural to turn first to those writers who are more concerned with ideas than purely literary aims. As representatives of the sixteenth century, marking recognizably different and successive phases, Rabelais, Calvin and Montaigne will hardly be challenged. For the seventeenth century, Descartes and Pascal come first to mind, with La Rochefoucauld and La Bruyère close behind, but here it seemed essential to cover as wide a selection as possible, so Corneille and Molière are included for having reflected, and also influenced, contemporary life in the field of entertainment, and Bossuet in that of religion. The choice of Retz imposed itself logically, for the volume of his work makes him more accessible than almost any other seventeenth-century historian, and his personal part in the events of his age is outstanding. There is no conclusive reason for closing the list at eight, except human frailty and a general desire to focus rather than diffuse such light as there might be. Some personal favourites were excluded with particular regret; Richelieu, for his *Testament Politique,* Rancé and Fénelon for their remarkable contributions to religious life and thought, Méré as a consultant on how to make friends and influence people, and others great and small. This is meant only as a reconnaissance; a boat's crew may go farther than an Armada.

The spokesmen chosen must then be made to speak, and to the point. Here the problem of definition is acute. The questions men asked about themselves have already been given as the basic subject under inquiry, but this needs to be explained further before the purpose and method of the inquiry can be appreciated. The conditions of modern life allow no one to be ignorant of the strains imposed on the human personality, and cases of maladjustment and breakdown are almost as familiar as rickets and cholera to an earlier epoch. This was not always so, and though it demands a considerable effort of detachment to imagine a human race free from the psychological preoccupations to which Western civilization commits us, that effort must be made if the barrier of history is ever to be crossed. Broadly speaking, what worries people today is status; the individual wants to know how he stands in relation to others, perhaps to God or some higher purpose, above all to himself. That is not to say that everyone is worried all the time, but rather that when thinking people write about the anxieties observed in themselves and others it tends to be in these terms. What gives this situation its characteristic shape is the concentration on the individual, on the single, isolated personality. It is at this point that the temptation to read history backwards is specially strong, and, with thoughts of human solidarity through the centuries, it is only too easy to translate the new anxieties of the sixteenth or seventeenth centuries into familiar modern terms, and see them as permanent and inevitable features of the human scene.

The individual normally finds himself fixed vertically and horizontally in a sort of spider's web of duties, privileges, interests, relationships. Sometimes he may feel like the spider in the web, sometimes like the fly, but most of the time he knows where he is. The web is constructed of sufficiently elastic threads to allow for expansion and normal wear and tear, but from time to time some sudden blow, or cumulative pressure on a weak spot, shatters it, leaving the individual temporarily in the air. This situation has been called the *moi désaxé*, and will be a recurrent theme of this study. It is human instinct to effect repairs with the minimum of delay, but after each catastrophe a certain amount of trial and error is necessary. It is claimed here that the sixteenth century represented one of these moments of catastrophe, and that throughout the seventeenth century efforts at repair were made with very varying success. Both diagnosis and remedy were subject to the most widely differing interpretations; the authors variously think the remedy will be found in the past, in the immediate present, in the future, or in eternity, and, depending on where they seek the remedy, so they will have diagnosed the ill. Most of them, allowing for chronology, comment on each other, and sometimes blame each other; one and all agree that there is something wrong. It is their questions and answers on this specific issue that are of immediate concern.

On a point of method this has one result which may lead to misunderstanding. The reasons for selecting these eight authors rather than others have already been given, but it should be emphasized that this is not intended as a study of the authors in the round, but of a problem (or series of problems) in the authors. No simple division between life and work has been made, nor has any comprehensive analysis of works been attempted. Each author stands in a special relationship to the central problem of the 'moi désaxé', but the method adopted in each case has been to examine how he sees the problem, how he tries to solve it and how he affects it. Thus portraits of very varying size and detail appear in the gallery. Descartes tackles the problem in laying down the first principle of his system, and had incalculable influence on his successors through his metaphysics, though the best of Cartesianism is in the method, to which almost no space has been allotted here. Corneille's psychology is central to his conception and execution of tragedy, and directly relevant here, but his dramatic technique and use of language must regretfully be left aside. Whereas the lives of Descartes and Corneille are virtually ignored in favour of their work, quite the contrary is the case with Retz, and to a lesser extent La Rochefoucauld. Retz made his impact on the century in real life, and his posthumous *Mémoires* are of interest not for their contemporary influence, but because they contain his own interpretation of that life, incidentally revealing the psychological and other values to which he subscribed. Both La Rochefoucauld and La Bruyère found themselves in a particular social situation which must be taken into account in discussing their view of the world around them, but autobiographical elements are quite secondary in *Maximes* and *Caracterès*. In dealing with Molière, as with Corneille, much of what is most precious must be sacrificed for the sake of relevance, and while the psychological pattern studied here is central to his comedy, the chapter on Molière has no pretentions to being a balanced exposition of more than one major aspect of his work. Bossuet may appear to come out rather badly, because the qualities for which he is justly admired have not on the whole seemed to be those which had the widest influence. The case of Pascal is a special one. In every way he is a central figure, coming historically between the four writers who grew up and flourished under Richelieu and Mazarin and the three who lived in the sunshine of

Versailles. He is able to comment on the trends represented by his predecessors, and to a large extent is prophetic of his successors. His work embraces science, religion, philosophy and morals, and can in this respect be compared only with that of Descartes. Though in his own day he probably had less influence than any of the others, except in the *Provinciales,* his analysis goes furthest. What is more, his remedy, alone of those discussed, has today an actuality amply demonstrated by publishers' sales. For these reasons, and also on grounds of personal predilection which it would be disingenuous to conceal, three chapters have been devoted to Pascal. Even so, not much more than a profile has been sketched.

Partly because of the prominence accorded to Pascal it may seem that too much emphasis has been placed on religion. While this must be a matter of individual judgement, the fact remains that however erratic the practice of Christianity in the seventeenth century, France was a nominally Christian country, so that even those who were neither *croyants* nor *pratiquants* knew very well what it was they were rejecting. Any serious discussion of the *condition humaine* had to deal with Christianity, and even those who were most hostile had no other vocabulary to hand for most of the things they wanted to say than that used by Christians. It is perfectly obvious that a full treatment of this whole problem would have to pay far more attention to social and economic factors than has been possible here, and the particular aspects emphasized have been given priority simply because they happen to be the aspects which seemed important to the men of the seventeenth century. No doubt they would have taken a different view of their predicament if they had been able to read some modern historians, but they did not, and this is no time to put them right.

All the texts examined, with insignificant exceptions, have been chosen because they are generally well known and readily available. It is recognized that this reduces the chances of saying anything novel, and increases those of offending cherished convictions in almost every reader. Despite the brilliant and indispensable work of such men as MM. A. Adam, Bénichou, Hazard, students still seem to be baffled and scholars interested when faced by these problems, and this seems sufficient justification for sticking to the highway.

The line of the argument is historical, with minor overlapping, and the chapters follow a plan imposed by the material. The book begins with a brief survey of sixteenth century developments, and goes on in more detail through the seventeenth century, with the Fronde as the half-way mark from many points of view. It will be seen that Descartes, Corneille and Retz all represent an attitude that is specifically denounced by La Rochefoucauld and Pascal, while Molière, Bossuet and La Bruyère advance views that have much in common, and in general oppose the first three. The pattern is capable of many formulations, of which one might be that the generation that fought the Fronde tried to orientate the individual *moi* on its own axis after the anarchy brought about in the previous century, while those who came after were concerned to curtail the demands of the *moi*, at least outwardly, in favour of society. For the first three, *gloire* was the end, and the will the means; this was denounced by La Rochefoucauld and Pascal as *amour-propre,* and contrary to true *honnêteté*, which is stressed as the ideal by the last three, and linked with their recommendation of moderation, conformism and obedience. This development comes out clearly from vocabulary, particularly in the different meanings and emphases attached to *honnêteté* throughout the century. Everyone knows that *le grand siècle* revolved round *le roi soleil*; it is the contention of these pages that it only settled on that axis after an abortive attempt to fix it on *le moi soleil.*

1: THE SIXTEENTH CENTURY BACKGROUND

IT must not be inferred from what has been said above that the Middle Ages were a period of tranquil security, rudely broken by the Renaissance. The seventeenth century followed a catastrophe in the sense that the sixteenth century had shown whole areas to be full of problems which had previously been taken for granted. The notion that the 'Ages of Faith' are some sort of historical Eden from which modern man is excluded by his impiety is as silly as that which treats 'medieval' as a synonym for Dark Ages. Men had plenty to worry about in the Middle Ages, and from some points of view life must have been a perpetual nightmare for many. The facts of physical existence were brutal enough, with war, famine, pestilence always round the corner, if not actually raging. Superstition added unseen terrors to those which visibly threatened, and where sheer ignorance veiled so much of the truth, speculation often arrogated the place of knowledge. The fifteenth century in particular was not a gay time, and the *danse macabre* is a representative enough legacy of generations beaten down by the Black Death and the Hundred Years War. It is an absurd simplification to compare Villon and Ronsard as spokesmen for their respective centuries, simply because each is the best poet of his time, but behind the absurdity there is an element of truth. One of Villon's principal themes is death, which also inspires some of Ronsard's best work. They both write movingly of the transience of earthly beauty, of the decay of flower and flesh, but there is a basic difference, going beyond Villon's insistence on corruption and Ronsard's greater delicacy; for Villon the real worries begin with death, for Ronsard poetic fame already offers a guarantee of immortality. Whatever might worry medieval man on earth, one anxiety took precedence over all others; judgement. The Crusades, the flagellant movements, the pious trinkets of Louis XI are three examples taken at random of how bodies of men, as well as individuals, took to heart the truth that in the midst of life we are in death, and went prepared for instant summons, variously fortified by hope of a martyr's crown, the stripes of penance or just talismans. Sudden death was so frequent an occurrence that the luxury of a deathbed repentance was not to be counted on. Hellfire was no Sunday bogey; as one preacher put it 'Non est jocus, non est fabula/Car il faut passer par là.'[1] and in this at least he was preaching to the converted.

The concern with life beyond the grave was constant and real, as chantry chapels and even great churches testify to this day. Great men sought as the ultimate privilege that of being buried in the habit of some religious order, as oblate or tertiary. Lepers shunned by society were not denied spiritual consolations, and no one thought they were irremediably lost, as were those who died excommunicate, kings or princes though they might be. The Dies Irae awaited all.

This overriding preoccupation with the afterlife left the individual with one problem of abiding force: how did he stand with God? Eternity lasted so long that one could not afford to take the same chances with it as with worldly matters. Happily the Church which so effectively preached the terrors offered a sure way to felicity, though it was no part of the bargain that the way should be smooth. Provided men had faith, hope and charity, made proper use of the sacraments and performed such works as their priests recommended all would be well. An emergency service for soldiers left nothing to chance; as one can see from the *Chanson de Roland,* men went into battle after general absolution, and, if they had time, made an act of contrition as they lay dying. The perils of travel were hardly less, and spiritual first-aid posts on road or mountain-pass, even on bridges, were numerous. There is no need to go on; the point is familiar enough. Salvation was the great problem throughout the Middle Ages, and questions of earthly status were negligible beside it. There was no hiding from God the truth about oneself, and therefore no point in self-deception.

Another aspect of medieval life is stranger, but no less charac-

[1] The Franciscan, Olivier Maillard, at Paris, Lent 1498.

teristic. Huizinga's admirable *Waning of the Middle Ages* depicts the love of ritual which is a constant feature of all medieval activity. In its later form this led to an emphasis on ceremonial and etiquette which quite disguised origins going back to a practical code of chivalry. Ritualistic, formalistic, legalistic, all these words amount to saying that there are proper ways of doing everything, a proper time and place and person for the accomplishment of every important act. Church and state alike had their hierarchies, in which the status, duties and privileges of each man was precisely laid down. This does not mean that there was uniformity; quite the contrary. The complexity of customs and relationships offered every opportunity for indulging in the universally popular sport of litigation, but the mere fact that the sport was so widespread indicates the conviction that sooner or later the rules would be found for establishing the right answer, which existed all the time, though hidden.

Respect for a man's office might well be accompanied by contempt for his person, and the same was true of institutions. Ideally the Church should have been full of virtuous men, conscientiously discharging their pastoral or other functions, and recruited on purely spiritual merits. The reality was as imperfect as human reality usually is, but while there were plenty of reformers, only occasional fanatics seriously thought of setting up a rival body. There were disputed elections at every level, but the most disreputable anti-Pope clung to the legal fiction of a valid election. Sooner or later reform 'in the head and in the members' would have to come, and meanwhile the legal forms were preserved, continuity was unbroken and permanent schism avoided at all costs. Civil government slowly evolved from military feudalism to something more sophisticated, but the ladder led as it always had done from the monarch at the top, through the great vassals to the country squires and their dependants. In the country land was still the basis of most relationships, and the principle of heredity ensured continuity. Even in the towns, where the rise of a merchant and professional class was well advanced by 1500, Parlements, universities, guilds, corporations and so on put virtually everyone in his place. Society was certainly not stagnant, but it was stable, moving forward on an even keel. This situation is reflected in the thought of the period, strongly inclined to classify and systematize everything. The hierarchies of Church and state are matched in the created world, in the cosmos and even in the angelic host, assigned to its duties of protection according to rank in the nine choirs. The heavenly bodies pursued their majestic course around the earth, stablished fast by the Psalmist, and in the microcosm of his body man mirrors the celestial order of the macrocosm. Everything was accounted for, world without end, primarily on the authority of Scripture as interpreted by the accredited doctors of the Church, failing that on the authority of 'the Philosopher', Aristotle, as 'baptized' by St. Thomas. It is easy enough to laugh at medieval *naiveté*, but it is only too easy to forget that medieval thinkers took eternity seriously, regarding this world as the realm of illusions and comparative irrelevance. It was much more important for them to chart the way to an everlasting kingdom than to America, to Heaven than to the moon.

It can be seen from all this that the 'moi' had an axis embracing this world and the next, relations with God and with man. There was no shortage of problems, but they could basically be reduced to survival in this world and salvation in the next. As has been said, there was no uniformity, but there was unity. The wider unity of Christendom was politically a mirage, but French unity was real enough, social cohesion was strong and, above all, every man, woman and child was assigned for spiritual care to his *persona,* or parson, by the one universal Church which presided over the lives of all from birth to death.

This was the world into which Rabelais was born in 1494, but it was not that which he left in 1553. The first cracks appeared while he was still at school, and the first extant document referring to him is his letter to Budé, showing him already engaged in the fight for the New Learning. Erasmus first challenged the Schoolmen, by showing how Philologia, the scientific study of language, could revolutionize exegesis, and thus undermine the whole basis of Scholastic authority. The knowledge of Greek opened up new vistas, as we find Rabelais telling Budé, but his generation remained faithful to the Christian heritage of their master Erasmus, and Bible study was always in the forefront of their programme. The treasures of Greece and Rome were copiously available, disseminated rapidly and widely thanks to printing. Plato and the neo-Platonists, a new 'unbaptized' Aristotle, above all Cicero and Plutarch gave a new direction to thought and culture, allegedly ruined for centuries past by the 'Goths and Vandals' of the Middle Ages. With a fresh and purer understanding of the Bible, based on textual study, the men of the early Renaissance had literally the best of both worlds, Christian and pagan.

The classic expression of this first exhilaration is to be seen in Gargantua's splendid letter to his son, written in 1532 (*Pantagruel*, ch. VIII).[1] What stands out is the sense of rebirth, of recovering, rather than discovering, a treasure thought to be lost. Paradoxically their idea of progress was largely to put the clock back, to establish continuity with a more glorious past so that they could disown the Gothic centuries of their immediate forebears. Even so, on the social and political level the break with the Middle Ages was more apparent than real. Rabelais's ideal of kingship comes in practice closer to the traditional ideal of St. Louis, dispensing patriarchal justice under the oak at Vincennes, than to any vague Platonic philosopher-king, let alone the sort of modern political thought represented by Machiavelli, proverbially anathema to the French throughout the century.

The axis of medieval man was in the last analysis theological, and the justification for the complex machinery of the Church and the authority claimed for her teaching was that it helped men to salvation. Unfortunately ideas have their own form of moth and rust which corrupt, and Rabelais and his friends found that the old ideas would no longer serve. Their solution was a synthesis of pagan and Christian wisdom, which preserved and strengthened the axis by changing the perishable human element. They argued that Scholastic teaching had run into the sands of pointless disputation, empty dogmatism, excessive subtlety, and, instead of helping men, put up a barrier between them and Scripture. By firmly basing their religion on the Bible the Christian

[1] *Œuvres complètes*, in *Bibl. de la Pléiade* 1934.

humanists claimed to substitute for the fallible human authority of theologians a divine authority which everyone could understand for himself, given adequate linguistic tools. On the human side, they offered the sum of wisdom achieved without benefit of grace or revelation by pagan authors. They argued that Greece and Rome show unaided human endeavour at its best, and that the Christian should model himself on these most admirable specimens of humanity, secure in the faith that the New Testament teaching would enable him to surpass his models in the one respect where they fell short. This is humanism as it was first understood, a heightened respect for human dignity, rooted in the achievements of the Classical past and preserved from arrogance by a constant awareness of man's dependence on God.

The philosophy of Pantagruelism in which Rabelais offers a full and balanced way of life has been qualified as *un stoïcisme gai*, and while it is this, it is still more a Christian Stoicism. God helps those who help themselves, but Rabelais's heroes implore his aid before every crisis, and only then go out to earn it by their own unsparing efforts. The usually rather donnish Epistemon plays so manful a part during the storm that he tears his hand on the rigging, and afterwards explains in typically Pauline terms his guiding principles: 'Icelluy [Dieu] fault incessamment implorer, invocquer, prier, requerir, supplier. Mais là ne fault faire but et bourne: de nostre part convient pareillement nous evertuer . . . estre co-operateurs avecques luy.' (*Quart Livre,* ch. XXIII)

Self-help must not lead to self-sufficiency, nor dependence to inertia; a proper balance must be maintained. The hero Pantagruel, whose gigantic stature is forgotten in the later books so that he can be a more human figure, is 'l'idée et exemplaire de toute joyeuse perfection,' and 'toutes choses prenoit en bonne partie, tout acte interpretoyt à bien . . . car tous les biens que le ciel couvre et que la terre contient . . . ne sont dignes d'emouvoir nos affections et troubler nos sens et esprits.' (*Tiers Livre,* ch. II) The most succinct formulation of this philosophy echoes the Stoic 'contemptus rerum fortuitarum': 'une certaine gayeté d'esprit confict on mespris des choses fortuites.' (*Quart Livre,* Prologue.)

The balance of Pantagruelism may be partly due to Rabelais's medical vocation and to the therapeutic claims he made for his book. Health of body and mind come from self-control, not from the moderation of mere timidity. Like Socrates, patron saint of the Renaissance, Pantagruel was capable of drinking level with his companions or totally abstaining at will, but he allows neither over-indulgence nor negative asceticism to vex his body. What is less often noted by critics who talk of Pantagruel's Stoicism is that his attitude to others is consistent alike with Christian charity and Stoic ideals of the brotherhood of man. As a prince he comports himself with dignity and restraint, commanding by his personal qualities a respect which his rank would in any case have earned. As a son he shows towards his father the deepest respect and affection. As a companion he treats those around him with courtesy and forbearance, patient even with the regrettable Panurge. All this is not unlike the traditional picture of St. Louis, but there is one great difference. One might expect to find this difference in the *abysme de science* which Gargantua urges his son to fill in with encyclopedic learning, but the same respect for equally godly learning led St. Louis to support the foundation of the Sorbonne, soon to become the ornament of intellectual Europe. The decisive difference is in the attitude of Pantagruel, and, through him, of Rabelais, to the Church. His dissatisfaction with existing practices is expressed often and clearly, so is his insistence on the necessity for private prayer, for the responsibility of each man to seek his own salvation without trusting to the intermediary of any person or institution. Obedience does not absolve men from the duty of initiative, and there is no doubt that whatever form of church Rabelais had in mind would have exercised a much looser control over doctrine. There is no reason to suppose that he had presbyterian views in any sense, but the whole tone of his work suggests that a reformed episcopate would have been composed of pastors rather than masters, almost certainly organized on a national basis independent of Rome. There is a marked 'squarson' element in his teaching, which lends colour to the view that he might have felt at home in the Church of England.

While there is protest, if not actually revolt, against the Church, as it is, the rest of Rabelais's thought shows that he was by no means opposed to the principle of authority. The first generation of the Renaissance rejected the dogmatic authority of the Schoolmen, and many of them for national reasons were unenthusiastic about papal supremacy, but they substituted other authority which they respected and expected others to respect. Thus, against the weight of tradition and institutional authority, they set up that of the Classics, based, as they were convinced, on the highest degree of excellence ever attained by man unaided, and to the centralized Roman authority they preferred that of rulers brought up to enlightenment by the New Learning. In this insistence on the near-sanctity of Classical authors Rabelais is of his generation, as he is in his essentially aristocratic view of life. Birth and education, not dogmatism or brute force, are the criteria for his ruling class, which comprised individuals commanding respect in themselves, not an institution whose representatives are obeyed *ex officio*. A second point is connected with this; personal responsibility and initiative are the basis for the moral law and for the spiritual life. The letter of the law, mere ritualism, means nothing. A king is as good as his deeds, a soul as healthy as its faith. There is striking emphasis on the liberty of conscience, but it is the liberty of responsibility, not of anarchy. Even the fantasy society of Thélème, with its rule *Fay ce que voudras,* is governed by unanimity of free choice. Much used to be heard about the cult of the individual and the secularization of culture as the hallmarks of the Renaissance, but this is putting the emphasis in the wrong place. For Rabelais, who speaks for his generation, the individual comes first, after God, but only on condition that heredity, education and environment guarantee integrity and responsibility; culture is secular when it affects things of this world, and is no longer subordinate to the man-made study of theology, but it is still dominated by true religion, based on Scripture. The axis is the same as it had been in the Middle Ages, but the lines of force have been changed and strengthened. The institution has been devalued in favour of the individual.

The last word on Rabelais comes from the posthumous Fifth Book, and despite the contested authenticity of the text, the views are unquestionably his: 'Car tous philosophes et saiges anticques, pour bien surement et plaisamment parfaire le chemin de cognoissance divine et chasse de sapience, ont estimé deux choses necessaires: guyde de Dieu et compaignye d'homme.' (*Cinquiesme Livre,* ch. XLVII)

This noble and balanced philosophy shirks none of the problems of man's nature, and successfully overcomes bigotry or bawdy. It incorporates much of what is best in the Middle Ages with the classical tradition, making the most of man without ever losing sight of eternity. One may well ask why things turned out so differently from the optimistic dreams of *Gargantua* and *Pantagruel*. It is a commonplace of history that revolutions are made possible by moderate reformers who pave the way for root and branch extremists, whose first victims they often are. The pacific Erasmus died (1536) full of misgivings as to the consequences of his early skirmishes with authority, but almost until the moment of his death it looked as though France at least might see the triumph of moderation. To this hope Rabelais still clung when he died in 1553, but events had long since overtaken him. The course of French history was changed literally overnight when on 18 October, 1534, posters were put up in public places in Paris and elsewhere, and fatally on the very door of the King's bedchamber at Amboise, attacking the Mass and other Catholic practices. This affair of the Placards, as it is called, was the work of French exiles living in Switzerland, and had consequences out of all proportion to its real significance. Overnight the King, François I, previously disposed to favour a reform without schism, became convinced that heresy meant sedition, that those who held the views to which his sister, Marguerite de Navarre, had almost won him, would extend their challenge to the authority of Rome by challenging that of the Crown. From that moment on the possibility of any form of Protestantism becoming the religion of France was permanently excluded.

An immediate result of the Placards was intensified heresy-hunting, the flight of some of those most heavily compromised and the prudent silence of the moderates who remained. Among those who fled was a clever young *protégé* of Marguerite, a lawyer and classicist called Jean Calvin. In 1536 the disorganized and intimidated minority of French reformers found suddenly that they had a leader and a programme, when the first (Latin) version of his *Institution Chrétienne* appeared, with an appeal to the King for tolerance. (An enlarged version was translated into French in 1541). Calvin did not win immediate recognition and had to leave Geneva for a while before returning there as undisputed master, but his book replaced the work of Luther, and of earlier reformers like Farel, and Viret, within a few years. It was not long before his authority at Geneva rivalled that of the Pope at Rome. The authoritarian climate of Geneva proved even less congenial to moderate men like Rabelais than that of Rome, and with mental reservations they stayed where they were. The opening of the Council of Trent in 1545 put a premium on neutrality, and moderation soon gave way to disillusionment. Disillusionment in its turn gave way to bloody partisanship when the Wars of Religion began in 1562.

It is essential for an understanding of the seventeenth century not only to remember the horrors of this civil war, but also its causes as they then appeared. Without Calvin there would have been continued persecution, but almost certainly no war, and no Protestant party strong enough to fight one. If it all comes back to Calvin, some special characteristic must be sought in his teaching to explain his motive force. It is not easy to look back beyond the political struggle, beyond the Edict of Nantes and its Revocation, to the religious issues from which it all began. The story is further complicated by the Jansenist controversy, which imparted a quite different colour to a number of Augustinian doctrines which might in other circumstances have been associated with Protestants. There is no point here in trying to disentangle specifically Calvinist from specifically Jansenist interpretations of Augustine, since the psychological impact was so similar, despite the very different theological and institutional implications, but this rather technical complication shows how hard it is to be sure, beyond a certain date, that it is Calvinism rather than more general Augustinianism that is in question. There are so many things Calvin did not do; he did not split the unity of the Church, that had already been achieved by Luther, Zwingli and others; he did not lead a crusade of arms, though he just lived to see the outbreak of war; he did not even originate any striking theological doctrine. His contribution lies in his logical, even legalistic, exposition of certain points of view which he took to their inexorable conclusion, and in the successful practical application of many of these ideas. His was the force of those who refuse to compromise on what they regard as the truth. For his contemporaries, friend and foe alike, his most characteristic and impressive work undoubtedly seemed to be the theocratic state of Geneva and his doctrine of Predestination.

All writers on Calvin stress the inexorable logic, perhaps encouraged by his legal training, with which he presents his case. The classification and systematization of medieval thinkers had still left them room for manœuvre, at the price of excessive complexity and subtlety, but Calvin manages to combine their powers of logic with a rigorous simplicity, allowing a single answer to any given question. He saw his, the Christian, position as perfectly straightforward. To put the case in extreme, but not inaccurate, terms, for the Catholic before Luther there was no salvation outside the Catholic Church, for Calvin there was no salvation within it. He could not deny the possibility completely on theological grounds, but for all practical purposes he acted as if the case were proven. The shift of emphasis is absolute; to leave the Catholic Church meant not only to break with ecclesiastical authority, but to cut adrift from the continuity of the past and the daily society of the faithful, no mere Sunday matter. That is why critics of the Papacy before 1517, vehement as they might be and jealous of national rights, had never advocated schism as a solution to the Church's ills. The political position of both Henry VIII and Luther enabled schism to become a national norm, so that a sense of isolation was by no means a necessary or even usual consequence of following one's lawful sovereign into revolt. Calvin's situation is quite different. A junior among his fellow-exiles, permanently estranged from his own country, at loggerheads with Luther and other reformers, he claimed that he alone was right. In a similar position, Luther might of course have acted in a similar way, but the Elector saved him the necessity. It may well have been the fact of Calvin's isolation which forced on his logical mind the theory of isolation. Setting at naught the centuries of Catholicism, Calvin claimed to be returning directly to apostolic times, to the Bible (some would unkindly say that he goes even farther back than the Gospels), and supports his claim on that justification by faith to which the conscience of each man must testify.

It is just possible to imagine the Catholic Church going most of the way with Luther, and until Trent this was not so wilfully far-fetched as it may sound, because Luther saw no virtue in a minority religion, rather the contrary. Calvin, by contrast, was obliged after the rejection of his initial appeal to the King to recognize that his followers must always constitute a minority. It could be said that such recognition is making a virtue out of necessity; it could also be argued that from the first version of the *Institution* to the last Calvin developed only in the sense of becoming more exclusive and attaching more importance to the austere virtue of being always in a minority. The rules for life at Geneva (for its earthly citizens, that is) make it look as if here, let alone hereafter, as few people as possible were to be admitted to the privileges of election. For Calvin's own generation, each of whom had been personally converted from Catholicism, some personal spiritual experience provided the confidence necessary for breaking away from the mass of the reproved into the remnant of the elect, but for those born into the new religion it must have been hard to resist the hope, and perhaps the belief, that the hereditary principle might apply to election.

This point is inseparable from another. Whether one agrees with Calvin or not, there is no escaping the fact that his life and teaching constituted a deliberate revolt against an established authority, whose shortcomings, in his view, absolved him from obedience. When he in his turn had to take over the reins of government, spiritual and temporal, he had the frightful example of such risings as that of the Anabaptists at Münster (1533–5) to remind him that rebellion breeds rebellion. He had therefore to found his own revolt from authority on an authority still more rigid, and maintain his rule with such inflexibility as to prove his respect for the law, when, according to his lights, it was rightly established. Hierarchical authority was rejected in favour of Presbyterianism, and only Scripture, or the direct inspiration of the Holy Spirit, acknowledged as valid authority. In practice there was no more latitude for interpreting the Bible in Geneva than there had been in Rome, probably less, but the principle of an ultimate appeal to the individual conscience remained, and applied with peculiar force to these still living in France, who had to decide what risk to take as between their mortal bodies and their individual souls. It is obvious enough that this doctrine of appeal to the individual, combined with the reiterated assertion that the elect will be in a small minority, imposed strains of a quite new kind on religiously minded men.

Rabelais despised the corruption of Rome, but he resented the puritanism of Geneva, and what offended him most was what he considered Calvin's inexcusable presumption in daring to predict the course of God's justice. He twice refers to the impostures of Calvin, in a context unmistakably connected with Predestination, and in addition to what has already been said of Calvin, something must now be added about this doctrine as it was understood, or misunderstood, by his contemporaries. Luther had already taught the inefficacy of works for salvation, but basing himself on an extreme Augustinian view of the irremediable corruption of human nature since the Fall, Calvin went further. For him man is so sinful as to deserve nothing but damnation, but God in His mercy bestows as a free, unearned gift the blessing of election on a chosen few, abandoning the rest to their fate. An apparently virtuous life might, in Calvin's view, merely be adding fuel to the eternal flames awaiting the victim of God's just punishment, and conversely, though for obvious reasons the point is not laboured, a scandalously profligate life is not in itself an impediment to election, though it is most unlikely to be a sign of grace. The justified sinner will demonstrate his possession of God's grace by living a good life, the good life can do nothing to earn him this grace. The implications of this doctrine of so-called double predestination are appalling, but need not be argued here; what must be stressed is that practical considerations militate against pure logic. In theory neither Calvin nor his followers could be certain of final election, despite what they took to be the irresistible illumination of the Spirit, but in practice, as he won adherents at some cost to themselves, it became necessary for an ever growing number of people to convince themselves that they were immune from the eternal fate to which they sadly consigned the rest of mankind.

Calvinists never attained more than a local majority in France, and it is a curious historical fact that all the countries in which they were numerous were themselves small and vulnerable, like Holland, the Swiss cantons and Scotland, so that a sense of minority was encouraged by both theological and political factors from the start. The effect of the Reformation on men's lives was much less drastic in other Protestant countries, where Lutheranism or Anglicanism did little to destroy national and religious unity, once the initial upheaval was spent. For the Frenchman in the sixteenth century the strain was different and greater than that imposed on most of his neighbours. For centuries men had been Catholic because there was nothing else to be, and social and religious cohesion had gone together; now they saw that men of the highest principles were ready to break every tie at the prompting of conscience. By the time the first Huguenots' children were growing up, they had the same agonizing choice as their fathers, but in reverse. Conscience could lead a man over to Geneva, or back to Rome, or confirm him in his present faith; reason might tell him that there were grievous wrongs in Rome, but that things in Geneva were far from good; desire for conformism might stifle conscience and reason, so that he would go through appropriate motions until forced by circumstances to reconsider his position. It had so long been taken for granted that the axis was unshakable that it was hard to accept the idea that protest had at last irrevocably led to Protestantism.

It was particularly unfortunate, and genetically fortuitous, that so acute a religious crisis should have coincided with a dynastic one. The weak and morally wretched sons of Henri II hardly seemed the best argument for continuing the Valois line on the throne, and yet it must have seemed that their worst fault lay in their common failure to produce an heir. It was bad enough that a religious dispute should have been exacerbated into civil war, that factional rivalries should reinforce doctrinal differences, but it was downright disaster that the guarantee of stability represented by a visibly continuing dynasty should suddenly lapse and that the only heir in sight should be a heretic. Even if Henri IV had not been a Protestant, his succession would have strained the principle of legitimacy to the utmost. The fact that, as a man, he was almost certainly the best king France could have had at the time did not diminish the shock administered to those for whom the hereditary principle of monarchy had long seemed the only sure thing in a distraught world. It is hard to be enthusiastic about a family tree quite so intricate as that of the Bourbons, but the alternative was anarchy, or Spanish domination, or both.

It is suggestive of the age that Henri IV is popularly remembered for two sayings; one is a declaration of principle, 'Paris vaut bien une messe', the other of policy, that on Sunday every peasant should be prosperous enough to have his 'poule au pot'. These proverbial remarks show a realistic approach to the post-war world, but add a rather sorry postscript to the Renaissance fervour of Gargantua, the burning zeal of Calvin and the tragedy of St. Bartholomew. There was hatred and intransigence on both sides, but in terms of causation rather than blame it can hardly be denied that but for Calvin Henri would not have had to choose between losing Paris and a Mass, and thousands of his subjects might have escaped sword and fire, at least in this world.

Montaigne did not live to see Henri restore peace and order, and his *Essais* reflect the reactions of a humane and cultured man to the tormented world around him. Rabelais just missed the war, Montaigne just missed the peace, and their different experience explains their different outlooks. Born in 1533, the year between the publication of *Pantagruel* and that of *Gargantua*, Montaigne came to manhood in an age when many questions that had long been open ceased to be so. It was clear, long before the first

Essais were published in 1580, that no peaceful solution to religious differences was in sight, and that ideals which fell between the intransigence of a post-Tridentine Catholic Church and a militant Protestantism had no hope of fulfilment. His apprehension of practical Christianity was overcast by the sight of armies laying waste the countryside and slaughtering helpless civilians in the name of two rival dogmas, each claiming exclusive right to the Saviour's name. Each denounced the faith of the other as prejudice, works were treated respectively as shibboleth and superstition. Montaigne was a practical man, not an abstract thinker, and he saw in this sorry state of religious affairs a proof that whichever side might prevail militarily or have the strongest arguments theologically, neither produced the fruits of true Christianity. As no alternative to the two embattled factions was feasible, it is not surprising that he should decide that institutional Christianity just does not work.

Small wonder then that he turned back from his own age to seek peace and wisdom in the writers of the past, that for his supreme example of virtue he should choose Socrates, to whom half a century before Erasmus had addressed the half-jesting invocation 'Sancte Socrates, ora pro nobis.' Practical as he was, Montaigne was like his contemporaries of what M. Febvre calls 'un siècle qui veut croire', and needing religious forms from time to time he lived as a modest *pratiquant,* using Catholic prayers and quite sincerely believing in a creator, who combined goodness and power. While there need be no hesitation in describing him (in sixteenth century terms) as a Catholic, it does seem almost impossible to regard him as a Christian, in the sense of one believing in Christ. An instructive comparison may be made between Rabelais's faith, eccentric as it is in details, and Montaigne's by looking at the remarkable chapter on Pan (*Quart Livre,* ch. XXVIII), published within a year of his death and thus representing his most mature thought, and then seeking anything remotely analogous in Montaigne. The quest is fruitless. A new element has appeared, which may be called de-Christianized Catholicism, conformism without conviction, fideism with a difference.

Another difference between Rabelais and Montaigne lies in

their attitude to the new horizons, physical and intellectual, which the Renaissance promised to open up. It took a long time for Columbus and his followers to impress the men who stayed at home, but already by mid-century, in Rabelais's last books for instance, discovery is a popular theme, usually associated with dreams of wealth, on *El Dorado* lines, but genuinely connected with a belief in human progress. Similarly the stirrings of scientific discovery, partly stimulated by re-reading the Classics, aroused real hopes for the improvement of human life, especially through medicine. By the time Montaigne wrote, many of the first travellers were already dead, and their experiences had passed into history. Wealth had indeed been found in the New World, but at a price in human squalor, rapacity and brutality that sickened men of conscience. New frontiers had been drawn, and had promptly shifted European rivalries across the sea, so that even refugees from religious intolerance found persecution catching up with them in Brazil. As for progress, civilized Europeans had come with cross and sword to share their benefits with naked savages, but enlightened priests had been among the first to realize, and protest, that all the moral virtues of simplicity, good faith, kindness were on the side of the so-called savages. Science seems largely to have been a closed book for Montaigne, and as it failed to cure his stone he is unlikely to have seen in that direction any panacea for human ills. The main lesson he drew from such discoveries as he knew of was that of relativism, which it would be wrong to write down as purely negative, but is at best noncommittal. Indeed, he draws some consolation from the fact that there were somewhere in the world men untouched by civilization, proving by their virtue that human nature is not irremediably corrupt (and by their nakedness that Edenic shame was not universal), but it would be the grossest anachronism to attribute to Montaigne any starry-eyed philosophy of the noble savage.

On the intellectual horizons the progress of Montaigne's thought is more complex and more important. He began, like so many humanists, by accepting rather uncritically the authority of the ancients, and particularly the Stoics. His main concern was always how to get through this life satisfactorily, how to deal with the daily problems imposed by war and the burden of official duties, and it is therefore with moral philosophy rather than theories of knowledge or metaphysics that he is first preoccupied. The example of his best friend, Etienne de la Boétie, whose premature death (1563) was the greatest sorrow of his life, persuaded him that pain and death could be conquered, and that true wisdom lies in conquering them, 'philosopher c'est aprendre à mourir.' In writing his earlier essays he was strongly influenced by Plutarch's *Lives*, recently translated, which show how pagans met death with fortitude, proving the efficacy of the Stoic philosophy which many of them professed. This early reliance on Classical authority was modified both by his own growing experience and by what is often called the 'sceptical crisis' of 1575–6, which bore primarily on questions of knowledge, but inevitably affected all his thought.

The *Apologie de Raimond Sebond* (II/xii) is from many points of view an unsatisfactory work, but, like Plato's *Timaeus*, similarly muddled and obscure, was taken by later generations as typical of the author's thought and exercised an influence disproportionate to its real place in the whole corpus. One is frequently moved to echo Gibbon's stricture on Augustine: 'His learning is too often borrowed, his arguments too often his own,' but the sheer bulk of the *Apologie* compels attention. The greater part of the essay consists in a detailed attack on human presumption, directed at its very foundation, human reason. Montaigne is indignant that rational arguments for the existence of God, such as those used by Sebond, should be dismissed by superior reasoning, and then turned against their user, to demonstrate the fact that God's existence is not only not proven but not provable. He makes much of the classic definition of man as *animal rationalis,* that is distinguished from the beasts by reason alone, and gives a lengthy catalogue of highly improbable stories tending to show that animals are cleverer, kinder, fairer, in every way superior to man. He exploits the other Scholastic tag, *nil in intellectu quod non prius in sensu,* by pointing to the countless errors to which our senses are liable, and thus to the fallibility of the very instrument on which reason itself depends. He makes fun of the dogmatic pretentions of philosophers, who in the course of two thousand years of dispute between the wisest men of every age have proved conclusively that where all claim the monopoly of truth, none can be believed. His answer to the question of truth is to suspend judgement, as his famous medal, struck in 1576, tells us; his answer to human arrogance is humility before the inscrutable face of the Creator. He agrees with Heraclitus that the world is in a state of flux.[1]

Finallement il n'y a aucune constante existence, ny de nostre estre, ny de celuy des objects. Et nous, et nostre jugement, et toutes choses mortelles, vont coulant et roulant sans cesse . . . Nous n'avons aucune communication à l'estre, par ce que toute humaine nature est tousjours au milieu entre le naistre et le mourir, ne baillant de soy qu'une obscure apparence et ombre, et une incertaine et debile opinion. (II/xii, p. 589)

So much for any *abysme de science*. His final words put Seneca in his place for suggesting that man must rise above humanity: 'C'est à nostre foy Chrestienne, non à sa vertu Stoique, de pretendre à cette divine et miraculeuse metamorphose.' (II/xii, p. 592)

Unfortunately the appeal to faith falls on ears already deafened by the assault on reason, and the *Apologie* established Montaigne as the sceptic *par excellence* for generations to come.

He is, however, remembered for a contribution to the history of ideas more original than scepticism and more relevant to the present study: what Pascal calls in exasperation 'le sot projet qu'il a de se peindre.' Faced with the impossibility of attaining certain truth, because of the fallibility of reason and the relativism of custom, Montaigne cast around for the field of inquiry in which the risk of error would be least and the authority of the inquirer consequently greatest. This field he found in himself: 'Je m'estudie plus qu'autre subject. C'est ma metaphisique, c'est ma phisique.' (III/xiii, p. 1042) No one could know more about 'mon estre universel, Michel de Montaigne', than himself, nor was the study of purely private relevance for 'chaque homme porte la forme entiere de l'humaine condition. (III/ii, p. 779) The precept

[1] References are to pages in the 1937 edition of the *Essais* in *Bibl. de la Pléiade*.

'know thyself' had been familiar from Greek times, but Montaigne gives it a new twist by claiming that publication of his own detailed self-portrait would actually contribute to the self-knowledge of each reader. Other writers had written about themselves, St. Augustine, for example, or Villon, but always with some larger end in view, whether the conversion of others through the autobiography of a convert or simply to enlist sympathy in distress; Montaigne is the first to make self-portraiture an end in itself. This apparently gratuitous concentration by one individual upon himself is the most striking feature of the *Essais*.

This is the beginning of real egocentricity, the cult of the individual carried to its logical conclusion. The background of external events and ideas had forced Montaigne by a process of elimination to hold fast to the only spar he could salvage from the general wreck, 'la forme sienne, la forme maitresse'. His philosophy is personal, but above all practical: 'Toute ma petite prudence en ces guerres civiles où nous sommes, s'employe à ce qu'elles n'interrompent ma liberté d'aller et venir.' (III/xiii, p. 1041) Though Socrates remains his ideal, his previous hero-worship of the great Classical figures becomes modified by years of experience in both public and private life: 'Les plus belles vies sont, à mon gré, celles qui se rangent au modelle commun et humain, avec ordre, mais sans miracle et sans extravagance. (IV/xiii, p. 1088) His *summum bonum* is clear enough: 'c'est une absolue perfection, et comme divine, de sçavoyr jouyr loiallement de son estre.' (ibid.) In the final sentence of his last essay he seems to come near Pantagruelism in his commendation of his declining years 'à ce Dieu, protecteur de santé et de sagesse, mais gaye et socialle' of the Horatian Odes, but the resemblance is only superficial.

Priority in Rabelais's thought goes to 'guyde de Dieu et compaignye d'homme', with self-control to rule the inward life and cheerful tolerance the outward. Calvin would probably have accepted the priority, but he denied man any power of self-control, and he is not generally associated with either cheerfulness or tolerance. Montaigne is very different; he says, and there is no reason to doubt his sincerity: 'Mon cathedrant, c'est l'authorité de la volonté divine, qui nous reigle sans contredit.' (II/iii, p. 334) He says too: 'j'estime tous les hommes mes compatriotes, et embrasse un Polonois comme un François postposant cette lyaison nationale à l'universelle et commune. (III/ix, p. 943) Both these sentiments can be amply supported by texts in the *Essais,* but the most ingenious exegesis cannot locate the priority in Montaigne anywhere but where he tells us to look for it: in himself. His humanity and his religion are interesting as aspects of his 'estre universel', his experience and habits make up his 'forme maitresse', to which he remains true, but he offers no general prescription to his reader beyond a self-knowledge similar to that of the *Essais*. It must be said at once that Montaigne is no solipsist; the moving essay 'de l'Amitié' (I/xxviii) shows his confidence in the possibility of a perfect understanding between individuals, rare as it may be, and if, as is sometimes claimed, he ended his self-exploration by discovering mankind, he had learnt the vital lesson through La Boétie. Not everyone has a Boétie, though, and the egocentricity of the *Essais* is an easier lesson to impart than that of ideal friendship. For Montaigne, 'mon metier et mon art, c'est vivre', and he was concerned only that his philosophy should work practically. Those who came after him had very different problems, and applied his methods with very different results. Scepticism and egocentricity fall into proper perspective within the whole spread of Montaigne's life and work, but abstracted from his book their implications are very different.

For Rabelais the individual is still bound by indissoluble bonds to God above, through Christ, and to men around him, through family, country, community of ideals. The cosmos is as firm as ever, and a fruitful field for the adventure of human progress. In this world and the next Rabelais speaks to and for the majority of mankind, all except the bigots and other enemies of nature attacked in the *Thélème* and *Physis-Antiphysie* episodes. Calvin has no interest in the cosmos, but if the web he spins is immeasurably more restricted, it is all the tighter. The chosen few could rely on support from their fellows in the minority, and above all from the Spirit acting on the individual conscience, but neither historical continuity, nor social traditions, nor the weight of numbers have any more a part to play. The axis is still God-centred, but the human element is irrevocably changed, with the individual exposed to quite new strains. With Montaigne, God is no longer at the centre, though He is above, remote in His majesty, and the minority has dwindled to one, representative of all mankind. The 'moi' is 'désaxé'; with unity disappear respect for authority and custom, replaced by automatic obedience and conformism outwardly, scepticism and relativism inwardly. Henceforth the measure of truth is I, human solidarity becomes an act of hope rather than of faith. Disillusioned by the failure of so many promises, Montaigne made a signal success of his attempt to find consolation within rather than without. The 'moi' now has itself for axis, and if its course is at first erratic, it has yet to encounter its most serious strains and stresses. Montaigne indefinitely suspends judgement, but his successors have had enough of flux, and the seventeenth century presents the 'moi' with critical hazards, as yet unsuspected.

2: DESCARTES

WHAT happened in the sixteenth century may be regarded, according to one's point of view, as a *felix culpa* or a *damnosa hereditas* for the seventeenth century. For Descartes it no doubt seemed to be both. But for the vigour of the Counter-Reform, the Jesuit school of La Flèche would not have been able to offer the young Descartes the best education then available in Europe; but for that same vigour Galileo might have escaped condemnation and Descartes might not have found prudence commanding him to spend his life in voluntary exile. Unsatisfactory as the lingering Scholasticism was, a century of revived classical philosophy proved no better alternative, so that even before he left school Descartes was impressed more than anything else by the *doutes et erreurs* which the current state of philosophy inspired. Anyone who has had to tidy a lumber-room will appreciate the sheer relief of deciding that chaos has now passed the point where the labour of sorting is justified. There is a dustbin for ideas as there is for other junk. Seeing that things could be no worse, Descartes felt confident enough to scrap the lot and start afresh, prepared to salvage anything which might subsequently come in handy. If this is the *felix culpa,* there is also the *damnosa hereditas* of civil and religious strife which is never far from his mind. In his refusal to run the slightest risk on this account, he made difficulties for his growing system which ultimately led to graver risks than those so carefully avoided.

Descartes starts where Montaigne leaves off, with doubt. Anyone who questions the importance of doubt in his thought, should conduct a pilot survey of Descartes's main works.[1] The obsessive fear of all that is doubtful or false is referred to in the opening lines of every one, and the words 'doute, erreur, faux, tromper' continually recur up to the point in each one where

[1] All references are to pages in the 1937 edition of Descartes, *Œuvres,* in *Bibl. de la Pléiade.*

they are finally banished by the discovery of certainty and truth. Montaigne had done his work well; his scepticism remained an obstacle which any pursuer of certainty had to overcome, or remove. As the primary negative stimulus in Descartes's thought, doubt plays a decisive role, and one that can be followed in varying forms in all his main works.

There is, however, a positive stimulus of no less importance which the works do not reveal, and which we know only from autobiographical fragments. The very nature of this stimulus precluded its publication, but its importance demanded that the effects which it produced should be motivated acceptably, that is rationally, in the published work. This positive stimulus is Descartes's famous dream, of which the effects can hardly be exaggerated. The actual details are related by Baillet, Descartes's biographer, from an account left by Descartes himself, and the important point is Descartes's own interpretation. According to him, he had been charged with the mission of founding a universal science, which would link together all branches of knowledge. Later on he came to see mathematics as the key, but the abiding memory of the dream concerned not so much the method as the fact that he, René Descartes, had been chosen for this unique task. He seems never to have doubted the divine origins of this dream, and at once made a vow to go in thanksgiving on a pilgrimage to Loretto, a vow actually performed some years later. This mysterious, perhaps mystical experience (which, incidentally, baffled Freud when submitted anonymously to him for analysis) took place on the night of 10 November, 1619, when Descartes was in winter quarters in Germany, on not very active service. It occurred when he shut himself up alone all day, for peace and warmth, in a room heated by a large Bavarian stove, *le poêle* of his account. It is this inner, though unpublished conviction of his divine personal mission which gives to Descartes's system its characteristic tone, both dogmatic and subjective.

In his best-known work, the *Discours de la méthode*, written in French for the widest possible public, Descartes gives what purports to be some autobiographical details of his development.

Although the inaccuracy of this account is patent, it does have the considerable merit of making clear what Descartes wanted his readers to think about him and, up to a point, what he wanted to think about himself. He begins with a fairly detailed description of his early years, of which the salient facts are that he had, by any standards, a very good education, that his own academic performance was distinguished and that it left him, at the end of it all, beset with 'tant de doutes et d'erreurs' (93). He then spent a short time travelling, seeking in 'le grand livre du monde' (97) that certain knowledge which had thus far eluded him. Failing there as well, he concludes his first part with the resolve to 'étudier en moi-même' (98), salvaging nothing from his education save a liking for mathematics, 'à cause de la certitude et de l'évidence de leurs raisons' (95). Except for the significant attraction to mathematics, his situation is similar to that of Montaigne, and for similar reasons.

The second part opens with a reference to the *poêle*, and proceeds to give rational arguments aimed at producing the same effect as his private experience, namely that the works of one man (in e.g. architecture, town planning) are superior to those of many, and that he will therefore rely on his sole unaided judgement. 'Le bon sens,' according to the opening sentence of the *Discours,* 'est la chose du monde la mieux partagée,' and it means 'le pouvoir de distinguer le vrai d'avec le faux' (91). Rejecting all book-learning, authorities or second-hand information of any kind, Descartes resolves to base his method solely on this power which he shares equally with all other men (since the standard Scholastic definition of man was *animal rationalis*), and thus to put the fruits of his work within the grasp of all endowed with 'la lumière naturelle de la raison.'

There follows the method itself, originally applied to mathematics, as we see in the unfinished *Règles*, but later given universal application. Four rules are given, of which the last three, Analysis, Synthesis, Enumeration, do not concern the present study, together with a preliminary condition effectively having the force of a rule: 'pourvu que je prisse *une ferme et constante resolution* de ne manquer pas une seule fois à les observer' (103). (My italics.)

In a moral context this apparently innocuous proviso is to play a leading part.

What is now the first rule of method had been in the mathematical *Règles* founded on 'intuition', for which the same condition was demanded. The purpose in each case is the same, to arrive at first principles from which all subsequent steps can be deduced 'sans aucune crainte d'erreur'. The *Règles*, written probably in 1628, give the first version of an idea which remains unchanged in all essentials from then on. Compare the texts, first of the *Règles*:

> Par *intuition* j'entends, non pas le témoignage changeant des sens ou le jugement trompeur d'une imagination qui compose mal son objet, mais la conception d'un esprit pur et attentif, conception si facile et si distincte qu'aucun doute ne reste sur ce que nous comprenons; ou, ce qui est la même chose, *la conception ferme d'un esprit pur et attentif, qui naît de la seule lumière de la raison.* (My italics.) (11–12)

then the *Discours*:

> Le premier [précepte] etait de ne recevoir jamais aucune chose pour vraie que je ne la connusse *évidemment* être telle; c'est-à-dire d'éviter soigneusement la précipitation et la prévention, et de ne comprendre rien de plus en mes jugements que ce qui se présenterait si *clairement et si distinctement* à mon esprit que je n'eusse aucune occasion de le mettre en doute. (103.) (My italics.)

At first reading these two texts look innocent enough, but in fact they contain the greater part of the Cartesian revolution. The vocabulary can easily be misleading; *évident* is for Descartes the highest degree of certain knowledge, a truth so true that it needs only to be enunciated to be accepted, and it is equivalent to a combination of *clair et distinct*; the definitions of these two words are given in *Principes*, 1/45 (453) where *clair* is defined as '[une connaissance] qui est présente et manifeste à un esprit attentif' and *distinct* as 'celle qui est tellement précise et différente de toutes les autres, qu'elle ne comprend en soi que ce qui paraît manifestement à celui qui la considère comme il faut.'

The historical context must also be recalled; the Scholastics had never denied the value of human reason, but in contrast with the certainty of revealed truth, they recognized in the created world a realm of contingent events, where man's knowledge can generally aspire only to a high degree of probability. Since the highest degree of probability is still in Descartes's absolute terms logically open to doubt, he is in effect rejecting *all* merely probable truths. The reference to 'la seule lumière de la raison' which is explicit in the *Règles*, and implicit in the *Discours*, is making a claim for human self-sufficiency of the most radical kind. Nor must the place assigned to the will be overlooked. Preconceived notions ('prévention') and over-hasty judgements ('précipitation') have to be avoided by constant exercise of the will, thus keeping the 'esprit pur et attentif.' Finally the explicit rejection of the senses and imagination (in Cartesian terms, the faculty which deals with sense impressions left in the mind when immediate sense stimuli are absent) takes us straight to the *Cogito*.

This method applied to mathematics proved of immediate and striking benefit, helping Descartes to perfect co-ordinate geometry and make notable advances in scientific inquiry. The irony of history has made us forget today that the method, which we see as a preparation for the *Cogito*, was originally simply a preface to the three essays which followed on *Dioptrique, Géométrie, Météores*. The scientists, who are competent to judge these essays, are not usually interested, and those on the arts side who might be interested are not usually competent. However that may be, it is the *Cogito* which rightly engages our attention, because in retrospect it can be seen to have affected all subsequent thinking.

His success in the abstract study of mathematics led Descartes to seek a more concrete application to the world of nature, but to make the transition he needed a first principle, which would not only satisfy the demands of his rules of method, but would also incorporate a truth concerning something actually existing; technically speaking, his original first principle needed an existential reference. This he provides in the *Cogito*, by a process rather sketchily described in the *Discours*, and at greater length in the first two *Méditations*.

It so happened that about the time when his thoughts had taken definite shape in his mind, he found himself one day, in

1627, at a social gathering, attacking some of the then prevalent free-thinking objections to religion. His eloquence and cogent argument were heard and appreciated by the Papal Nuncio and by Cardinal de Bérulle, founder of the French Oratory, and these two eminent persons seem to have persuaded him to apply his talents without delay to defending the cause of the Church against the onslaughts of free thought. This official encouragement, added to his private sense of mission, had several curious effects, one being his eventual condemnation for proposing a doctrine of Transsubstantiation, which he believed immune from the damaging criticism levelled at the (still) orthodox doctrine, and another being his prompt and permanent removal to a Protestant country. Here this champion of Catholicism took a Protestant mistress, whom he might perhaps have had to marry but for the difference of religion, and had by her a natural daughter, Francine, to whom he was devoted, and who was brought up as a Protestant (her death in childhood was one of the great sorrows of Descartes's life). A more philosophical result was his realization that the true enemy not only of his own system but also of the Church, to whose cause he was now committed, was scepticism.

The destructive work of Montaigne led Descartes to an argument designed to outflank the sceptics by a *reductio ad absurdum*. The dangers of the full so-called hyperbolical doubt employed in the *Méditations* (originally written in Latin for professional scholars) are somewhat toned down in the *Discours*. In the *Méditations* he rapidly resumes the stock arguments against the senses—since they can sometimes be shown to deceive me they must be regarded as always potentially fallible—about sleeping–waking and so on, and then hastens to a conclusion by deciding not to examine all such propositions one by one, but all at once in their basic principle. He supposes, for the sake of argument, that instead of God there is 'un certain mauvais génie, non moins rusé et trompeur que puissant, qui a employé toute son industrie à me tromper (165). If this *malin génie*, as he is generally called, can be conquered, scepticism will be disarmed, since it could never go to greater extremes. Considering all the propositions which this nightmare creature may submit to him, he finds that if he is to avoid error his only recourse is to withold assent, to doubt. Happily there is a loophole; 'qu'il me trompe tant qu'il voudra, il ne saurait jamais faire que je ne sois rien, tant que je penserai être quelque chose' (167). The triumphant conclusion of this argument is always known as the *Cogito,* from the Latin version of the 'Je pense donc je suis' (113) of the *Discours.*

This then is the first principle he has been seeking, beyond the reach of doubt and *clair*. He goes on at once to make it *distinct* and thus fully *évident* by affirming, in the *Discours,* 'ce moi, c'est-à-dire l'âme par laquelle je suis ce que je suis, est entièrement *distincte* du corps' (114). This proposition he now describes as unshakable by the 'plus extravagantes suppositions des sceptiques' (113), a periphrasis in the *Discours* for the *malin génie* who does not appear there.

His very clarity of expression makes Descartes a trap for the unwary, and even the simplest word suddenly turns out to have unexpected implications. In the *Méditations* (in general the most reliable exposition of his metaphysics) he answers his own questions: 'Mais qu'est-ce donc que je suis? Une chose qui pense . . . C'est-à-dire une chose qui doute, qui conçoit, qui affirme, qui nie, qui veut, qui ne veut pas, qui imagine aussi et qui sent.' (170)

The last two verbs refer not to the outside world, whose existence is still under the spell of doubt cast by the *malin génie* on every proposition besides the *Cogito*, but to those activities of the mind, as yet unexplained, but normally associated with outside stimuli. It is the other categories of *penser* that are so revealing. Thought suggests intellect, but if one looks at the first six verbs, only one, *conçoit*, concerns pure intellection, the others all refer to different operations of the *will.* The actual mental operation with which Descartes challenged the *malin génie* was doubt, and generalizing from *douter* to *penser* he arrives at the *Cogito*. It is time to say that this doubt is not what it seems, the *nescio* of Montaigne, but an *active* doubt, a *nolo credere, nolo falli*, in a word an act not of the intellect, *entendement*, but an act of will.

This is not just a quibble. The primacy of the will in Descartes is a point not stressed by most critics until they come to his psychology, but if the definition of thought quoted above means anything, it means that from first to last Descartes is asserting his personality through his will, and that his first principle derives from this faculty rather than from that of intellect. The immediately subsequent steps may obscure this point for some readers of Descartes, and perhaps even for Descartes himself, and it is worth disposing of them before returning to a more detailed consideration of the *Cogito*.

From his first principle, Descartes extracts his criterion of truth: 'Je pouvais prendre pour règle générale que les choses que nous concevons fort clairement et fort distinctement sont toutes vraies.' (114) So far he has arrived at a certainty henceforth unassailable, but at the cost of isolating himself completely within his own disembodied mind. He is, in technical language, in a solipsist impasse. To escape he must exorcize the *malin génie*. For this he must prove the existence of a veracious, omnipotent God, without whom his criterion of truth cannot be applied, because his memory too needs an external guarantee. By his own definition, deduction lacks the immediacy, and thus the unshakeable validity, of the first principle, the *Cogito*, actually present to the mind, because the recollection of having once conquered the *malin génie* depends on memory, which depends on the continuity of time still to be guaranteed (i.e. that it is not a discrete series of moments). He therefore proceeds to prove that God exists by the only version of the standard proof, from effects to cause, then open to him, from his own existence. Among the facts of this existence is that of his own imperfection, revealed by his doubt; to know one's own imperfection one must have an antecedent idea of perfection, but this can come only from a truly perfect source, which is God; QED. *Douter* is here used in its more common, passive, sense of *nescio*, and thus provides the argument neatly summarized as 'dubito ergo Deus est'. It cannot be too strongly emphasized that God is *not* necessary to prove the *Cogito*, but is proved by it, and moreover, as we shall see in a moment, it is quite false to Descartes's intentions to suppose that the doubt (imperfect knowledge), by which God is proved, corresponds with that desperate act of will, the active doubt, by which Descartes's existence is proved.

God's existence once proved, Descartes can now reincorporate the world of non-mind, including his own body and the rest of matter, into his system. According to a famous passage in the Preface to the *Principes*, philosophy can be likened to a tree, of which metaphysics are the roots, physics the trunk. This is illustrated by the rather unexpected nature of the link between Parts IV and V of the *Discours*. Descartes begins his survey of the physical world by speaking of: 'Certaines lois que Dieu a tellement établies en la nature et dont il a imprimé de telles notions en nos âmes, que . . . nous ne saurions douter qu'elles ne soient exactement observées en tout ce qui est ou qui se fait dans le monde.' (119–20) Thus at the very moment when he is about to leave his solipsist sanctuary for the world outside, Descartes discovers *within his mind* notions of the laws of nature. A little farther on he explains that these derive in fact from 'aucun autre principe que les perfections infinies de Dieu'. Anyone who might be tempted to regard this as a mere form of words should turn to *Principes,* II/37–42, where a scientific exposition of the three laws of motion (of inertia, linear movement, conservation of movement) is opened by the words: 'De cela aussi que Dieu n'est point sujet à changer . . .' (495)

Since the definition of God's attributes is solely the work of Descartes's reason (and excludes, for instance, mercy) this line of argument explains two typically Cartesian phenomena. One is the error into which such *a priori* reasoning led him, as in his theory of the circulation, based on the assumption that the heat within the heart acts as a sort of internal combustion engine, or the activity of the pineal gland, a somewhat furtive rendezvous for mind and matter. The other is of immense importance for the later development of materialism, and is the claim, made in the last part of the *Discours*, that by following out Descartes's method men can become 'maîtres et possesseurs de la nature'. (134) This claim derives from man's *possession* of the laws of nature within his mind (whether put there by God or not hardly matters now) and his ability to manipulate them as a master.

Solipsism had thus given way to a man-centred system, in which nature is reduced to the status of object, and made the servant of man's will, guided by his trained intellect.

The last words bring us back again to the *Cogito*, and man's personal situation. This may be seen in three aspects; intellectual, moral, psychological, closely interconnected. Having proved to his own satisfaction that God exists as a principle of veracity, Descartes asks how the existence of such a good creator is compatible with the fact of Descartes's own fallibility; where does error creep in? His answer is simply that God made everything for the best. To man as a finite creature, he gave a finite understanding, (*entendement*), but an infinite will, and it is when man exercises this will in the absence of adequate information from intellect that error occurs. This leads him, in *Méditation* IV, to a discussion of free will, which further illustrates the special position of the will in the Cartesian system. He writes of the will: 'C'est elle principalement qui me fait connaître que je porte l'image et la ressemblance de Dieu'. (196) One of its principal attributes is liberty: 'Et certes la grâce divine et la connaissance naturelle, bien loin de diminuer ma liberté, l'augmentent plutôt et la fortifient.' (197) In other words, the more clearly the truth is seen the freer one is to follow it. The mention of 'grâce divine' may be regarded as a purely formal courtesy, for numerous other texts make it clear that it is 'la connaissance naturelle' in which Descartes is interested. What this amounts to is that our quasi-divine wills are only misused because of the limitations of finite intellect, but these limitations can be minimized by the right use of reason, that is the Cartesian method. Reason will then serve to reinforce will. To the claim offered to his followers of being 'maîtres et possesseurs de la nature' may now be added an older one: 'eritis sicut dei'.

When one comes to ask what kind of moral life the 'moi' leads, a formal difficulty arises. Descartes is precluded by his own logic from having a definitive system of ethics, for he tells us that the topmost branch of the tree of philosophy mentioned earlier is 'la plus haute et la plus parfaite morale, qui, présupposant une entière connaissance des autre sciences, est le dernier degré de la sagesse.' (428) However, while making his way to the top, the philosopher must still live. To that end he needs a rule of life, 'une morale provisoire', whose chief function will be to leave him free from inward and outward disturbances during his task. The first draft of this is to be found in the third part of the *Discours,* and a later, though still not definitive, version in some letters he wrote to the Princess Elisabeth, daughter of the dispossessed Elector Palatine, in 1645.

The first rule is one of Conformism, to come to terms with the established order and when faced with a choice always to take the middle way. The second is Constancy, to pursue a course once chosen to the end, on the grounds that pending the attainment of perfect certainty, still in the future, all choices are merely probable, and it is not justifiable to exchange one merely probable course for another no more certain. The third is Self-Control, 'de tâcher toujours plutôt à me vaincre que la fortune, et à changer mes désirs que l'ordre du monde.' (108) In the later version the first rule is amended to a recommendation to be guided as far as possible by reason, which is a somewhat more dignified way (more suited to a princess at any rate) than the wholly non-moral counsel of expediency given in the *Discours.* The second rule remains substantially the same, but contains a gloss which links it up with other texts already quoted; referring to 'une ferme et constante résolution' he says 'et c'est la fermeté de cette résolution que je crois devoir être prise pour la vertu'. (954) The frequent references to this as a prerequisite to the method are now given in the clearest terms a moral significance. The third rule is virtually unaltered, but in the *Traité des Passions,* composed for the same princess at about the same time, it receives a most illuminating commentary; in Article 152, 'Pour quelle cause on peut s'estimer', Descartes writes of 'l'usage de notre libre arbitre, et l'empire que nous avons sur nos volontés . . .; il nous rend en quelque façon semblables à Dieu en nous faisant maîtres de nous-mêmes.' (629) The recurrence in so many contexts of words like *maître, empire, vaincre* speaks for itself, and heralds Corneille. Once again, this time in a moral context, the claim for the will is the same: 'eritis sicut dei.'

With the *Traité des Passions* we come to the psychological aspect of the 'moi'. The irreconcilable dualism set up between mind and body is no accident, it is an integral part of the system. For Descartes, the human body is an inseparable part of the world of matter, and this is ruled by mathematical-mechanical laws in a totally deterministic way. It is indeed through our knowledge of these laws that we can claim mastery of nature. The one field in which this dualism had to be reconciled was that of psychology; if our bodies are really *automata* (Descartes uses this very word) such an act as murder, for instance, will be no more than an encounter between two physical machines, devoid of moral significance. Moreover, passions, defined by Descartes in terms stressing their external, physical origin, should logically rule the body and have no effect on the mind. These difficulties Descartes attempted to solve by locating in the pineal gland the point where mind and matter interact, regardless of the fact that mind has by definition no extension, and can thus occupy no place. His choice of the gland was based on typically *a priori* arguments; it is small mobile, central, single, unlike most parts of the brain which are double, and even today its functions are uncertain. Granted the inconsistency of the theory, it proves useful. Descartes's theory of control is attractively simple; messages originating from the body travel, in a physical sense, to the brain, and then back again to the appropriate part of the body, causing a reflex action. Thus stimuli provoking the passions (described in precise physiological terms) of, for example, anger or fear, will be automatically translated into assault or flight. This process can be interrupted by originating a message in the mind (*not* the brain) and conveying it through the pineal gland instead of the usual automatic, i.e. unthinking, response. The most effective way of doing this is to prepare oneself in the absence of stimuli by reflecting on the morally desirable course of action, thus training the will to give the desired response, when the stimuli actually come from outside. Thus a reflex, conditioned by rational preparation, replaces the former automatic, because physical, reflex. The key-text for Descartes's psychology, and in so far as self-control is moral, for his ethics, is Article 50: 'Qu'il n'y a point d'âme si faible qu'elle ne puisse, étant bien conduite, acquérir un pouvoir absolu sur ses passions. (582) It must be remembered that passions are for Descartes purely external, so that amour-propre, the desire for self-fulfilment or *libido sciendi* are not concerned. Once again the will makes us masters, this time of our bodies and their passions. Once again the machinery involved has the effect of concentrating all the initiative *within* us, of making the 'moi' not only the centre, but almost its own universe.

One result of this is that the morally desirable course of action just referred to is not properly moral at all, but simply prescribed on 'moral' grounds from completely arbitrary premisses discovered within myself. Another result, not discussed as such by Descartes but no less implicit, is the difficulty of finding a place for a Mediator between the *moi pensant* and God, principle of veracity, revealed not by Scripture but 'la lumière naturelle de la raison'. It is indeed impossible to see how Descartes's attitude to the world of matter, including human bodies, could be made to square with a belief in the Incarnation, let alone the resurrection of the body. This is not to cast doubt on the sincerity of, for instance, his apparently edifying death in Stockholm, but as the critic Laberthonnière says 'il fut un croyant sincère, mais banal.' Recalling his intimate associations with Protestantism in Holland, and the somewhat off-hand statement of the *Discours*, 'Je révérais notre théologie, et prétendais autant qu'aucun autre à gagner le ciel', (96) we may reasonably accuse Descartes of that form of fideism known as the doctrine of the two truths; for purposes of salvation he accepted those revealed doctrines which in philosophy his reason would lead him to reject.

This great emphasis on the 'moi', and on the will within the 'moi', prompts a further question, concerning the status of other people. Here, perhaps more than anywhere else, Descartes's philosophy betrays his self-sufficient temperament. Except for his mistress and Francine, his personal attachments were few, and if he chose exile and renounced the solace of family life the reason is to be found clearly expressed in the 'morale provisoire': 'Et particulièrement je mettais entre les excès toutes les promesses par lesquelles on retranche quelque chose de sa liberté.' (107)

It is thus no surprise to find that others enjoy a status hardly more substantial than that of the shades in ancient Hades. Their bodies are part of the deterministic world of matter, and their minds (or souls) by which they can claim to be persons, exist solely by analogy with Descartes's own. In strict logic he need not postulate minds for the other bodies he sees around him any more than for animals. Since modern science has invented machines that talk and others of universal adaptability, his two main criteria for distinguishing between men and animals are of little value.

Bertrand Russell tells the story of an American lady who once wrote to him complaining that she had been a solipsist all her life and had never found anyone to agree with her. Descartes is not a solipsist in such a naïve sense, if only because he was passionately concerned that his mission should win converts, but it may be that he is a solipsist *malgré lui*, or something very like it. As he puts it, anyone can produce his own solipsist situation through his own personal *Cogito*, essentially a non-transferable asset, and so the world consists logically of as many solipsist systems as there may be people thinking them. Apart from logic, however, there is the general tone of Descartes's work, which suggests that all men are equal except only for Descartes, a sort of first-class citizen with special relations with an invisible head of state, God. Just as motives of prudence, not philosophy, led Descartes to exclude at the start from his inquiry political and religious institutions, accepted as they stood, so the existence of other people proves a convenient, if unproved, assumption. It is hardly going too far to say that the result of thus omitting from an otherwise comprehensive system all examination of the mainsprings of society reveals a mentality with disastrous bias.

Before leaving this point, one should, in order to be quite fair to Descartes, quote from a letter to Elisabeth, written 15 September, 1645, and worthy of study as a piece of unusually moving eloquence:

> Et il faut toujours préférer les intérêts du tout, dont on est partie, à ceux de sa personne en particulier; toutefois avec mesure et discretion . . . ; si un homme vaut plus, lui seul, que tout le reste de sa ville, il n'aurait pas raison de se vouloir perdre pour la sauver. (967).

Granted the nobility of the opening words, one would like to know who is to be the judge in the subsequent proviso.

The implications of Cartesianism are so many and so rich that they are still today far from exhausted, and the preceding pages have attempted only to give some idea of a set of themes lying at the heart of the system. The starting point is that of Montaigne; finding all other knowledge exposed to 'doute et erreur' Descartes resolves to study himself. Unlike Montaigne, however, his aim is not to limit the field of uncertainty, but to found a whole system of certain knowledge. Within himself he finds a proposition which resists the most desperate assaults of scepticism, and, in the act of will by which he refuses to be deceived, he discovers the unshakable truth of his own existence. This existence is purely non-material, it refers to his 'esprit ou âme', and quite specifically excludes his body, let alone the rest of the outside world. Within the solipsist situation of the *Cogito* he discovers a criterion of truth, the purely subjective recognition of ideas as clear and distinct. Only then does he leave his solitary eminence to prove the existence of God, external guarantee of all his subsequent ideas. On the validity of these proofs of God depends the escape from solipsism, and if they are not accepted, he must remain alone for the rest of thinking time. With God admitted to share his empire, Descartes can now proceed to *a priori* physics, to his mastery of the world of nature and to his alternative blueprint for the creation in *Genesis* in case God should ever decide to create another world.

In all this his will is supreme, quasi-divine. Through his will, guided by the right use of reason, he can infallibly avoid error; he can achieve that firm and constant resolution later identified with moral virtue; he can subdue and then control the importunity of his own passions. Real morality never makes an appearance, the preliminary studies are still incomplete, but 'ce n'est que le provisoire qui dure', and the maxims of Conformism, Constancy and Self-Control are not effectively supplanted. It is ironic to see how the first, the most temporary of all, eventually becomes the guiding rule for the century. All the emphasis is on mastery, of mind over matter, of the 'moi' over everything else. The dualism was not easily resolved, what Descartes had put asunder perhaps no man has yet succeeded in rejoining permanently. The world of nature was reduced to numbers, and science became accessible to all. God became a convenience, necessary for a specific purpose, and thereafter buried with the rest of the roots of the tree (the Edenic apple-tree?). The revolution is complete, the 'moi' has become its own axis, self-sufficient, free, independent of other persons and things, contemptuously emancipated from the body, spurred on by the whisper 'eritis sicut dei . . .'

This was Descartes's legacy. If much of it was already in the air, his is the credit and responsibility of putting it all into a system, expressed lucidly enough for all to follow. He sowed the seed in ground well prepared for it, and for an understanding of both ground and harvest we must turn to his contemporaries in other fields. It is not from them either that we shall hear 'guyde de Dieu et compaignye d'homme.'

3: CORNEILLE

MORE than half a century has passed since Lanson first made his challenging comparison between the psychology of Descartes, as represented by the *Traité des passions*, and that of Corneille in his dramas. The question of reciprocal influence is easily settled by chronology, which shows that at all relevant times neither Descartes nor Corneille could have copied the other, but the question of common influences remains worthy of investigation. Both men had received a Jesuit education, and the cultured society in which both grew up was roughly the same, but above all it was the circles in which their influence was felt that were closely related. Philosopher and dramatist alike may be said to interpret the same *Zeitgeist*, each depending on his chosen medium, reflecting and transforming the historical image.

Descartes's philosophy starts from a position of confident strength and looks forward to a horizon of unclouded optimism, but behind this confidence and this optimism lie potential dramatic tensions of a high order. Claiming like a new Archimedes that with the lever of his thought he could move the world, Descartes exhibited hubris of authentically tragic significance. Though he himself remained unpunished, very many of those who heeded his prompting: 'Eritis sicut dei . . .' knew a full measure of tragedy. Even without his presumptuous claims on the universe, Descartes had in his dualism sown the seeds of conflict within the very heart of man. The *Cogito* is achieved at the price not only of severing all the traditional bonds by which man had been joined to other men and to the world around him, but also of splitting in two the personal union of mind and body and expelling the instincts of the latter. In his *Discours* Descartes warns weaker spirits that the path he is about to follow is perilous and testing; looking back the way we have come we cannot pretend ignorance of its dangers. For all this, as it stands Cartesianism is not a dramatic, let alone a tragic, philosophy, but its stability depends entirely on its foundations, the 'moi', which in turn can last just as long as the will holds it together.

It may be presumed that both Corneille and Descartes wrote about the world as they found it and also as they were content to find it. It will be recalled that Descartes explicitly removes religion and political institutions from the scope of the otherwise total revaluation he is about to undertake, so that in fact he concentrates on the one hand on the 'moi', pure spirit, and on the other on the world of matter, impersonal and mechanistic. A curiously similar pattern can be observed in Corneille; the sincerity of his religious beliefs is no more in question than Descartes's, but from his theatre he completely excludes problems of true, that is Christian, religion, with the notable but debatable exception of *Polyeucte* and the regrettable lapse of *Théodore*. Moreover, and paradoxically for a dramatist so closely associated with political themes, he allows virtually no free outcome to political discussion, since the inevitable result of his numerous political dramas is the assertion of an already established order.

For Descartes as for Corneille the role of the will is decisive and dominant, though it could perhaps be argued that they do not necessarily mean the same thing by the same word, and whatever one may think of Lanson's thesis as a whole, it seems perverse to deny the parallelism between the training recommended in the *Traité de passions* and the measures actually taken by so many of Corneille's characters. It remains to be seen how far Corneille shared that unclouded optimism mentioned above. A dramatist without a sense of conflict would seem to be a contradiction in terms, and it is therefore necessary in the first place to define the area in which Corneille recognized conflict as possible, and then the means by which he thought it could be resolved.

In his illuminating and highly important *Discours* (1660), Corneille explains quite clearly what he had been trying to do for thirty years and what he continued to attempt for fifteen more. Above all he reminds us of his exceptional credentials for formulating such views[1]; 'Le commentaire dont je m'y sers le

[1] Corneille, *Œuvres,* (Paris, 1862), vol. I, p. 51.

plus est l'expérience du théâtre et les réflexions sur ce que j'ai vu y plaire ou deplaire.'

This statement enables us to see both in the *Discours* and in the plays a social document, a record of public taste, no less than the expression of the author's own views. Indeed, there are reasons for supposing that Corneille's views were considerably modified in the light of public reaction, and that he might have written differently had not the fate of actual productions been his prime consideration. However that may be, his own words and the testimony of all his contemporaries agree on the fact that some themes were consistently more popular than others.

Two capital texts are these, from the *Discours du poème dramatique*:

> Sa [la tragédie] dignité demande quelque grand intérêt d'Etat, ou quelque passion plus noble et plus mâle que l'amour, telles que sont l'ambition ou la vengeance.[1] [La tragédie] veut pour son sujet une action illustre, extraordinaire, sérieuse; [la comédie] s'arrête à une action commune et enjouée.[2]

A great deal of Corneille's theatre is covered by these two sentences, and they have far-reaching implications. The major political interest recommended in the first part is by no means an open problem, nor does it involve a genuine conflict at the personal level; the rule of law will prevail, and in most cases this rule corresponds so closely to the form of government existing in Corneille's France that in his day it could hardly be challenged on moral grounds. Some of the early great plays slightly obscure the point; in *le Cid* the tragic knot is lossed by the just and wise king, in *Horace* the same, in *Cinna* it is the emperor who has become just and wise during the play, in *Polyeucte* it is Sévère, himself just and wise and legal representative of a man who, though bad, is legal emperor, but in all these cases they are acting in their official capacity, and not as mere individuals endowed with justice and wisdom. Perhaps the most striking example is *Suréna* whose eponymous hero accepts death rather than rebel against a ruler whom he despises, but who is legal king. The rebel hero of Romanticism is far away (think of Cinna's conversion

[1] op. cit. p. 24. [2] op. cit. p. 25.

from conspiracy); the lesson taught here by Corneille's heroes is the value of *discipline* in self and state.

A distinction must be made between discipline and blind obedience. *Rodogune* illustrates the point very well, and apart from being one of Corneille's own favourite plays is the only one of the early great tragedies whose strongest character is wicked. Cléopâtre, though *de facto* queen, is a murderess, and has thus no claim *de jure* to her subjects' allegiance. Her son Séleucus says:

> Lorsque l'obéissance a tant d'impiété,
> La révolte devient une nécessité.
>
> (III/v)

Here revolt is not illegal, but against illegality, and thus re-establishes the rule of law.

The difference between Cléopâtre, a common criminal, and Auguste, a legal ruler, disgusted at his own tyranny and self-reformed, brings home the point: 'Mais quoi? toujours du sang, et toujours des supplices'. (*Cinna*, IV/ii)

Since the emperor has taken himself in hand, the conspirators have no longer any right, legal or moral, to interfere, and must therefore be either destroyed or themselves reformed.

The political issue is one of great simplicity. Already in his first tragedy Corneille makes king Créon say:

> Mais le trône soutient la majesté des rois
> Au-dessus du mépris comme au-dessus des lois,
> On doit toujours respect au sceptre, à la couronne.
>
> (*Médée*, II/iii)

In his very last play, *Suréna*, the same point is made, more subtly and more regretfully, but no less cogently. For all the greatness of his services to the crown, Suréna remains a servant, and bows to royal authority, though:

> Mon crime véritable est d'avoir aujourd'hui
> Plus de nom que mon roi, plus de vertu que lui.
>
> (*Suréna*, V/ii)

Here 'crime' must be taken not as mere rhetoric, but as painful fact.

Nowhere more plainly than in *Horace* is the true political issue revealed. In a series of lines, which should be taken together, Corneille betrays the fundamental moral (for want of a better word) assumptions on which so many of his plays are based. Speaking of kings in general and Tulle in particular Camille says:

> De qui l'indépendante et sainte autorité
> Est un rayon secret de leur divinité [des dieux]
>
> (III/iii)

Tulle himself has no doubts on this score:

> J'aime à la [justice] rendre à tous, à toute heure, en tout lieu.
> C'est par elle qu'un roi se fait un demi-dieu;
>
> (V/II)

Finally old Horace expresses his creed, speaking of kings (as opposed to 'le peuple stupide'): 'C'est d'eux seuls qu'on reçoit la véritable gloire.' (V/iii)

There is no need to labour the point; time after time the legal ruler acts as *deus ex machina*, and the only requirement of legality is that the ruler should officially dispense justice, which often amounts to no more than tidying up dramatic loose ends. In the authoritarian days of Vichy the slogan was 'Travail, Famille, Patrie'; Corneille's heroes aristocratically ignore the first of these categorical imperatives, but the implications remain much the same.

From the first the individual has to come to terms with certain arbitrary and wholly external rules, which constitute his 'devoir'. Not morality, but legality, is the basis of political 'devoir', and in the last analysis the individual must bow before established order. There are, of course, other 'devoirs', equally external and arbitrary. The most famous is that 'honneur' of which don Diègue reminds his son, commanding him to ignore the moral law by inflicting death to avenge a slap, to break royal law by duelling and the law of love by killing his lover's father. The only justification for this particular 'devoir' is paternal insistence on the code of the small group to which they all belong by rank. The moral content of this is inferior even to the pure expediency of Descartes's maxim of Conformism, but is no less compulsive for that. It might obviate much misunderstanding if 'devoir' in Corneille were translated, at least mentally, not by 'duty', which has noble overtones, but simply by 'must'. In this case of Rodrigue, however, a still more compulsive 'devoir' is supplied at the end by the king: 'Pour vaincre un point d'honneur qui combat contre toi,/Laisse faire le temps, ta vaillance et ton roi.' (v/vii)

In the face of such inevitable submission, it may well be asked how the hero becomes heroic and wherein his conflict lies. The answer lies essentially in the relationship between 'devoir', an external, impersonal concept, and that other Cornelian keyword 'gloire', than which nothing could be more personal. Since the end of Cornelian drama demands the continuance of established order, the subject's ultimate 'devoir', and since the aim of the hero is the satisfaction of his 'gloire', which means public recognition of his heroic qualities, the solution of the play clearly consists in reconciling the two ideas, and such conflict as there will be on the *external* plane will derive from temporary, or apparent, incompatibility between them.

At this point the second of Corneille's phrases about tragedy becomes relevant. The first, concerning the 'intérêt d'Etat', is purely external, the second specifically excludes love as a tragic theme and insists on 'une passion plus noble et plus mâle', for example ambition or vengeance. Ambition, which makes of others stepping-stones or stumbling-blocks, and vengeance, which sees them only as targets for the knife, are isolating passions. They share precisely those characteristics which are represented by the impersonal and external demands of the state, and at the same time are sharply distinguished from the only passions, namely love and pity, which demand that other people should be recognised as persons, not things. Two quotations from *Médée*, his first, and *Suréna*, his last, tragedy express just this attitude in tones of equal cynicism:

JASON: Aussi je ne suis pas de ces amants vulgaires:
J'accommode ma flamme au bien de mes affaires.
(*Médée*, I/i)

ORODE: La seule politique est ce qui nous émeut:
On la suit, et l'amour s'y mêle comme il peut;
S'il vient, on l'applaudit; s'il manque, on s'en console.
(*Suréna*, III/iii)

Neither of these remarks is put into the mouth of a hero, but hey show sufficiently the sordid egoism and heartless statecraft aturally encouraged by such a conception. On the political plane he treatment of persons as things approaches what we could peraps call totalitarian psychology; on the individual, even heroic, evel the affinities with the solitary grandeur of Cartesianism can ardly be mistaken. It is particularly interesting to find the first, nd in some ways plainest, statement of what was to be a guiding heme for most of Corneille's drama not in a tragedy at all, but in he comedy *la Place Royale* (1634). This play is of considerable nterest in itself, as having affinities with the theme of Molière's *Aisanthrope*, but the hero, Alidor's, concluding words show a very ifferent reaction from that of Alceste; having lost his lover, ngélique, largely through his own fault, he cries:

> Je cesse d'espérer et commence de vivre;
> Je vis dorénavant puisque je vis à moi,
> Et quelques doux assauts qu'un autre objet me livre,
> C'est de moi seulement que je prendrai la loi.
>
> (v/viii)

Polyeucte is in many ways a test case. At first sight the problem or Polyeucte seems to lie in the irreconcilable claims of love for auline and obedience to his new-found God, and illustrates the amiliar love and duty conflict which scholarship candidates so eadily find in Corneille. Things are not, however, what they eem. Already on the question of obedience there is a suggestive erbal parallel; both Auguste and Tite, good emperors, apply to hemselves the ritual phrase 'maître de l'univers', but since Décie, he emperor here, is not only like them pagan, but also bad, we nd Polyeucte underlining the legal aspect of the case: 'Je n'adore u'un dieu, maître de l'univers. (v/iv)

This may be just an unconscious reminiscence, though probably ot, but it draws attention to the fact that Corneille sees Christiany as having already a *de jure* supremacy, above the *de facto* rule of agan emperors. The problem does not in fact arise again, but it ould have been odd if a writer with such an acute sense of galism had not covered his position by making God's law upreme on earth as in heaven.

Apart from this significant legal point, there are serious ground for questioning the status of religion in the play. In terms of a the other plays of Corneille, the hero risks and often suffers deat in pursuit of 'gloire', public self-justification. When Polyeuct vehemently insists on destroying the idols within moments of hi baptism, and while his wife and her former (and for all Polyeuct knows, constant) lover are together with all the local notables a an official ceremony, this is undoubtedly consistent with the pur suit of 'gloire', and though equally consistent with the operatio of divine grace, cannot be shown necessarily to derive from it. I weighing up the probabilities, it must be remembered that Poly eucte is already at the opening of the play disturbed in his honey moon happiness by his wife's dreams of Sévère and of his ow death, and that his decision to court martyrdom follows im mediately on the unexpected meeting of Pauline and Sévère, wh heroically renounce each other. On the moral plane Polyeuct cannot compete with such sublimity except by some such cours of action as he proposes and then carries out.[1]

When he says, on the news of Pauline's approaching visit t him in prison: 'Et je ne regarde Pauline/Que comme un obstacl à mon bien', (IV/ii) it is clear from the context that we are intende to interpret the last word in the theological sense of salvatio but such an interpretation is not strictly necessary within th framework of Cornelian psychology; his 'gloire', quite distin from his salvation, demands that he shall show himself capabl on the human plane of an act of renunciation not inferior to th already made by Pauline and Sévère. This is not to deny th sincerity of his conversion (the century of Rancé knew ho violent such conversions could be), still less the sincerity of Co neille's own religion, but simply to contend that there is nothin in Polyeucte's conduct which cannot adequately be motivated b the notion of 'gloire', without recourse to any supernatur elements. One has only to reproduce the same situation of a her risking death by defying an official religion, but this time sub

[1] In an admirable chapter on *Polyeucte*, Eugene Falk (*Renunciation as a Tragic Foc* Minneapolis, 1954) presents detailed textual evidence for which there is no spa here, and comes to conclusions which carry conviction, and are quite independe of the kind of thesis being advanced here.

stituting for Christianity a pagan cult (or even agnosticism) to see how exactly this play follows the pattern of all the others, with no need of theological support. A reservation should probably be made in favour of Pauline, whose cry: 'Je vois, je sais, je crois, je suis désabusée!' (v/v) is in every way more convincing, untainted as it is by considerations of 'gloire'.

Dead, Polyeucte earns a love which in life had been more dutiful than emotional, and this too is compatible with his desire for self-justification. On the evidence of the play, everything he does can be motivated by pursuit of 'gloire'; this may well be a heroic love of virtue for its own sake, of the kind that leads to martyrdom, but it is certainly not love of another person for her own sake. This should dispose of the love–duty interpretation of the play, and also give us pause before accepting it as Christian. While Christianity is certainly shown as the supreme authority in the play, it cannot be said to have any demonstrable moral superiority, for the heroic renunciation of Pauline and Sévère, prompted solely by 'gloire', is achieved without benefit of clergy, whereas even after conversion Polyeucte conspicuously falters.

It is instructive to turn back to Alidor's words quoted above from *la Place Royale* and compare his sentiments with Polyeucte's. Making every allowance for the difference between comedy and tragedy the similarity of psychology can hardly be missed. It is worth adding Angélique's farewell words, for she, like Pauline, arouses fewer misgivings than her lover:

> Un cloître est désormais l'objet de mes désirs:
> L'âme ne goûte point ailleurs de vrais plaisirs:
> (v/vii)

On this basis *Polyeucte* no longer appears the exception to the general run of Corneille's plays; the religious element can only be termed secondary. In view of this, too, it is fair to generalize from Corneille's endorsement of certain passions rather than others and to say that only those passions or affections which enable the hero to ignore the rights of other individuals as individuals, are acceptable in tragedy. *Amour-passion* is a weakness to be overcome, but selfless devotion to another is an aberration not even to be mentioned. This must not be confused with *générosité*, ideally a love of virtue (not of others) for its own sake, in practice usually meaning a passion-free state which enables the individual to go through certain outwardly laudable motions, with no necessary implications of inner benevolence, but rather of a kind of Stoic ataraxia.

Coming to the heart of the matter, the area of tragic conflict may now be defined as the exercise of the will in the pursuit of 'gloire', through the exclusion of other factors and persons. External authority, of family or state, is accepted without question, other people are to be overcome or ignored. In his last play Corneille puts into the mouth of Suréna words which fit his whole conception of the hero: 'Mon vrai crime est ma gloire, et non pas mon amour.' (v/iii) At the end of his career, again, Corneille used the by then familiar idea of La Rochefoucauld in his formulation of a truth which can be applied in retrospect to the plays of the preceding forty years: 'L'amour propre est la source en nous de tous les autres.' (*Tite et Bérénice*, I/iii)

On the internal plane this reduces the conflict simply to the elimination of all weaknesses and distractions, normally represented by the passion of love, a permanent challenge to the would-be solipsist. On the external plane, public (though not popular) recognition is an essential feature in the pursuit of 'gloire', so that the Cornelian hero is only genuine when wearing his medals, often posthumous. Inner righteousness in the face of public reprobation is as alien a concept to Corneille's drama as is unresolved mental conflict. Saint Joan and Hamlet have seen through 'gloire' in their different ways, and neither the market-place at Rouen (which he knew so well) nor the battlements of Elsinore would have suited Cornelian tragedy.

The actual terms in which characters describe what is going on inside them before they win the conflict are of considerable significance. Pauline uses a striking phrase: 'Ma raison, il est vrai, dompte mes sentiments . . . Elle n'y règne pas, elle les tyrannise.' (II/ii) And earlier: '. . . sur mes passions ma raison souveraine.' (ibid)

Séleucus, in *Rodogune*, uses the same metaphor: 'Et ma raison sur moi gardera tant d'empire,/Que je désavouerai mon cœur s'il en soupire.' (I/iii)

Auguste expresses his final triumph over cruelty, vengeance and other passions in similar words: 'Je suis maître de moi comme de l'univers;/Je le suis, je veux l'être.' (V/iii) And thirty years later Tite echoes him in expressing his own failure: 'Maître de l'univers sans l'être de moi-même.' (II/i)

Finally, to illustrate the permanence of the victory once gained, the hero looks back with lucidity and no regret. Both Rodrigue and Polyeucte (and no doubt others as well) look back on their critical decisions and each says: 'Je le ferais encore si j'avais à le faire.' (*le Cid*, III/iv and *Polyeucte*, V/iii)

With this the process is complete; first the senses and the passions they arouse must be met and neutralized by 'raison'; the clash will at first be disagreeable, but then with the elimination of the invading outer world self-mastery proves so satisfactory that no other state appears desirable; at last the hero can look back dispassionately on the struggle which was so painful while it lasted.

It will be seen that 'raison', not *volonté* is Corneille's chosen term, and in view of Descartes's equally critical use of the word, and the very different usage of other writers, this calls for some comment. For Descartes 'raison' is the same as *lumière naturelle*, that is *le pouvoir de distinguer d'entre le vrai et le faux*, short of revelation the only reliable authority and custodian of truth. Its proper use depends on eliminating *préventions et précipitation* by the constant exercise of the will, which must ensure *une ferme et constante résolution* in the faithful application of the rules of method. If all this is done, then the result will appear *clair et distinct* and can be trusted as the basis of a subsequent chain of deduction. After the *Règles*, Descartes does not seem to have used the word 'intuition' to express the type of immediate apprehension which alone reveals first principles, but he held to the notion of a privileged form of knowledge, by which, for instance, logical or other axioms are intuitively known, his *innéisme*. 'Raison' is not, therefore, *raison raisonnante*, and thus far Corneille follows Descartes, nor is it just common sense for either of them, still less the golden mean. For both it is that faculty by which man can free himself from the tyranny of the body and senses to which all animals are subject, and for both it depends intimately on the energetic use of the will. There is, however, a decisive difference, which can best be grasped by considering in each case the truths revealed by 'raison'. For Descartes, all first principles, self-awareness, logical and mathematical axioms, the nature of God, and presumably certain moral truths are intuited, and being *clair et distinct* need no further scrutiny. The Cornelian character is not a philosopher seeking for abstract truth, but a person urgently requiring guidance in a course of action which brooks no delay. What comes to such a person through 'raison' is a recognition that, for instance: 'L'amour n'est qu'un plaisir, l'honneur est un devoir,' a realization and acceptance of a categorical imperative, not a reduction of love or duty to clear and distinct ideas.

What logical axioms are to Descartes, 'devoir' is to the Cornelian character, equally self-evident, equally compulsive, but the former come from within, the latter from without. There are certainly moral implications, but not moral sanctions, in the duty imposed on the hero by environment and heredity, but in some cases the course prescribed for him is positively at variance with normal moral concepts. The duel in *le Cid*, the detestable nationalism of *Horace*, the very questionable ethics of *Cinna*, to take only the first three great plays, all have the status of moral absolutes, the 'raison' in every case accepts the situation, but for no other reason than the pressure of public convention, the Conformism of Descartes's *Morale Provisoire*. *Famille*, *Patrie* . . . are unquestionable axioms, not only for Corneille's heroes, but, as far as one can judge, for the author himself.

This being so, there is never any question of a hero being left to work out his own salvation; liberty of indifference does not exist. In place of *grâce divine et connaissance naturelle*, which help Descartes to the highest degree of liberty, the Cornelian hero need only eradicate from himself all desire except to follow the dictates of his group, 'devoir', on his way to 'gloire'. This may entail suppressing not just the distractions of the passions, but also surrendering the individual's right (if he has one) to enquiry and challenge: 'Their's not to reason why . . .'

No modern reader can fail to see the contemporary application of these rules. For the ruler, hedged with his own divinity, there is freedom, total freedom for his will, for the subject little enough. Self-mastery is the prerequisite for an acceptable sacrifice on the altar of 'gloire', external difficulties constituting no more than an obstacle race, not a conflict. Self-sacrifice in this context is a sacrifice of the weaker (more human?) to the stronger self, proper object of amour-propre.

It is time to come back to the *point de départ* for this study of Corneille. In tragedy he was explicitly aiming at *une action illustre, extraordinaire, sérieuse*, leaving to comedy *une action commune*. Contrast this with the opening words of the *Discours de la Méthode*, expressly offering a philosophy suitable for every man endowed with *bon sens*. In his theatre Corneille was writing of characters far exalted above ordinary men, to whom the rules of ordinary life need never apply, any more than they did on the stage. A nagging wife, or just indigestion, would soon make nonsense of *une action illustre*—Félix is so ordinary that he is almost comic, don Diègue is not far behind, Prusias really is comic—but the implications of this drama are that not only the heroes, not only their social group, but also the audience will subscribe to this view of how to behave in a crisis. Here is the real point; the very bourgeois Corneille, with all the careful traditions of a Norman lawyer family, himself a good family man and sound Catholic, looked up at the aristocratic world above him and was dazzled. For them to behave with lofty egoism, invoking the honour of their noble families, or the debt their country owed them, seemed to him as natural as it would be unspeakable in himself and his kind.

This situation may perhaps be best described as a theoretical moral dualism based on class, and on something that looks perilously like a fallacy; all tragic heroes are of noble birth, they all obey certain rules peculiar to themselves and ignore those of ordinary men, therefore all those who want to qualify as heroes in real life must ignore ordinary rules. At times it looks almost as though one could add; all those who are of noble birth can automatically regard themselves as above ordinary moral codes.

'Gloire' is not bourgeois respectability, self-mastery is not bourgeois temperance, great nobles are not always good citizens. This view was compounded of several elements: the cult of the great man, specially inspired by Plutarch, natural snobbery, respect for authority, reverence for royalty, and a fair share of flattery no doubt all enter into Corneille's view of the tragic hero. It is these factors, from which Descartes, for example is free, which probably account for Corneille's distinctive contribution to the development which may conveniently be traced from the *Cogito*. Conformism for Descartes had been only *faute de mieux*, and though this particular maxim was never supplanted, he never endows it with a higher moral value than that of expediency. Corneille, as has just been seen, extends the notion of conformism by making obedience to an *aristocratic* code a pseudo-moral imperative, a 'devoir' with no hint of the provisional. In addition, like Descartes he stresses the importance of the will in furthering the supreme aim of self-fulfilment, but while paying lip-service to reason, in practice he equates virtue with effort, and makes its sole justification public acclaim. Thus he has the best of both worlds; the solipsist hero is honoured by the world he rejects. In external matters, the acceptance of legal authority, in internal ones single-minded pursuit of 'gloire', are the axes prescribed by Corneille. Neither true morality nor balance has any place in the system.

The fact that philosopher and playwright offer a substantially similar picture, despite differences in temperament, working conditions and medium, suggests that the real world of history in which they both lived provided a background too emphatic to be ignored. It is neither the abstract 'moi' nor the tragic hero who rubbed shoulders daily with Descartes and Corneille, but men of flesh and blood, and it is to them and the records they left that we should turn for a fuller perspective.

4: RETZ

THE close connexion between Corneille's drama and the real life of his day is vividly brought out in the *Mémoires* of Paul de Gondi, Cardinal de Retz.[1] This remarkable man combined a high degree of literary felicity with an unrivalled experience of political intrigue, but foremost among his qualities is lucidity. The events of the Fronde, in which he played a leading part, and which make up the bulk of his *Mémoires*, are presented in much the same spirit as one of Corneille's plays, and indeed on at least two occasions Retz actually quotes Corneille (*Horace* on p. 310, *le Cid* on p. 745) at an interlocutor. The *Mémoires* are addressed to a lady, whose identity remains conjectural, but who is generally thought to have been Mme de Sévigné, a more than usually fervent admirer of Corneille. On numerous occasions some new development is presented in theatrical terms, variously revealing Retz as heroic actor and producer. Retz, like Descartes and Corneille, had been a pupil of the Jesuits, in his case at the Collège de Clermont, and this 'âme peut-être la moins ecclésiastique qui fût dans l'univers' (3), as he describes himself, proved himself none the less a competent theologian when the profession he had been unable to escape demanded public display of his talents. Retz was in every way a man of parts. His *Mémoires* treat with equal lucidity and skill the exploits in which he was involved, be they amorous, martial, political or even religious, and show from the inside the workings of one of those aristocratic spirits which Corneille had perforce observed from without. Though each man was fully acquainted with the person and work of the other, there is no more need than in the case of Corneille and Descartes to postulate direct influence; once again it is the spirit of the age manifesting itself in different ways according to the context. The behaviour of Retz and his fellow Frondeurs, together with his retrospective analysis, may be seen as a practical experi-

[1] All references are to pages in the 1956 edition of Cardinal de Retz, *Mémoires*, in *Bibl. de la Pléiade*.

ment where Cartesian philosophy and Cornelian drama had been rather the theoretical formulation of certain rules and reactions.

As one would expect, the work is intensely personal, constituting as it does a sort of *apologia pro vita sua*, and more objective historians of the Fronde have found it hard to share Retz's assessment of his own part. In writing his account of what he did and why he did it, Retz is motivated at all stages by concern for his 'gloire', and when he suppresses or falsifies facts this is to be attributed less to defects of memory than of probity. In the general scheme of the development being studied in these pages, Retz's self-analysis and self-justification may be taken as an unusually detailed portrait of a 'moi', whether 'désaxé' or not remains to be seen. His own character and conduct form the framework of a structure into which he incorporates his judgements on others and on the wider problems, particularly political, of his age.

A man can of course be devout without wanting to make the Church his career, but Retz makes it abundantly clear from the first that his soul was anything but ecclesiastical. Forced into the Church by considerations of family pride, for the see of Paris had been in the family ever since the favour of Catherine de Medicis had first drawn them to France, and his uncle, the present incumbent, had been the first to enjoy archiepiscopal dignity, Retz began building up a *persona* of his choice. By accompanying his pious and charitable aunt, Mme de Maignelais, on her rounds of almsgiving he became identified in the minds of the poor and needy with that good woman's virtue and much better-known than most prelates of the century. Going even further 'Je faisais même un peu le dévot, et j'allais aux conférences de Saint-Lazare' (27), given by Monsieur Vincent (de Paul), former preceptor in his parents' household and now supported by them in his good works. Aged about twenty-five, he found that the prospect of succeeding his uncle as Archbishop flattered his vanity: 'Je me résolus donc, non pas seulement à suivre, mais encore à faire ma profession.' (30) An early example of his candour follows as he tells how he lost two prospective mistresses, one to Port Royal, the other to a rival, and comments:

'Voilà de quoi devenir un saint.' (ibid) He was, however, careful not to overdo it, and did not become a 'dévot' for fear of being unable to continue the act: 'mais j'estimais beaucoup les dévots; et à leur égard, c'est un des plus grands points de la piété.' (ibid.) So the build-up continues, and the first brief part of his *Mémoires* ends with the death of Louis XIII, Mazarin in power and Retz assured of the Coadjutorship. He concludes:

> Il me semble que je n'ai été jusques ici que dans le parterre, ou tout au plus dans l'orchestre, à jouer et à badiner avec les violons; je vas monter sur le théâtre, où vous verrez des scènes, non pas dignes de vous, mais un peu moins indignes de votre attention.(43)

His description is fully justified by what follows. His ambition could only be fulfilled by being a successful Archbishop of Paris, and this he recognized as presenting peculiar difficulties to one of his temperament. The scandalous follies of his uncle were a potent warning of the dangers threatening his own career:

> . . . tous les obstacles et de conscience et de gloire que j'opposerais au dérèglement ne seraient que des digues très mal assurées. Je pris, après six jours de réflexion, le parti *de faire le mal par dessein, ce qui est sans comparaison le plus criminel* devant Dieu, mais ce qui est sans doute le plus sage devant le monde . . . parce que l'on évite, par ce moyen, le plus dangereux ridicule qui se puisse rencontrer dans notre profession, qui est celui de mêler à contretemps le péché dans la dévotion (italics in original.) (44)

A few lines later he explains and justifies himself: 'Je pris une ferme résolution de remplir exactement tous les devoirs de ma profession, et d'être aussi homme de bien pour le salut des autres, que je pourrais être méchant pour moi-même.'

These startling sentiments speak for themselves. It is odd to find the vocabulary of Descartes and Corneille put to such use, but it is the same vocabulary, *gloire*, *devoir*, *ferme résolution*, with the same meaning. Exclude the mention of God and salvation and the argument is not unfamiliar. Like any Cartesian or Cornelian hero Retz fears to fall a prey to passions which might compromise his ambition; his reason holds up to him the example of his uncle as one to be avoided at all costs, and at the same time warns him that he can only fail in any attempt to repress the carnal appetites of which he has so far been the willing victim; there is then nothing left but to plan rationally a course of action to be implemented by firm resolve. The result is a dualism more bizarre than anything yet seen, but still the natural product of tendencies already observed in Descartes and Corneille when applied to the problems of daily life. Lucidity could hardly go further, but in Retz's defence it should be emphazed that the only evil contemplated was that of sexual licence, and that the example of piety, charity and discipline which he proposed to set in public, for whatever motives, was sorely needed in Paris. There is a certain bravado, or at least panache, about this profession of cynicism which should not be allowed to obscure the logic of Retz's position. The divorce between public 'devoir' and private indulgence marks a turning-point in the development of the 'moi', for Retz claims to believe in God and yet *deliberately* (after six days thought) makes a choice, which, as he says himself, will offend God and may damn himself. It is, of course, true that no pupil of the Jesuits would regard salvation as irretrievably lost until the end, when timely repentance might avert the full consequences of such a choice and enable a man to have literally the best of both worlds. The point did not escape Pascal.

This double scale of values becomes a main theme as Retz launches into his account of the Fronde, beginning with a description of how Mazarin collected the strings of power into his hand. The conduct of his fellow-clergy is thus described: 'Le clergé, qui donne toujours l'exemple de la servitude, la prêchait aux autres sous le titre d'obéissance.' (51)

The *mot* should be recalled when we come on to Bossuet.

When events seemed to offer him the chance he had been seeking, Retz speaks again of the fundamental dualism of his character and his office:

> Je rappelai tout ce que mon imagination m'avait jamais fourni de plus éclatant et de plus proportionné aux vastes desseins; je permis à mes sens de se laisser chatouiller par le titre de chef de parti, que j'avais toujours honoré dans les *Vies* de Plutarque . . . Les affaires brouillent les espèces, elles honorent même ce qu'elles ne justifient pas; et les vices d'un archévêque peuvent être, dans une infinité de rencontres, les vertus d'un chef de parti. (96)

These heroic aspirations can be compared with Cornelian pursuit of 'gloire', likewise inspired by Plutarch, but if one sometimes wonders what happens to the Cornelian hero when he is being neither tragic nor heroic the last phrase suggests an answer.

M. A. Adam has a telling comment on the *élite* of this generation: 'Elle veut être lucide, et dans ses plus grands désordres elle s'observe et se raille.'[1] It would be natural to equate *lucide* with something like Cartesian *clair et distinct* or Cornelian *raison*, but it is the last word, *qui se raille*, which shows the essential difference between philosopher and dramatist on the one hand and Archbishop on the other. Cartesian dualism is so radical that it is hard to realize that a man of Descartes's intelligence should be so carried away by enthusiasm and a sense of mission as to ignore this glaring defect in his system. Cornelian heroism is so singleminded that the hero is blind to the logic of events and makes a categorical imperative of his own wishful thinking. Neither Descartes nor Corneille is lucid as Retz is, because neither is willing to abandon high seriousness for a moment's self-mockery. This is particularly striking in Corneille's case, since his competence as a comic writer is outstanding, and he must have known better than most tragic authors how narrow is the gap between high tragedy and farce. Matamore is uncomfortably near the *Cid*, but the distance is maintained, Félix is almost a figure of fun, Prusias still more, but by and large the hero in Corneille is insulated from banality. He acts according to his 'devoir', which is so presented as to appear respectable, even when its implications lead to the sort of disaster seen in *Horace*. For Corneille 'devoir' is an imperative, as it is for Descartes, even if it no longer has any moral content, and 'gloire' is the ultimate self-justifying goal, to be reconciled with 'devoir' as the curtain falls. Retz sees things more realistically, perhaps more cynically. 'Devoir' for him means performance of prescribed functions, and praise goes to efficiency rather than conviction. 'Gloire' is paramount, and it is better not to search too diligently into its foundations. The motive in Corneille is often no more laudable than it is in Retz; the difference is that Retz sees it more clearly

[1] *Histoire de la Littérature française au* XVIIe *siècle*, vol. II p. 19.

and records it dispassionately. The will plays the same part in all three authors, but only in Retz does reason recognize the moral bankruptcy of a voluntaristic ethic.

Having decided to make a bid for this role of leader, *chef de parti*, Retz gives some idea of how he thought it should be played. At an early stage in hostilities, when the question of leadership had still to be settled, the duc d'Elbeuf, of the House of Lorraine, fancied himself for the part, but Retz had other ideas. He wanted Conti as titular leader, and to that end persuaded M. de Longueville, M. de Bouillon and the maréchal de la Mothe to support his candidate one after the other. He explains why:

> Nous avions concerté de ne faire paraître sur le théâtre ces personnages que l'un après l'autre, parce que nous avions considéré que rien ne touche et n'émeut tant les peuples, et même les compagnies [Parlement] qui tiennent toujours beaucoup du peuple, que la variété des spectacles. (149)

These words recall those which close the first part of his book, and show Retz this time as producer rather than actor. In fact his candidate won, but Retz had no illusions about his character. After a long list of portraits he writes:

> J'oubliais presque M. le prince de Conti, ce qui est un bon signe pour un chef de parti. Je ne crois pas vous le pouvoir mieux dépeindre qu'en vous disant que ce chef de parti était un zéro, qui ne multipliait que parce qu'il était prince du sang. (155)

Elsewhere he elaborates on the *chef de parti* notion:

> L'on ne connaît pas ce que c'est que le parti, quand l'on s'imagine que le chef en est le maître: son véritable service y est presque toujours combattu par les intérêts, même assez souvent imaginaires, des subalternes. (574)

This last statement sounds like an almost peevish complaint that in real life the interests of others can not only not be ignored but may even restrict the hero in the exercise of his will.

The theatrical metaphors of Retz have a significant echo in a scene he describes just after his successful conflict with Elbeuf. Pursuing his advantage, Retz accompanied Mme de Longueville and Mme de Bouillon to the Hotel de Ville, where their beauty

s they stood on the steps, each clasping her child, moved the
eople to wild enthusiasm. That evening, Noirmoutier returned
rom leading a skirmish into the suburbs and, still in fighting rig,
nd accompanied by three other officers, came into Mme de
ongueville's room in the Hôtel de Ville: 'Ce mélange d'écharpes
leues, de dames, de cuirasses, de violons, qui étaient dans la
alle, de trompettes, qui étaient dans la place, donnait un spectacle
ui se voit plus souvent dans les romans qu'ailleurs.' (151)

Retz and Noirmoutier then jestingly identify the situation and
haracters with those described in d'Urfé's best-selling novel,
'*Astrée*. This readiness to see life, and civil war at that, in terms
f drama and fiction is most revealing. It is natural enough that
etz should draw such comparisons when he came to write after
he events, but all the evidence suggests a conscious awareness of
he similarity at the time.

Retz is sometimes attractive in the brazen audacity with which
e admits to playing a part. On one particularly solemn occasion
n the Parlement he had to reply to a violent attack, purporting
o emanate from the Queen. He recounts the episode in terms of
la pièce qui s'allait jouer' and 'la comédie que vous allez voir'
428), decides to treat the letter as coming from Mazarin, and
hen: 'Comme ma mémoire ne me fournit rien dans l'antiquité
ui eût rapport à mon dessein, je fis un passage d'un latin le plus
ur et le plus approchant des anciens qui fût en mon pouvoir . . .'
431) Called upon to answer the attack he says: 'Je n'y répondrai,
Messieurs, . . . que par un passage d'un ancien qui me vient dans
'esprit.' (432)

Though he enjoyed pulling wires behind the scenes, Retz is, as
ere, perfectly at ease in the limelight. We see him at his best in
nother incident in the Parlement. (553) He tells how a heated
xchange ends with La Rochefoucauld pinning him between the
eaves of a double door, and how he would probably have lost
is life but for the intervention of Champlâtreux, son of the
Premier President, Molé, who despised him but whom he
espected. A few moments later a hired assassin almost reached
Retz, who was protected at the last moment by his friend Argen-
euil's diversion. These incidents are important, because they

show Retz cool and courageous in the face of real and imminen danger, and remind us that he was running no idle risk. Havin behaved so creditably in what might have been tragedy, Retz wa able on the following day to add a comic epilogue. This time h was passing near the Parlement, in his official capacity of Archbishop-Coadjutor rather than politician, at the head of a processio of clergy, when he met Condé, his assassin's paymaster, with L Rochefoucauld and others, in his coach and accompanied b armed men. Some menacing cries were heard, but Condé to knew how to play a part: 'Il fit taire ceux de sa suite qui avaient commencé à crier; il se mit à genou pour recevoir ma bénédiction; je la lui donnai, le bonnet en tête, je l'ôtai aussitôt, et je lui fis un très profonde révérence. (561)

This constant play-acting and concern for visible effects is th keynote of all Retz's behaviour as he describes it in his *Mémoires* It hardly matters whether he acted as he says or for the reasons he gives, the impression he wants to convey is what counts. His 'gloire' demands that he should be by turn witty, brave, unscrupulous and gallant. No other rule is admitted save that of success, no other judge qualified save himself. Morality and truth have become simply irrelevant to a self-gratification which knows no such bounds.

His attitude to others is quite in line with what has already been said. Like Corneille, but for different ends, he preferred 'quelque passion plus noble et plus mâle', and love for him seems to mean no more than that 'dérèglement des mœurs' which an archbishop should take pains to conceal. Not the least entertaining part of his book is that dealing with his numerous amours, and one could quote extensively to show how light-hearted and agile Retz proved himself in such affairs. A single sentence gives the measure of the man. Writing of Mme de Longueville, on whom he had looked covetously for some time, he says: 'Le bénéfice n'était pas vacant, mais il n'était pas desservi. M. de la Rochefoucauld était en possession; mais il était en Poitou.' (132)

The ecclesiastical turn of phrase assorts well with the realism of outlook.

Most of the time other people are for Retz tools or puppets.

Inhibited by his cloth from total freedom of action, Retz needed a man of straw to do what he was told. Beaufort was just the man:

Il me fallait un fantôme, mais il ne me fallait qu'un fantôme; et par bonheur pour moi il se trouva que ce fantôme fut petit-fils d'Henri le Grand; qu'il parla comme on parle aux Halles, ce qui n'est pas ordinaire aux enfants d'Henri le Grand, et qu'il eut de grands cheveux bien longs et bien blonds. Vous ne pouvez vous imaginer le poids de cette circonstance, vous ne pouvez concevoir l'effet qu'ils firent dans le peuple. (159)

More often than not Retz's judgements on others are lapidary rather than profound. The death of Louis XIII was followed by an attempt by Beaufort to govern 'dont il était moins capable que son valet de chambre' (42), assisted by the Bishop of Beauvais, 'plus idiot que tous les idiots de votre connaissance' and 'une bête mitrée' (48). Mazarin's ally, M. de Candale, 'n'avait rien de grand que les canons' (345), another, Provost, 'chanoine de Notre-Dame et conseiller au Parlement, autant fou qu'un homme le peut être, au moins de tous ceux à qui l'on laisse la clef de leur chambre.' (734) Sometimes, though, the criticism is directly relevant to the events in which the characters are concerned. Thus the failure of Parlement to exploit the arrest of Broussel, which precipitated the first Fronde, is explained by the character of the leaders: 'Le président Violé avait toute sa vie été un homme de plaisir et de nulle application à son métier; le bon homme Broussel était vieilli entre les sacs, dans la poudre de la grande chambre, avec plus de réputation d'intégrité que de capacité.' (103)

The balance is a nice one; remembering Retz's own decision to combine business with pleasure, one can understand his scorn for a man who had not bothered to acquire professional competence, and at the same time for one whose honesty did not redeem dullness. A very similar point is made in a judgement Retz quotes on Richelieu: 'aussi pédant en amour qu'il était honnête homme pour les autres choses.' (564)

It would be hard to associate Retz with either of the characteristics imputed to his fellow Cardinal, but his use of the word 'honnête' is by no means self-evident. Mere pleasure seeking or mere integrity are as incompatible with what he calls 'honnêteté' as the pedantry just mentioned. His portrait of Gaston d'Orléans adds something to the conception:

> M. le duc d'Orléans avait, à l'exception du courage, tout ce qui était nécessaire à un honnête homme; mais comme il n'avait rien, sans exception, de tout ce qui peut distinguer un grand homme, il ne trouvait rien dans lui-même qui pût ni suppléer ni même soutenir sa faiblesse. (152)

The theme of Gaston's notorious cowardice recurs several times and gives Retz the chance of another quip: 'Je crois que vous êtes moins surprise de la conduite de Monsieur en voyant ses principes; ceux de la peur se peuvent encore moins attaquer que tous les autres: ils sont inabordables.' (739)

The pattern becomes clear enough when these strictures on Violé, Broussel, Richelieu and Gaston d'Orléans are related to the portrait Retz offers of himself: painstaking attention to the details of his calling, both theological and charitable, impetuosity and wit in affairs of the heart, intrepidity and resource in the face of danger. One is invited to see in Retz's extended self-portrait, as it appears on every page of the book, that of the perfect *honnête homme*, and that is why those defects from which he knew (or thought) himself to be free are so much emphasized when he comes to criticize others.

A very complete picture can be filled in by collating the good and bad points ascribed to his sitters in what he calls his gallery of portraits. Condé is praised for his genius as a general, criticized for the narrowness of his intellectual training; his brother-in-law, Longueville, is praised for some obvious good qualities but finally condemned 'parce qu'il eut toujours des idées qui furent infiniment au-dessus de sa capacité' (153); Elbeuf 'le premier prince que la pauvreté ait avili; et peut-être jamais homme n'a eu moins que lui l'art de se faire plaindre dans sa misère' (154); Bouillon and Turenne both come in for warm praise as men of solidity and judgement; La Rochefoucauld is criticized for 'une irrésolution habituelle' and, improbable as it may seem coming from Retz, for his '*Maximes*, qui ne marquent pas assez de foi en la vertu' (155); Molé is put in the highest class, with Condé, for courage, but 'il s'en est fallu beaucoup que son esprit n'ait été si grand que son cœur' and, still more significant:

> il jugeait toujours des actions par les hommes, et presque jamais des hommes par les actions. Comme il avait été nourri dans les formes du Palais, tout ce qui était extraordinaire lui etait suspect. Il n'y a guère de disposition plus dangereuse en ceux qui se rencontrent dans les affaires où les règles ordinaires n'ont plus de lieu. (157)

It is obvious enough how the positive qualities can be applied to Retz; for the rest the remark about Elbeuf must be read in the context of Retz's own fall from prosperity, and the strange comment on the *Maximes* is probably best explained by remembering that Retz was perfectly prepared to acknowledge the existence of virtue in others, M. Vincent is an obvious example, so long as he did not have to practise it himself, and so long as it was not identified with the claims of 'honnêteté'. The last judgement, on Molé, is particularly relevant to this study, for Molé belonged to just the same background of *noblesse de robe* as Corneille, but did not in real life expect to deal with the supermen or 'actions éclatantes et illustres' with which the tragic theatre was concerned. The distinction comes out largely as a social one, with Retz plainly seeing himself as one of the warrior caste, a born leader by blood if not by profession. As for judging men by their actions, the test of the Fronde proved the strength and weakness of all the participants, and it is in the light of their record on this active service that Retz judges his contemporaries.

In this connexion he makes two remarks of a general and most revealing nature to show that he was sufficiently lucid to make allowances for his own errors of judgement whether they arose from good or bad qualities within himself. Of his friend Noirmoutier, who let him down badly, he writes: 'L'inclination naturelle que nous avons pour quelqu'un se glisse imperceptiblement dans le pardon des offenses, sous le titre de générosité.' (327)

Again, speaking of an interview between Gaston and the Queen he observes: 'La plus grande imperfection des hommes est la complaisance qu'ils trouvent à se persuader que les autres ne sont pas exempts des défauts qu'ils se reconnaissent à eux-mêmes.' (589)

This is as true of Retz as anyone else, and no doubt explains the comparative failure of a man so brilliant. Some of his post-mortems on his own conduct seem to bear out this statement. His own courage led him to put too high a price on sheer audacity, and at the same time his rather devious mind attributes too much credulity to the general public. Thus the incident of the door, described earlier, he blames partly on his own error of judgement. Asked just before the incident whether he was armed, he did not deny it, and this he finds unpardonable for a cleric, though his reasons may not convince everyone:

> Il y a des matières sur lesquelles il est constant que le monde veut être trompé. Les occasions justifient assez souvent, à l'égard de la réputation publique, les hommes de ce qu'ils font contre leur profession: je n'en ai jamais vu qui les justifient de ce qu'ils disent qui y soit contraire. (553)

The picture so far traced has few elements which cannot be related to what has already been seen in Descartes and Corneille. Ambition is Retz's end, skill his means, other people either obstacles, puppets or conquests, depending on sex and status, almost never equals. The will sets the pace; reason steers; morals and scruples are thrown overboard. 'Gloire' is, as ever, the ultimate goal, 'honnêteté' the quality of the acceptable man; acceptable, that is, in battle, in Parlement, in salon or in bedroom. The 'moi' in Retz appears more nakedly arbiter of its own conduct than in the others, because no cloak of fiction or abstraction covers its identity. God is not called in even as a convenience, he is relegated to the background together with such other irrelevant factors as respectability, a bourgeois weakness, and civic duty. More lucid than Descartes and Corneille, Retz shows the *reductio ad absurdum* of a voluntarist ethic based on individual self-sufficiency.

It must be said for completeness that by the time Retz came to write his *Mémoires* disgrace had taught him that there is more to human relationships than just buying and selling. On the last page of his book he tells how Noirmoutier, whom he had rewarded, deserted him, and comments of all who act thus:

> Leur première application est de jeter dans le monde des bruits sourds de mécontentements qu'ils feignent avoir de ceux qu'ils veulent

abandonner; et la seconde est de diminuer, autant qu'ils peuvent, le poids des obligations qu'ils leur ont. (882)

The voice is that of La Rochefoucauld, though the hand is that of Retz, but the paragraph ends in a different vein:

L'unique remède contre ces sortes de déplaisirs, qui sont plus sensibles dans les disgrâces que les disgrâces mêmes, est de ne jamais faire le bien que pour le bien même. Ce moyen est le plus assuré: un mauvais naturel est incapable de le prendre, parce que c'est la plus pure vertu qui nous l'enseigne. Un bon cœur n'y a guère moins de peine, parce qu'il joint aisément, dans les motifs des grâces qu'il fait, à la satisfaction de sa conscience les considérations de son amitié.

This then is the faith in virtue which Retz finds lacking in the *Maximes*, but he waits until the end of the book before professing it.

There is one aspect of Retz's work which sets him apart from most of the other authors of his day, and which reveals him as an unusually acute political observer. The 'moi desaxé' is, by definition, that of the individual, and those authors who are primarily concerned with the individual have little or no time for the mass. It is very much to Retz's credit that he not only recognized, but tried to exploit the mass of the Parisian people at a time when most men of his birth and breeding regarded them as unworthy of consideration.

One of the main disruptive elements facing the individual in the seventeenth century was the collapse of the feudal hierarchy and power and its replacement by the absolutism, first of Richelieu and then of Mazarin. Across the Channel protest had come from Parliament, but in France the Parlement, never a comparable institution, had become further debased as a mere rubber stamp for the will of the minister. Retz, who had himself paid for logs to warm the exiled Queen of England, freezing in destitution in the Louvre, knew well enough the realities of revolution, and that, with no effective Parliament to lead, the Paris mob could assume the same importance as in the days of the League, when Guise, Henri III and Henri IV had fought for its favours. It is too early to speak of class warfare, but it is on the horizon. All this Retz saw and understood.

Explaining how previous rulers, right back into the Middle Ages, had bowed before the law, except when inspired by ignorance or wickedness to defy it, Retz shows how the present state of anarchy has come about:

> Le cardinal de Richelieu leur succéda, qui fit, pour ainsi parler, un fonds de toutes ces mauvaises intentions et de toutes ces ignorances des deux derniers siécles, pour s'en servir selon son intérêt. Il les déguisa en maximes utiles et nécessaires pour établir l'autorité royale; . . . il forma, dans la plus légitime des monarchies, la plus scandaleuse et la plus dangereuse tyrannie qui ait peut-être jamais asservi un Etat . . . (64)
>
> Il n'y a que Dieu qui puisse subsister par lui seul. Les monarchies les plus établies et les monarques les plus autorisés ne se soutiennent que par l'assemblage des armes et des lois; et cet assemblage est si nécessaire que les unes ne se peuvent maintenir sans les autres. (65)

In the sphere of politics Retz is quite clear that this break with the legitimate principles of the past, and their replacement by power in its crudest form, is what is wrong, and in rebelling against the established order he did not consider himself bound by an authority which he repudiated. In the absence of any accredited representative of legitimacy, only anarchy could follow from the clash of selfish interests among the Frondeurs.

Much of what Retz then proceeds to say about Richelieu could equally be applied to himself, and also has affinities of an unmistakable kind with Cornelian tragedy: 'Il voulut régner selon son inclination, qui ne se donnait point de règles . . . Il aimait la gloire beaucoup plus que la morale ne le permet . . . Il avait assez de religion pour ce monde . . .' (66)

Thus far one Cardinal seems worth another, but Retz concludes that Richelieu's greatness earned him: 'cette sorte de respect . . . qui dans un Etat où il n'y a plus de lois, supplée au moins pour quelque temps à leur défaut.' (68)

One could not ask for a clearer exposition of the heroic principle and voluntaristic ethic as applied to politics.

When he comes on to Mazarin, Retz makes just the point we are trying to illustrate; successful heroics depend on real heroes. Mazarin, says Retz, lacked all greatness, 'il se moqua de la religion', and instead of dealing gently with the 'assoupissement' of the body politic, as befitted his meanness, tried to act like his predecessor. The result was the anarchy of the Fronde, which failed miserably, and indeed only intensified the moral anarchy, until the principle of legitimacy was at last reasserted with the reunion of power and crown under the personal rule of Louis XIV.

His insight extends to the common people and their reactions to events. Retz first came into prominence in 1648 by subduing the mob on the barricades thrown up in protest against the arrest of Broussel. He comments with rare realism:

> J'ajoutai tout ce que je crus pouvoir adoucir cette commune [i.e. the mob]; et je n'y eus pas beaucoup de peine, parce que l'heure du souper approchait. Cette circonstance vous paraîtra ridicule, mais elle est fondée; et j'ai observé qu'à Paris, dans les émotions populaires, les plus échauffés ne veulent pas ce qu'ils appellent se désheurer. (93)

Heroes may not take time off for meals, but Retz knows that the big battalions march on their stomachs.

Two odd facts reported by Retz suggest that the people had a sense of history and also that English affairs had not gone unnoticed. He speaks of finding an officer wearing a gorget with the image of Henri III's assassin on it and the inscription 'Saint Jacques Clément' (99). On another occasion he writes: 'Le peuple fit de grandes clameurs; nous entendîmes même quelques voix qui criaient: "République!" ' (247)

He seems to have been almost alone in taking note of public reactions, and on one occasion, when he tried to convince the Queen of popular feeling, admits: 'Je connus . . . qu'il est impossible que la cour conçoive ce que c'est que le public. La flatterie, qui en est la peste, l'infecte toujours au point qu'elle lui cause un délire incurable sur cet article.' (499)

He makes just the same point in describing the Court's return to Paris: 'Elle [la cour] y fut reçue comme les rois l'ont toujour été et le seront toujours, c'est-à-dire avec acclamations qui ne signifient rien, que pour ceux qui prennent plaisir à se flatter.' (299)

Remarks like these show how few illusions he had about the sort of popular support he himself courted, and how total was his absence of sympathy for the people, despite his insight into their minds and feelings. This is due primarily to his own pride as an aristocrat, as the following explanation of why he had not packed the Palais with his own men during the door episode shows: 'Il n'y eût rien eu de si odieux que de mettre les gens, ou du peuple ou du bas étage, dans ces sortes de lieux, où l'on ne laisse entrer, dans l'ordre, que des personnes de condition.' (555)

It is one thing to win the people's favour by bringing out on a balcony a blonde and handsome prince who speaks their language, quite another to let them into the home of privilege. The habit of treating people as things, which in his own class applied to individuals, in the classes below applied to the mass collectively. It is only right, though, to give Retz his due for seeing, however regretfully and with whatever qualifications, that politics was no longer a game for aristocrats alone, and that the rules which applied to the nobility were not those observed by the commoners.

In trying to assess the meaning of all that Retz did and wrote the surest method is to follow his own predilection for theatrical metaphors. The Fronde, the people in it and its various aspects are described in just the same way as Corneille describes his own successes and failures, as well as his guiding principle, in his *Examens* and *Discours* (published in 1660, and thought to be roughly contemporaneous with the composition of the *Mémoires*). Two principles are here involved: the right of self-criticism and the histrionic view of life. The latter is evident from the very beginning of the *Mémoires*, and has the effect of presenting Retz as actor-producer, the other main figures as rival actors or as puppets manipulated by Retz, and the mass of the people as the audience. To some extent the march of history favoured such a view, because the complete failure of the Fronde, and the death or disgrace of the leading characters, and above all the new régime at Versailles, enabled the whole episode to be seen with some detachment after ten years or so.

We have seen how the spur of ambition led Retz to make the most of the ecclesiastical role which had been imposed on him against his will, and how he prepared himself in private and in public for the opening night, so to speak. When, to use his own image, he steps upon the stage, his dual role of actor-producer emphasizes what he believes to be his complete control of his situation. He begins to write, as well as to act, his own part, with brilliant improvisations like the bogus Latin quotation. At the same time his presentation of Beaufort, blonde idol of the masses, on the balcony, or the beautiful and pathetically maternal Mme de Longueville and Mme de Bouillon on the steps of the Hôtel de Ville reveal him as a talented impresario. He is not only *maître de soi*, he has learnt how to make the crowd dance to his tune. The fact that he despises the dance, and hardly cares for the tune, adapted as it is to popular taste, does not detract from the sheer virtuosity of the performance.

Retz holds to no solipsism in the sense of a lofty isolation like that seen in either Descartes or Corneille, but his dependence on an audience reaction which he openly despises forces him back into a sort of isolation which is lonely without being lofty. The tragic hero is only concerned with 'gloire', he does not stop to analyse what it may be worth in itself. The realism and lucidity of Retz take full account of the audience and its weaknesses—who else would have allowed for a refreshment interval on the day of the barricades?—but he remains committed to a 'gloire' in which he can hardly believe, just as the actor once on the stage has to accept the play. Willpower drives him on to the only goal he knows, and he sees his rivals driven in the same way; it was La Rochefoucauld who described the whole affair which nearly cost him his life as 'une triste farce'.

This is where the importance of self-criticism comes in. Granted that one sometimes has no choice but to act foolishly or wrongly, it is always a consolation to be able to denounce one's error before anyone else. Very much as Corneille tended to disarm criticism by including comments unfavourable as well as favourable in his *Examens*, so Retz forestalls attack by claiming to know better than anyone else what he was about and how he slipped up. The posthumous publication of his book makes no difference to its role as long-term apologia. This defensive device operates in many different ways. It can be used subtly for transferring commendations of others to one's own account, or for inviting comparison between their defects and one's own qualities. Thus Retz's criticism of Gaston as lacking only courage to be 'honnête' invites comparison with his own often emphasized courage, and thus acceptance of his own claims to 'honnêteté'. A more oblique way of patting himself on the back is by ascribing mistakes to excessive generosity or boldness, qualities which elsewhere he warmly praises in others. So much candour may deceive, just as the supposed clarity of Cartesianism may make us doubt at first whether it is not we who are at fault in finding dualism there, or as the sublimity of tragic poetry may momentarily blind us to the brutality of a Horace. One must ask where Retz got his standards before accepting his version of 'honnêteté', 'devoir', 'gloire'. The answer seems to be that he either gets them from within, from the promptings of his own pride and ambition, or accepts, albeit with scorn, conformism in externals. 'Devoir' is a series of motions appropriate to one's office or position, devoid of moral connotation, 'honnêteté' is worldly success, extrapolated from what he considers his own best qualities, 'gloire' is the meaningless applause of people whom he treats as no better than *bêtes-machines* without intelligence. As no one else can know his motives better than he, no one can judge his measure of success or failure except by external criteria. Much of Retz's procedure of self-justification is closely similar to the technique of his Jesuit masters in *guider l'intention*: he cannot easily deny what happened (though he sometimes does even that) but he can ascribe other causes to the effects. At the heart of all this activity self-gratification is the only enduring reward. Lifemanship in externals, amour-propre for the rest are the twin poles of Retz's design for living. He rejects the authority of the state as usurped, the divine law as inconvenient and plays the hero with his tongue in his cheek. Despite all one cannot help liking him.

The Fronde neatly divides a century in which regnal years are just misleading. The sort of plays Corneille was writing up to his withdrawal from the theatre in 1652 owed their success largely to the fact that the audience was prepared to share the same heroic assumptions as the author. The Fronde put an end to such day-dreams and to such thin hopes of feudalism as had survived the

Wars of Religion and Richelieu. Though Corneille returned to the theatre in 1660 with *Œdipe*, and even in his last play, *Suréna*, showed his mastery, the Fronde which conveniently bisects his career marks for him a point of no return. People who had tried to act like Cornelian heroes in real life, willing their way to glory, and others who had seen them fail, were no longer in the mood for 'quelques passions plus nobles et plus mâles que l'amour'. When Racine gave them love, tragedy returned to favour, and Corneille fell into eclipse.

Adam writes[1] that 'vers 1652 la tragédie est morte', but it had not died alone. Descartes was dead, La Rochefoucauld seriously wounded and in disgrace, Retz in disgrace and soon to be a fugitive, Mazarin spinning out his last years of power with no one to hand over to except his rightful king. Though Louis XIII died in 1643, it is his age, that of the Three Musketeers, which comes to an end with the Fronde, and it is to that age that Corneille, La Rochefoucauld and Retz belong, though they live on for another twenty years or so after the Fronde. The dramatist depends on being in tune with his public, and it is to anachronism rather than to failing powers that Corneille's decline is to be attributed. The writer of memoirs or the *moraliste* has no such limitations, and in the writings of Retz and his rival we see the post mortem of the age in which all three had known fame and hope. Despite the apparent detachment of the *Mémoires* Retz does not seem to have learnt his lesson, he is still laying down his own law, putting tactics above motives. He does, however, seem to have learnt to distinguish tragic from comic heroes, and his ability to mock himself on occasion is a sign of grace.

For all that, neither high seriousness nor laughter is enough in such a cause. To treat the destiny of a nation as a theatrical performance is simply frivolous. Frivolity it is which above all characterizes the Fronde and explains why France had to wait 140 years for a real Revolution. These men and women are often called Cornelian figures, but it is well to recall that Corneille's genius was not limited to tragedy. A single episode suggests that if they are Cornelian they belong to the comic phase, and certainly

[1] op. cit., vol. II p.322.

typifies their frivolity. It is not particularly surprising that at the outset of hostilities Mme de Longueville should have lodged, as we have seen, at the Hôtel de Ville, nor that she should there have given birth to a son (29 Jan. 1649). In view of the times there is nothing specially unusual about the fact that the father should have been La Rochefoucauld, but when we learn that the child was christened, possibly in the presence of both husband and father, though this is uncertain, by La Rochefoucauld's greatest rival both in politics and for the lady's favours, by the Archbishop-Coadjutor himself, things seem to have got out of hand. This ceremony serves as a symbol for the Fronde, and should be borne in mind when we come on to La Rochefoucauld. Nobody, indeed, was ever quite the same after the Fronde.

5: LA ROCHEFOUCAULD

HOWEVER much one may disagree with the assumptions about life on which Corneille's characters base their conduct, it cannot be denied that even the less effective tragedies contain characters who arouse our admiration or, at the very least, our respect. Misguided as they often seem to be, they are trying to do something difficult, even though to us it may appear simply pointless, and in their attempt they sacrifice all other considerations. Single-mindedness and high seriousness are the marks of all Cornelian heroes, and the best of them (from a dramatic point of view) have a panache about them which more than anything else typifies the pre-Fronde age. Descartes's famous portrait by Hals and his reputation as a swordsman belong to just the same tradition. Unfortunately the inner man, on whom Corneille and Descartes alike lay constant stress, is inaccessible to public gaze, and it is a good deal easier to imitate panache, which by definition will not escape notice, than the moral qualities with which it should properly be associated. In their admiration for the type of behaviour which Corneille put upon the boards, and with which their ancestors had filled the pages of French history, the Frondeurs were not sparing in panache, but the christening ceremony just recalled, and in general all of Retz's *Mémoires*, make it impossible for us to see behind the *actions éclatantes* the *âme noble et généreuse* which alone can invest them with meaning. Anyone who has seen a modern revival of a Victorian melodrama, acted with all the emphasis of the original, will have a vivid mental picture of the borderline between pure tragedy, which bears constant repetition, and its near relative, melodrama, which does not. It is in no sense a disparagement of Corneille's art to say that a strong vein of melodrama runs through his tragic work, *le Cid* and *Rodogune* being two obvious examples, without in any way detracting from the genuine tragic content. It is not altogether unfair to see in the Fronde an attempt to reproduce the melodrama, not wholly without success, under the mistaken impression that tragic nobility would automatically be conveyed by a performance from which all seriousness was absent.

Accounts of La Rochefoucauld's serious wound at the barricades of St. Antoine show him to have been a man of extreme courage and moral constancy, risking death for a cause in which he had ceased to believe. If this is typical of one side of the Fronde, and such acts of great bravery were very numerous, the episode already referred to, when Retz was trapped by the door, offers a dramatic *tableau vivant* even more eloquent. The scene very well represents the untragic and very melodramatic (when not farcical) tone of the Fronde; in La Rochefoucauld's own words 'une triste farce'.

Even if the Fronde had not been defeated, it is arguable that after four years of sporadic anarchy, in which anyone who felt so inclined could try himself out as a hero, society would have worked heroic aspirations out of its system. La Rochefoucauld's works remind us that even the protagonists of the Fronde, and certainly the spectators, had other, more peaceful preoccupations. In Retz we have already seen that moral standards have given way to social ideas about 'honnêteté'. La Rochefoucauld goes a step further by devoting his *Mémoires* to much the same events and people as Retz, with a similar number of general reflections on character and conduct, while in his *Maximes* he combines the practical experience gained in the heat of conspiracy and rebellion with the more leisurely observation which his eventual return to the salon life of Paris permitted him. In a way the *Maximes* may be said to represent the post mortem of La Rochefoucauld's own generation, but they equally show the results of vivisection performed on that which followed, and combine the two findings in passing judgement on mankind in general.

For those who were afraid or unable to exercise the autonomy of the philosopher or hero, conformism was the prescribed course. What had originated in the first salons as a revolt against contemporary standards of boorish behaviour, the social aesthetic, gradually became a moral anaesthetic. Provided the rules were observed, social success could be expected, and with the growing domination of the salons in the latter half of the century, social success became a harsh necessity, now that political adventure was out of the question. The two chief rules have been summed up as *suivre nature* and *plaire*, the second depending on the first. A glance at Boileau's confident pontification on what constitutes nature, or at Molière's satire on the art of pleasing in *Le Misanthrope*, is sufficient warning that these rules cannot be interpreted at their face value. None the less, they correspond roughly to fairly constant social requirements. When Retz, after Descartes, rails at pedants, or praises social graces above mere honesty, he is thinking of these two rules. In another way, Philinte echoes Retz in showing the literal Alceste that the two rules must be brought into accord and that the only nature to be followed is that which will bring social acceptance. Inevitably the tendency towards playacting, noted before, was encouraged by the elaborate ritual of the later seventeenth century, and since applause was the only worthwhile measure of success, it was quite obvious that an increasing discrepancy was bound to arise between what the individual knew himself to be, what he wanted in his heart to be and what he wanted others to think of him. A certain amount of insincerity is normal in any age, but this discrepancy was far more serious in one where no alternative to individual autonomy, verging on solipsism, had yet been found for the 'moi désaxé'. The best anaesthetic wears off, and the *Maximes* show the patient as often as not painfully conscious of the canker within him.

It was bad enough that voluntarism should be utterly discredited, and that its former exponents should live on in their frustration. As a measure of collective security society had now to impose on all its members these rules in which no one fully believed but which could guarantee outward peace while perpetuating lethal inner conflict.

From whichever angle the problem is approached, the individual finds himself confronted with a situation over which he must, but cannot, regain control. Society lays down rules of conduct, based on the general needs of a rich and idle aristocracy, and sits in permanent judgement in its own cause; new fashions are checked when they lead to excesses, old ones mocked when they fall out of date. It is not enough that the individual should go through the motions of conformism; society begins to inquire into motives, to look for the 'nature' followed by the individual. Comedy, gossip, maxims are varying expressions of this tendency. On the other side, the individual who has the courage and the capacity for self-knowledge is constantly aware that private motives are as often as not belied by public performance; not only must the façade conform, but some attempt must be made to convince the outside world that the foundations are sound. Under such circumstances any appreciable degree of lucidity will tend towards cynicism and, if accompanied by conscience, to split personality, while refusal to look too deeply into an uncomfortably insistent question can only produce an impression either of stupidity or incurable frivolity or both.

The *point sensible* is where the inner and the outer inquiries meet, in those intimate relationships where mere outward conformism is inadequate and where some exchange of self-knowledge cannot be avoided. The sort of clumsy frankness represented by Alceste is, of course, no answer to the problem of mutual sincerity, but one can readily understand why people in general and the moralists in particular devote so much attention to love and friendship. If such relationships cannot be put on a viable footing there is no way out of the solipsist nightmare, except through religion or metaphysics, and that road had been heavily mined ever since the *Cogito*.

La Rochefoucauld had had more opportunity than most for putting friendship to the test. In the Fronde he had seen cowardice and duplicity on all sides, as well as real loyalty; in love he was no amateur, and apart from more ephemeral liaisons, there was Mme de Longueville, Mme de Sablé, Mme de La Fayette, not to mention his wife. Already provided with a solid fund of experience, prevented from further active participation in politics, and thus enjoying unrestricted leisure, he became connected with Port Royal and involved in discussions with such men as Arnauld and Jacques Esprit on questions of ethics and theology. It is in particular the debate on *vertu païenne* which inspired the series of reflections eventually published as the *Maximes*, and this theme which provides the theoretical basis and unity of the book.

Ever since the Renaissance the outstanding virtues of pagans like Cato or Socrates had been contrasted with those of the champions of Christianity, to whom grace should have granted a decisive advantage but who seemed less admirable. Many felt that the result of unaided human effort was a virtue both truer and more effective than that in practice demonstrated by most Christians. Adam expresses in a telling phrase the main theme and aim of La Rochefoucauld: 'Ce n'est pas la réalité de la vertu qu'elles nient [les *Maximes*], c'est qu'elle soit jamais "naturelle".[1]

Here, in advance, is the answer to the injunction *suivre nature*, while *l'art de plaire* forms a large part of the target at which the *Maximes* are aimed. It must be stressed that though the argument as it now reads appears to deal with purely human values, independent of theological considerations, the context is inseparable from Christianity. The people described belonged to a recently Christian society, the vocabulary of many centuries of Christianity was still current, and patterns of thought and conduct were still judged in Christian terms, even by those who had forsaken Christianity. Thus, even if one cannot absolve La Rochefoucauld from the charge of partiality, it is fair to say that his contemporaries could best be addressed in the terms he chose.

The *Maximes* are not arranged in any very rigorous order, and it is convenient to consider successively what they have to say about man in his individual nature, then in his personal relationships, especially love and friendship, and finally in his public relationships, in society, politics and so on.

The first casualty is the rule of reason; the early *Maximes* represent in various ways the multiplicity and force of the passions besetting man's spirit:

Les passions sont les seuls orateurs qui persuadent toujours. (8)[2]

Les passions ont une injustice et un propre intérêt qui fait qu'il est dangereux de les suivre, et qu'on s'en doit défier, lors même qu'elles paraissent les plus raisonnables. (9)

Il y a dans le cœur humain une génération perpétuelle de passions, en sorte que la ruine de l'une est presque toujours l'établissement d'une autre. (10)

[1] op. cit. vol. IV, p. 101.

[2] References are to the numbers of individual maxims. The edition followed is that of La Rouchefoucauld, *Œuvres complètes*, in *Bibl. de la Pléiade* (1935).

Thus far Descartes would have agreed, and the *Traité des Passions* diagnoses roughly the same morbid condition in prescribing as a remedy the proper use of the will. La Rochefoucauld speaks of what he has seen in practice, not of what ought to be in theory:

Nous avons plus de force que de volonté, et c'est souvent pour nous excuser à nous-mêmes que nous nous imaginons que les choses sont impossibles. (30)

Si nous résistons à nos passions, c'est plus par leur faiblesse que par notre force. (122)

The bankruptcy of voluntarism could hardly be more explicitly proclaimed. For those who feared the anarchy of conflicting wills, the cry had long been for moderation, the golden mean, but La Rochefoucauld leaves no room for illusions on that score either:

La modération est une crainte de tomber dans l'envie et dans le mépris que méritent ceux qui s'enivrent de leur bonheur; c'est une vaine ostentation de la force de notre esprit; et enfin la modération des hommes dans leur plus haute élévation est un désir de paraître plus grands que leur fortune. (18)

. . . La modération est la langueur et la paresse de l'âme, comme l'ambition en est l'activité et l'ardeur. (293)

On a fait une vertu de la modération, pour borner l'ambition des grands hommes et pour consoler les gens médiocres de leur peu de fortune et de leur peu de mérite. (308)

This has already made substantial inroads into the prepared positions of those who believe in the will, or simply in the security of a middle way, based on common sense and reason, but even reason has lost its dignity: 'L'esprit est toujours la dupe du cœur.' (102) 'Tous ceux qui connaissent leur esprit ne connaissent pas leur cœur.' (103)

The constantly changing passions to which man is the helpless prey not only prevent him from acting as he would wish, but, more serious still, prevent him from acquiring what all unanimously agree is the indispensable prerequisite of independent action; self-knowledge. *Le moi pensant* is only half, and not the stronger half, of man. If one could know the *cœur* as reliably as one knows *esprit* perhaps something could be done about it, but the *carte du cœur* is not to be drawn up as lightly as the *carte du Tendre*. The sands are continually shifting and changing shape: 'On est quelquefois aussi différent de soi-même que des autres.' (135) 'Il est plus aisé de connaître l'homme en général, que de connaître un homme en particulier.' (436)

On the basis of this analysis, human conduct is capricious, unpredictable and amoral, when it is not deliberately immoral, since the determining factors are the passions and momentary self-interest. The two Cartesian standbys, reason and will, are of no avail; reason is continually obscured by the passions, will is applied ineffectually or wrongly. Self-knowledge, the only firm starting point for improvement, is uncertain. It is not surprising under these conditions that La Rochefoucauld sees in selfish human behaviour an untidy jumble of virtues and vices. In some of his most characteristic maxims he describes his view of the moral position:

Les vertus se perdent dans l'intérêt, comme les fleuves se perdent dans la mer. (171)

Les vices entrent dans la composition des vertus, comme les poisons entrent dans la composition des remèdes; la prudence les assemble et les tempère . . . (182)

Le nom de la vertu sert à l'intérêt aussi utilement que les vices. (187)

Failing reason to distinguish vice from virtue, let alone will to follow one rather than the other, the purely subjective criteria of self-interest can only result in some such view of morality. The fugitive and cloistered virtue, like a buried treasure, yields no interest, so that it is fair to say that in this context La Rochefoucauld is speaking of virtue primarily in terms of its public appearance. As if to emphasize that this is not all, that besides the subjective criteria just mentioned there is to be found a positive and enduring standard, La Rochefoucauld gives an example of genuine virtue, the *acte gratuit* whose value derives from less ephemeral standards: 'La parfaite valeur est de faire sans témoins ce qu'on serait capable de faire devant tout le monde.' (216)

More often what passes for public exhibition of virtue is mere lip-service, inspired by motives which have nothing to do with virtue. A famous maxim serves as a heading for a whole group of others: 'L'hypocrisie est un hommage que le vice rend à la vertu.' (218)

Lacking alike the fortitude to follow true virtue and the conviction to follow vice, men take the line of least resistance which leads to hypocritical and self-deluding acts of feigned virtue. Grief, for example, covers a multitude of motives, not all honourable: 'Il y a dans les afflictions diverses sortes d'hypocrisie.' (233) Some mourn for themselves 'sous prétexte de pleurer la perte d'une personne qui nous est chère . . .' and thus 'on se trompe soi-même. Il y a une autre hypocrisie, qui n'est pas si innocente, parce qu'elle impose à tout le monde: c'est l'affliction de certaines personnes qui aspirent à la gloire d'une belle et immortelle douleur.' This applies mostly to women. He ends the catalogue of tears 'Enfin on pleure pour éviter la honte de ne pleurer pas.'

Generosity is no less suspect: 'Ce qui paraît générosité n'est souvent qu'une ambition déguisée, qui méprise de petits intérêts pour aller à de plus grands.' (246) 'La magnanimité méprise tout, pour avoir tout.' (248)

Goodness, like moderation, may be only a disguised defect of character: 'Nul ne mérite d'être loué de bonté, s'il n'a pas la force d'être méchant: toute autre bonté n'est le plus souvent qu'une paresse ou une impuissance de la volonté.' (237)

Thus the amour-propre to which the first maxims introduce us, so far from being a singleminded, and, if necessary, immoral quest for personal advancement is shown to be a hesitant, fumbling compromise. This analysis depends, of course, on La Rochefoucauld's chosen terms of reference, in the context of the *vertu païenne* controversy; it does not claim to be an exclusive or exhaustive account of human nature, just an account of what man is, left to himself. In one of the rare maxims directly touching on a religious subject (but published only after his death) he gives a fuller perspective: 'Dieu a permis, pour punir l'homme du péché originel, qu'il se fît un Dieu de son amour-propre, pour en être tourmenté dans toutes les actions de sa vie.' (509)

Simpler than some modern existentialists, La Rochefoucauld thinks that Hell is ourselves, not others. Looking back on the maxims already quoted, and the ideas they represent, these words are clearly of utmost importance, and demonstrate the link between the *Maximes* and the symptoms of the 'moi désaxé' discussed in earlier chapters. 'Un Dieu de son amour-propre . . .' is, after all, only another way of stating the solipsist position, but La Rochefoucauld is the first of the writers discussed to relate a philosophical (or religious) position to social phenomena. He will not be the last.

This maxim, by linking *intérêt* and amour-propre, brings home the fundamental nature of man's aberration. It is not merely transient selfishness, or miscalculation of moral values, but the permanent and radical reorientation of man's spiritual eye on to himself. There can be no religion when man becomes his own God, but equally there can be no ethics when man's self occupies the place properly taken by some transcendental, or at least, objective, standard. No standard, no moral certainty; no moral certainty, no firm act of will; no firm act of will and only the passions remain, ever changing, to obfuscate the light of reason. In the terms of the *Traité des Passions* this is the only way to express the chain of events.

It might be that amour-propre, or *intérêt*, eventually brings on a feeling of loneliness and a desire for company, and here the problem latent in Cartesianism is dragged out into the light of day. The individual who seeks company at once involves his amour-propre in conflict with another's, no less strong. On the basis of La Rochefoucauld's analysis of human nature such a conflict is unlikely to be resolved satisfactorily, and as in love the other person is not only a rival in selfishness, but also a woman, nothing but pain and disaster can be expected. He dwells at some length on the collision of egos, and given his definition of love, the rest inevitably follows: 'Il est difficile de définir l'amour: ce qu'on en peut dire est que, dans l'âme, c'est une passion de régner; dans les esprits, c'est une sympathie; et dans le corps, ce n'est qu'une envie cachée et délicate de posséder ce que l'on aime après beaucoup de mystères.' (68)

If this is so, there is no reason to query this: 'Si on juge de l'amour par la plupart de ses effets, il ressemble plus à la haine qu'à l'amitié.' (72)

There is perhaps more to it: 'Il est du véritable amour comme de l'apparition des esprits: tout le monde en parle, mais peu de gens en ont vu' (76), though the 'peu' almost amounts to a negative.

Thwarted love means wounded pride, and La Rochefoucauld's own amorous experiences had taught him all he needed to know about falling out of love, which he did with singular brutality. He writes: 'Plus on aime une maîtresse, et plus on est prêt de la haïr.' (111)

This must be interpreted in terms of amour-propre—the more one has committed ones amour-propre, the more it will suffer from defeat by another. Love, in fact, becomes not a substitute for amour-propre, but simple an extension of its frontiers.

Even if other factors were favourable, the incessant fluidity of human personality creates special difficulties for any kind of durable relationship.

La constance en amour est une inconstance perpétuelle, qui fait que notre cœur s'attache successivement à toutes les qualités de la personne que nous aimons, donnant tantôt la préférence à l'une, tantôt à l'autre: de sorte que cette constance n'est qu'une inconstance arrêtée et renfermée dans un même sujet. (175)

Il y a deux sortes de constance en amour; l'une vient de ce que l'on trouve sans cesse dans la personne que l'on aime de nouveaux sujets d'aimer, et l'autre vient de ce que l'on se fait un honneur d'être constant. (176)

On this view, love is no exchange, since neither side of the equation is fixed, but an opportunity for self-gratification, either by the satisfaction of a thirst for novelty, or by the pride of successful obstinacy. The real point remains the same; love is simply selfish. 'Il n'y a point de passion où l'amour de soi-même règne si puissamment que dans l'amour, et on est toujours plus disposé à sacrifier le repos de ce qu'on aime qu'à perdre le sien.' (262)

Equivocal though this definition of love may be, even were

man's reponsibility less, the woman's attitude ensures disaster. Self-deception allied to selfishness provokes the ultimate slander: 'Les femmes croient souvent aimer, encore qu'elles n'aiment pas: l'occupation d'une intrigue, l'émotion d'esprit que donne la galanterie, la pente naturelle au plaisir d'être aimées, et la peine de refuser, leur persuadent qu'elles ont de la passion, lorsqu'elles n'ont que de la coquetterie.' (277)

Feminine psychology is damned in a single phrase: 'Dans les premières passions, les femmes aiment l'amant; et dans les autres elles aiment l'amour.' (471)

Even so it is open to question whether this is not an improvement on the masculine situation previously described.

If the chapter on love is discouraging, that on friendship is well-nigh hopeless: 'Quelque rare que soit le véritable amour, il l'est encore moins que la véritable amitié.' (473)

The reason is not far to seek: 'Ce que les hommes ont nommé amitié n'est qu'une société, qu'un ménagement réciproque d'intérêts, et qu'un échange de bons offices; ce n'est enfin qu'un commerce où l'amour-propre se propose toujours quelque chose à gagner.' (83)

Once more exchange is not the aim; the friend is a projection of oneself, with no claims of his own: 'Nous sommes plus près d'aimer ceux qui nous haïssent que ceux qui nous aiment plus que nous ne voulons.' (321)

Intimacy and sincerity serve selfish ends: 'Le plus grand effort de l'amitié n'est pas de montrer nos défauts à un ami; c'est de lui faire voir les siens.' (410)

Two suppressed maxims stress once again the essential selfishness of the relationship:

Le premier mouvement de joie que nous avons du bonheur de nos amis ne vient ni de la bonté de notre naturel, ni de l'amitié que nous avons pour eux: c'est un effet de l'amour-propre qui nous flatte de l'espérance d'être heureux à notre tour, ou de retirer quelque utilité de leur bonne fortune. (582)

Dans l'adversité de nos meilleurs amis, nous trouvons toujours quelque chose qui ne nous deplaît pas. (583)

This gloomy tale is thus summed up: 'La plupart des amis

dégoutent de l'amitié, et la plupart des dévots dégoutent de la dévotion.' (427)

Another way of saying that most of what passes for friendship and piety is false.

There is a ray of hope, corresponding exactly to the scintilla of virtue admitted above: 'S'il y a un amour pur et exempt du mélange de nos autres passions, c'est celui qui est caché au fond du cœur, et que nous ignorons nous-mêmes.' (69)

Even friendship can exist: 'Nous ne pouvons rien aimer que par rapport à nous, et nous ne faisons que suivre notre goût et notre plaisir quand nous préférons nos amis à nous-mêmes; c'est néanmoins par cette préférence seule que l'amitié peut être vraie et parfaite.' (81)

These feelings restore grace: 'L'envie est détruite par la véritable amitié, et la coquetterie par le véritable amour.' (376)

Even so, the illusion is best preserved by ignorance: 'Dans l'amitié, comme dans l'amour, on est souvent plus heureux par les choses qu'on ignore que par celles que l'on sait.' (441)

Lucidity and contentment seem from all this to be virtually incompatible in personal relationships, and the small spark of residual faith in human nature is exceptionally modest. When La Rochefoucauld comes on to speak of daily relationships with other men, not specially chosen as intimates, but imposed in the very nature of society, the question of 'honnêteté' naturally comes first. The problem is, in a way, simplified, since it no longer involves compromise between two selves on fundamental issues, but rather the most effective presentation of oneself before society taken as a whole. The first essential is, as always, self-knowledge: 'Les faux honnêtes gens sont ceux qui déguisent leurs défauts aux autres et à eux-mêmes; les vrais honnêtes gens sont ceux qui les connaissent parfaitement, et les confessent.' (202)

With this necessarily goes a measure of humility: 'Le vrai honnête homme est celui qui ne se pique de rien.' (203)

But above all the essential is absolute honesty (in the modern sense) both to oneself and to others: 'C'est être véritablement honnête homme que de vouloir être toujours exposé à la vue des honnêtes gens.' (206)

Despite these solid moral foundations, in the last analysis La Rochefoucauld's *honnête homme* can only be recognized by the same sort of external signs as those mentioned by Retz: 'Un honnête homme peut être amoureux comme un fou, mais non pas comme un sot.' (353)

This seems to be another way of saying that intelligence, even obscured by passion, is an inseparable part of 'honnêteté', but clearly once this type of quality becomes necessary, the pretence of moral correlatives to social success cannot long be maintained.

Although the approach is of some antiquity, and indeed honoured by most of the medieval Doctors, a view of supposed moral worth which claims to establish woman's *a priori* inferiority must be in some sense suspect. 'Honnêteté' loses any serious moral connotation when associated with such generalizations as these: 'Il y a peu d'honnêtes femmes qui ne soient lasses de leur métier.' (367) 'La plupart des honnêtes femmes sont des trésors cachés, qui ne sont en sûreté que parce qu'on ne les cherche pas.' (368)

Unwilling or unwanted, virtuous women seem to be denied either moral or social approbation, and are subjected to quite different criteria from men. Hardly equal pay for equal work.

There is no need to labour the point. La Rochefoucauld clearly distinguishes, at least in his own mind, between the genuinely moral quality of 'honnêteté', based on harmony between private motive and public performance, and what he calls by the same name, but which is purely public and amounts to little more than *politesse mondaine*. There is something of Alceste in this. A letter by Méré,[1] claiming to reproduce what La Rochefoucauld actually said on a given occasion, puts the matter very well: 'Les faux honnêtes gens, aussi bien que les faux dévots, ne cherchent que l'apparence.'

This is the authentic Alceste, as is the alternative: '. . . la noblesse du cœur et la hauteur de l'esprit, c'est de là que procède la parfaite honnêteté, que je mets au-dessus de tout.'

Such a view unites moral and intellectual excellence in just the same way as Descartes, Corneille and Retz wished to see them

[1] La Rochefoucauld, op. cit., pp. 604-7.

united. In this same letter of Méré there is an even more significant and revealing passage, which illustrates beyond possibility of misunderstanding how la Rochefoucauld proposed to solve the problem of Conformism:

> . . . pour être effectivement vertueux, au moins pour l'être de bonne grâce, il faut savoir pratiquer les bienséances . . . rien ne me paraît de si mauvaise grâce que d'être un sot . . .
>
> Nous devons quelque chose aux coutumes des lieux où nous vivons, pour ne pas choquer la révérence publique, quoique ces coutumes soient mauvaises; mais nous ne leur devons que de l'apparence; il faut les en payer et se bien garder de les approuver dans son cœur, de peur d'offenser la raison universelle qui les condamne.

This is Philinte, not Alceste, and succinctly resumes the problem which every cultured seventeenth-century Frenchman had to face. For some, social pressure proved too strong, and having in any case to keep up appearances, they went no further, so that their *cœur* was simply left out of account. It is interesting that even here it is not in the name of morality, but of 'la raison universelle' that La Rochefoucauld takes his stand. It is rather hard to decide just what he had in mind by this expression, but it looks almost equivalent to the 'general consensus of *honnêtes gens*', that is, an externally voiced agreement rather than an inner light, let alone a transcendental value.

This reflection takes us back to the beginning of the argument. By cutting out all transcendental values, and confining his observations to the plane of unaided human nature, La Rochefoucauld shows without much difficulty that human conduct is neither virtuous nor reasonable. Constantly shifting interpretations of amour-propre derive from the passions, in the last analysis that which is least specifically human in us, because based on purely physiological factors. The body, the material world, is the realm of the contingent, in which man can only drift in the swirling currents of fortune until a lifeline rescues him from above. Temperament is decided by chemistry; indolence is the cause of the same moderation which in a fiery nature would be virtue. Pure chance, or an accident of birth, may provide the perfect setting for external generosity, clemency or valour, which in a humbler context would pass unnoticed. Once the will has abdicated, control and responsibility cease; the individual is the sum of the fortuitous and material influences which work upon him. A minimal effort of will can secure general approbation for acts which are morally neutral, but socially desirable. To be an *honnête homme* one has only to go through certain motions devised by society for its own protection. Human relationships of love and friendship which are never tested to breaking-point may well give the illusion of success, but morally they are without significance. In a word, human nature and human conduct are shown in this analysis to be part of a game of chance, wholly irrelevant to any higher purpose or design.

When this is said, one is still forced back to the argument of *vertu païenne*. Except for odd references to *dévots* there is virtually no mention of religion in the *Maximes*, and, more important, human conduct is condemned and praised in purely human terms. Sin is never mentioned, nor on the other hand those virtues which may be called specifically Christian (though, of course, not exclusively so), like humility, self-sacrifice, brotherly love. The reality of such virtues is not denied, it is not even discussed, but then they do not belong to the allegedly pagan (though nominally Christian) society of which La Rochefoucauld was aiming to give a picture. Man as portrayed in the *Maximes* is a sorry creature, but he is nowhere represented as the whole of man. Monsieur Vincent and Rancé of his contemporaries, St. Teresa or St. François de Sales a little earlier, fall quite outside La Rochefoucauld's chosen field of observation, and from the *Maximes* one could hardly infer the possibility of their existence. La Rochefoucauld shows mankind dedicated to the cause of Mammon, but omits to consider those who acknowledge another master, however unworthily they may serve him. Had he been a pagan this would have been fair enough, but since his privileged position of critic depended on his religious convictions, he cannot be absolved of failing to tackle his problem at its crucial point. In fact the morality of the *Maximes* is not only no *Introduction à la Vie Dévote*, not a lesson in *contemptus mundi*, but is scarcely even consistent with Christianity.

It cannot be denied that in some respects the *Maximes* retain elements reminiscent of Corneille. Unobtrusive though they are, La Rochefoucauld's occasional positive qualifications show that he recognized, even on the human plane, a class of individuals endowed with genuine virtue. Not only the controversial context of the work, but their whole tone, makes it impossible to regard the *Maximes* as a confession of the author's own weakness. He stands aloof and disgusted outside the society he condemns, and his own assumption of superiority is no less marked for being tacit. This is in line with Corneille's heroic view, which emphasizes the exceptional quality of the hero in contrast to the pathetically ordinary people who surround him. The difference is that Corneille had absolutely no personal reason for identifying himself with his heroes, indeed just the opposite, while La Rochefoucauld had and did. In the active period of his life he acted a typically Cornelian part, but by the time he came to write he had undergone the influence of Port Royal. The result is curiously paradoxical; like his Jansenist friends he takes a gloomy view of ordinary unregenerate humanity, and in condemning *vertu païenne* in such detail he makes nonsense of the claims to our admiration of, for example, Auguste; by suppressing all references to God and grace he seems to put his exceptional cases of true friendship, 'honnêteté' and so on into a superior category, but one apparently still based on human, not divine, gifts. The same curious paradox applies to his view of himself; originally deriving from pure worldly pride in his birth and breeding, in his sense of 'gloire' his conviction of personal superiority was only reinforced when it became spiritualized as a result of more recently acquired religious beliefs. The pride of a great noble and disillusioned hero would sufficiently explain his attitude towards the world he surveys, and though the picture is in fact used to illustrate the theme of 'misère de l'homme sans Dieu', one feels, as with the conversion of Polyeucte, that the *deus ex machina* is invoked to supply motivation for which natural means had already proved adequate. By exposing the nature of amour-propre La Rochefoucauld is the first of the writers here considered to describe the state of the 'moi désaxé', but both in his presentation of the

Maximes and in the picture he gives of himself in the *Mémoires* he shows how much easier it is to denounce the dangers of self-centredness than to avoid them. Whatever Port Royal may have taught him about election, one is left with the strong impression that in his heart La Rochefoucauld was convinced that in Paradise his name would win him the *tabouret* he had been denied at the Louvre.

6: PASCAL—*LETTRES PROVINCIALES*

THE picture of man and society variously presented in the authors so far discussed is both clear and extensive, but it is far from complete. One would not expect a dramatist, especially in tragedy, to deal with problems of every-day life, and Corneille explicitly excludes such questions from consideration as tragic themes. Descartes offers a philosophy for the *honnête homme*, and indeed left unfinished a presentation of his system specifically adapted to this type of reader (in *la Recherche de la Vérité*), but the discrepancy between Cartesianism and the daily life of ordinary people reflects its author's own preference for a life of isolation. Both Retz and La Rochefoucauld in their very different ways are concerned with practical problems, but both are so limited by circumstances of birth and breeding that their observations are quite one-sided; even when Retz, for instance, shows some intelligent awareness of the common people of Paris, it is from a position of complete detachment. The sum total of these authors' prescriptions and descriptions falls far short of a guide to the human predicament as such. Pascal's situation is not limited by the exigencies of *genre* or class-consciousness, nor does he offer a system, but of all these authors he is the one most deeply involved in the human predicament, because he feels himself essentially man, not *gentilhomme*, or *honnête homme* but just *homme*.

Impressive as they are, his technical qualifications come second to this almost obsessive consciousness of a humanity shared with all men. A scientist at least equal, perhaps superior to Descartes, a writer of French inferior to none, a propagandist as skilful as Retz, who pays tribute to the *Provinciales*, Pascal has always aroused the most intense feelings, whether of sympathy or antipathy, and defies classification. It could perhaps be claimed that this is a sign of greatness; it is only honest to recall that his greatest work was left unfinished, and that his other great literary work must inevitably be judged by the violently polemical context of its composition. The nature of the *Pensées* and the *Provin-*

ciales makes it most desirable that they should be studied separately, at any rate to begin with, and that one should as far as possible allow for the apologetic purpose of the one and the polemical purpose of the other. Pascal's enemies can hardly have been all he said they were, but the positions he chose to attack indicate clearly enough what he himself stood for and to a large extent also the image of his opponents which he succeeded in fixing in the public eye. Like St. Augustine in an earlier age, Pascal cannot be accepted as an entirely reliable witness to anything but his own preoccupations, but the difference is that, while we know well enough what Augustine thought of Pelagius, the converse is not true, whereas in Pascal's controversy with the Jesuits both sides are amply documented. Happily there is no need here to examine the accuracy or justice of Pascal's charges, it is enough that he made them, that he hated the things he was attacking, whether the Jesuits in fact represented them or not, and that whatever the details of the case, the Jesuits certainly did stand for principles radically opposed to those of Pascal and Port Royal. It cannot be too strongly emphasized that the chapters which follow concern Pascal, and not Jansenism in any technical sense, and that the judgements passed represent an interpretation of Pascal's indictment of the Jesuits, and not an historical assessment of the justice of that indictment. It would be too much to ask for objectivity on such a subject, and the following pages make no such unconvincing claim.

A factor of great significance is the enormous success of the *Provinciales*, which thus marked the course of contemporary events in a decisive way. They survive today as literature, but they were composed and published at some risk to liberty, and even life, during an unusually vehement battle, which soon overflowed from the sphere of theology into that of politics and social life. To some extent the success of this amateur intervention into a professional debate forced Pascal into a false position; committed to help his friends, and deeply compromised by what he had already done, he could not easily withdraw from the conflict, nor did he have time in the heat of battle to select, or even adequately to inspect, all the ammunition supplied by Port Royal. It would be foolish to deny the palpable faults of the book, some due to carelessness, some to prejudice, but it would be absurd to deny its abiding merit, which goes far beyond style. The immediate or proximate cause of the letters was the quarrel between Jansenists and Jesuits brought to a head by the Five Propositions. These were allegedly extracted from Jansen's *Augustinus*, but while both sides recognized them, with minor reservations, to be heretical, the Jansenists repudiated their authenticity as extracts. The ultimate cause goes farther back, and must be classed with other reactions to the moral theology and spiritual climate produced after, if not by, the Council of Trent.

The Society founded by Ignatius Loyola, contemporary at the University of Paris with Calvin and Rabelais, showed the world two very different spheres of activity; in foreign missions, especially in the Far East, the work begun by Francis Xavier, a founding father, prospered remarkably, and at a heavy cost in Jesuit martyrs, but in Europe, where equally dangerous missions to Protestant countries formed only part of the Society's task, Jesuits were found more often in positions of power than of danger. In France the beginning of the seventeenth century saw the establishment of Jesuit colleges which acquired from the start the reputation of providing the best and most up-to-date education. It is no accident that men prominent in such different walks of life as Descartes, Corneille and Retz should all have been educated at Jesuit schools. It is, however, an accident that in literary history these three names should be followed by those of La Rochefoucauld, Pascal and Racine, all closely connected with Port Royal in one way or another, and this rather misleadingly suggests that talent belonged alternately first to one party and then the other. A more correct view would be that Jesuit supremacy in the educational field continued (even Voltaire turns up as one of their pupils), but was challenged powerfully, though briefly, by Port Royal, whose writers strongly react against prevailing codes of social and religious behaviour. No less important than their schools were the numerous posts held by Jesuits as spiritual directors or confessors in the houses of the great, including the King, who initiated the long tradition of having a Jesuit as royal confessor. The influence derived from this contact with the great, even more than the formative influence of their schools, is the primary reason for the Jesuit clash with the Jansenists, and for their final inevitable victory.

The two main factors involved are theological and social. The authorized theology of the Society was Molinism (after the sixteenth century Spanish Jesuit Molina, not to be confused with the Quietist Molinos who came a century later), and its main characteristic was a doctrine of free will and grace temperamentally closer to the extreme of Pelagianism that to that of Calvinism, and no doubt devised as an antidote to the exaggerated Augustinianism of the Reformers. In simple terms the Jesuits were optimistic regarding the economy of salvation, making allowances rather than exceptions, and they went to the limit of orthodoxy (their enemies would say beyond) in the degree in which they stressed the value of human effort in earning salvation, thus almost allowing man to work his passage.

A famous scandal arose in the seventeenth century over accusations that Jesuit missionaries in the Far East allowed their converts to continue pagan customs, including idolatry, side by side with the practice of Christianity. Rightly or wrongly the Society was condemned for this, but the point of the reference is that something very similar can be seen in their activities in France at the same time. Their aim was to propagate Christianity or their brand of it, from the top, by influencing those who themselves had most influence. Since aristocrats and those of royal blood were naturally those for whom worldly temptations were strongest, and since the serious practice of Christianity demands a measure of discipline and responsibility, well this side of austerity, the Jesuits were faced with the problem of converting these influential people in some recognizable sense without alienating them by too insistent requests for a change in their way of life. Conversion had to be as painless as possible, therefore the promises must be attractive and the demands modest. It is often argued that it is easier to raise the spiritual standard of living once you have got your subject into a church than to lay down conditions for entry which will keep him out. As allegedly with the Chinese and their idols, so they acted with the aristocrats and their fleshpots.

The practical results of this policy were that within the Society discipline remained almost ferociously strict, but in dealing with their noble and wealthy clientèle the Jesuits displayed an attitude so sweetly reasonable and socially accommodating that no one would be frightened away. They would no doubt have argued that the end justifies the means, and their great success in this aristocratic ministry is an historical fact. Whether this particular end can itself be justified is another question, and one with which the *Provinciales* are concerned. The social aspect of their mission brought them down heavily on the side of Conformism and of the established order. In furthering their religious cause they not only tolerated but defended temporal conduct which was agreeable to those they had in view but obnoxious to many others. The *morale relâchée* imputed to the Jesuits is in many ways the theological counterpart of the ethical codes already seen in Descartes, Corneille and Retz, and it is an open question how far the connexion was causal.

The *Provinciales* go to the very heart of the problem, and examine in great detail both the practice of the Jesuits and the theological implications of their teaching. The first three letters deal with the highly technical arguments concerning grace, which the Jansenist controversy had aroused, and tend to show by brilliant satire that the Jesuits had won the support of the Thomists and others by using the same words as they with an entirely different meaning, that the condemnation of the Jansenists was purely formal, in the sense that, whatever they had actually taught, a formula would have been found to secure their condemnation, and, generally, that the whole affair was a logomachy devoid of real content. The theological issues involved in any discussion of grace are of the utmost complexity, but in these first letters Pascal is trying not so much to prove his opponents wrong as dishonest.

With his Fourth Letter Pascal brings Jesuit moral teaching under fire, and here, where immediate practical questions are at stake, he presses the attack home. In their relations with the high-born the Jesuits most often played the role of confessor or spiritual director, and in this role the general argument about getting people to church first and then preaching to them takes on a somewhat deeper significance. The sacramental discipline of the Catholic Church presents in the sacrament of penance a very real obstacle to easy conversion; the sinner is called effectively to repent, and absolution at the hands of a priest is an indispensable preliminary to further participation in the sacramental life of the Church. The aim of the penitent is salvation, the means is sacramental grace, and this derives in the first instance from absolution. It is not therefore difficult to see how absolution and salvation could become confused in the minds of theologically naïve people, to the extent that the first becomes a guarantee and not a condition of the second. The Jesuits had to make things as easy as possible for men and women whose normal lives entailed a generous ration of indulgence in a variety of sins. Their penitents required present assurance without the demand for future amendment; in a word, salvation on easy terms. The easiest terms of all are those by which the possible number of sinful acts, and the gravity of that small number, is reduced to a minimum. It is the various devices employed by the Jesuits to effect this reduction which Pascal examines and condemns.

The first such device is the doctrine of *grâce actuelle*. Its exponent, Père Bauny, was addressed by an adversary with the words: 'Ecce qui tollit peccata mundi', for this doctrine laid down that before an act can be called sinful such conditions have to be fulfilled as virtually to eliminate sin. The first general principle runs:[1] '. . . une action ne peut être imputée à péché si Dieu ne nous donne, avant que de la commettre, la connaissance du mal qui y est, et une inspiration qui nous excite à l'éviter.' (*Lettre* IV, p. 462)

The dialogue continues to explore this line further and shows that the greater the ignorance, or even indifference, of the individual, the less his acts of omission and commission can be regarded as sinful. An actual desire to avoid sin by praying

[1] All references are to the 1936 edition of Pascal, *Œuvre*, in *Bibl. de la Pléiade*. In the case of the *Pensées*, the numerical classification of that edition is given first, indicated by 'P', and followed by the corresponding number in the Brunschvicg classification.

against it, followed by failure, is the last of five conditions laid down by M. le Moine, who further says there is no sin in those who:

'. . . n'ont jamais pensé à désirer la santé de leur âme, et encore moins à prier Dieu de la leur donner . . . Ils n'ont jamais eu de pensée d'aimer Dieu, ni d'être contrits de leurs péchés'; de sorte que, selon le Père Annat, ils n'ont commis aucun péché par le défaut de charité et de pénitence. (id. p. 464)

As the Jesuit spokesman exclaims, this doctrine means that the less one loves God the less one sins. The Lutheran injunction 'Pecca fortiter' takes on an unexpected significance, as the interviewer says:

Point de ces pécheurs à demi, qui ont quelque amour pour la vertu; ils seront tous damnés ces demi-pécheurs. Mais pour ces francs pécheurs, pécheurs endurcis, pécheurs sans mélange, pleins et achevés, l'enfer ne les tient pas; ils ont trompé le diable à force de s'y abandonner. (id. p. 465)

This is good fun in the Rabelaisian tradition, but it is a travesty of the Jesuit position. The letter carries the discussion much further, and the main point made is the distinction, already in Aristotle, between knowledge (or ignorance) of general principles of right and wrong, and of the good and evil consequences of a particular act. In the latter case some quite unforseen circumstance may provoke an accident which may be fatal but cannot be imputed as a crime or sin against the doer; ignorance in this case absolves from blame. Quite different is the former case, and it must be remembered that the context of the discussion is not that of a pagan society, but of one in which Christian teaching is universally available, and even hard to avoid. Failure to acquaint oneself under such conditions with moral and religious principles is only excusable on grounds of diminished responsibility, through mental deficiency or the like, and failure to undergo some elementary form of moral development would hardly excuse a person of sound mind from bearing the responsibility for his actions. *Omnis peccans est ignorans* expresses a familiar truth, and avoidable, let alone deliberate, ignorance increases rather than reduces guilt. The doctrine of *grâce actuelle* will in practice cover almost all acts save those of careful premeditation, as, for instance, Retz's decision 'de faire le mal par dessein', and will excuse all sins of surprise, of the kind that could be affected or eliminated by 'une ferme et constante résolution'. The doctrine, in a word, encourages irresponsibility and discourages contrition.

This is an example of Jesuit casuistry, but it should be said that Pascal is not attacking casuistry as such. In a church which demands of its adherents that they should go regularly, if not frequently, to confession, some guide for the confessor is essential if the sacrament is to be effectively administered from a disciplinary point of view; rules should be as uniform as possible, a firm standard should be laid down to take account of the peculiarities of over- and under-sensitive consciences, and the ordinary priest, in the seventeenth century by no means a scholar, should be able to feel that there is some authority behind the decisions he makes, even though in the last analysis responsibility must, God aiding, be his alone. All these needs are better met by some system of case-law than by a fixed code, and this is what the science of casuistry aims to provide. It is up to the penitent to confess what may be troubling his conscience, how often and in what circumstances he has committed or omitted particular acts, and to express his regret at what has offended God, together with his readiness to make amends, as appropriate, and do such penance as his confessor may prescribe. It is up to the confessor to assess the gravity of the offence, to offer counsel and encouragement, or admonition as necessary, and to grant absolution if he is satisfied that the penitent has made a confession both true and contrite. An obvious risk arising from the sheer weight of numbers passing through the confessional is that the process of judging individual cases may well become very perfunctory, but in the nature of things anyone sufficiently troubled in conscience is likely to say so, and true contrition on the penitent's part is more important than expertise in the confessor. A more serious danger arises once absolution is regarded as a right and repentance ignored as a duty. The analogy with case-law then puts the confessor in the position of defence counsel and judge together, against a feeble prosecution put up by conscience and, it must be said, the word of God in Scripture. The moment that confession becomes simply an occasion for getting the penitent off, its penitential aspect disappears, and with it all encouragement to contrition and the love of God. It is this aspect of casuistry, and the spirit behind it, that Pascal so vehemently condemns, for such an attitude ends by cutting man off from God on the pretext of abolishing the barrier of sin.

These are no doubt over-simplifications, but this is more or less how Pascal saw the problem, and explains his selection of particular Jesuit practices for criticism. It is common ground that though good and evil are fixed by immutable decree of the divine will, human interpretations of specific issues may vary widely. If, however, it is accepted that man is cut off from God by sin, and goes to confession to be cleansed and reconciled with God, it is clearly better to err on the side of caution than to take an over-favourable view which may only perpetuate separation. As soon as penitent and confessor conspire to secure an acquittal, instead of to earn a pardon, the situation changes, the need for caution disappears and any legal argument, no matter how rare or abstruse, may be proposed. This is where the doctrine of Probabilism comes in. 'Je ne me contente pas du probable, lui dis-je, je cherche le sûr.—Je vois bien, me dit le bon Père, que vous ne savez pas ce que c'est que la doctrine des opinions probables . . . C'est le fondement et l'ABC de toute notre morale.' (*Lettre* V, p. 479)

The Jesuit explains that according to this doctrine a minority opinion, even a minority of one, can legitimately be followed in favour of the penitent. One doctor, Emmanuel Sa, writes: 'On peut faire ce qu'on pense être permis selon une opinion probable, quoique le contraire soit plus sûr.' (id. p. 481) Another, Filutius: 'Il est permis de suivre l'opinion la moins probable, quoiqu'elle soit la moins sûre.' (ibid.) Finally Bauny: 'Quand le pénitent suit une opinion probable, le confesseur le doit absoudre, quoique son opinion soit contraire à celle du pénitent . . . Refuser l'absolution à un pénitent qui agit selon une opinion probable est un péché, qui de sa nature est mortel.' (ibid.)

On one view these arguments might seem consistent with the

claim that Christian charity should give anyone the benefit of any possible doubt, but on another it is hard to reconcile the spirit of penitence with a desire for self-justification which goes to such extremes. By advancing a single opinion in his own support, against the unanimous verdict of other doctors, a penitent is substituting wishful thinking for conscience and common sense and is claiming that the needs of his case present him with an opinion so convenient as to be necessarily certain. 'Clair et distinct' was subjective enough for Descartes, and as a criterion it led him into some absurdity, but this theory of Probabilism is applied on an equally subjective basis not to the problems of philosophy, but to the relationship between man and God. One process claims to offer certainty *ici-bas*, the other salvation *là-haut*.

In the next letter Pascal puts into the mouth of his Jesuit a plea for justification which deserves attention:

> Hélas! me dit le Père, notre principal but aurait été de n'établir point d'autres maximes que celles de l'Evangile dans toute leur sévérité. Et l'on voit assez par le réglement de nos mœurs que, si nous souffrons quelque relâchement dans les autres, c'est plutôt par condescendance que par dessein. Nous y sommes forcés. Les hommes sont aujourd'hui tellement corrompus, que ne pouvant les faire venir à nous, il faut bien que nous allions à eux: autrement ils nous quitteraient; ils feraient pis, ils s'abandonneraient entièrement . . . Car le dessein capital que notre Société a pris pour le bien de la religion est de ne rebuter qui que ce soit, pour ne pas désespérer le monde. (*Lettre* VI, p. 489)

The similarity between this attitude to religion and the temporary ethic adopted by Descartes, lest any precipitate decision should hamper his ultimate freedom of action, is a very real one. The danger is that, as always, *ce n'est que le provisoire qui dure*. Bringing people to church by judicious dilution of Evangelical precepts may or may not be wise, but it is unquestionably disastrous if the compromise Gospel becomes permanent. Religion, like manners, then becomes a matter of etiquette, the performance of socially desirable gestures, *l'art de plaire*, and eventually just *politesse mondaine*. To the objection that it need not develop thus, one can only say that it did.

So far all the doctrines mentioned, as distinct from their abuses, have something to be said for them, even if one may dislike their implications. When Pascal comes on to his next charge, a new element is introduced, which strains impartiality to breaking point. 'Sachez donc que ce principe merveilleux est notre grande méthode de *diriger l'intention*, dont l'importance est telle dans notre morale, que j'oserais quasi la comparer à la doctrine de la probabilité.' (*Lettre* VII, p. 498)

There follow several improbable, though apparently authentic, examples to show that if man cannot attain to Evangelical purity, Evangelical purity can be conveniently adjusted to suit human self-interest. The absurdity of the examples given, repugnant alike to sense and decency, should not be allowed to obscure the fundamental principle involved. The moral quality of an act depends on intention, and if it is once admitted that history may be rewritten so that honourable motives can everywhere be substituted for the real promptings of passion and selfishness, conscience may make cowards of us all, but with skilful direction of the intention we can become heroes, if not saints. As we have seen, Retz interprets his own motives in the most favourable light possible, after the event and behind a smokescreen of frankness; so too does La Rochefoucauld in his *Mémoires*, and they are at one in attributing the worst motives to their contemporaries in general and each other in particular. This is a practical illustration of how the method works. In his *Maximes* La Rochefoucauld shows that it can also work to the detriment of man in general, when he explains all motivation in terms of amour-propre. Jansenists as a group followed this path of pessimism and rigour, but there is all the difference in the world between extreme or excessive accusation, of oneself or others, used as a preliminary to penitence, and systematic exculpation, designed to avoid all need for penitence. Corneille's heroes 'dirigent l'intention' when they look back on their actions, and seek to make self-interest respectable by identifying it with the common good, as expressed in social demands. Cartesian psychology recommends mechanical deployment of certain passions to neutralize the effects of others, but the incentive is psychological equilibrium, not moral virtue. A man who knows that a tendency to rage is the greatest threat to his philosophical equanimity may embrace his enemy in an attempt to redress the balance, but the act, though commendable as being in the best interests of society, is actually motivated by pure self-interest and not by love of his neighbour. The *Traité des Passions* expounds at length and in detail the view that what is good or bad for the *moi pensant* is in itself good or bad. When applied to religion such moral subjectivity and relativism becomes anarchy, for the individual penitent who submits his past intentions to the direction of his confessor is abdicating both will and intelligence in the cause of self-interest, here served by absolution. '. . . quand nous ne pouvons pas empêcher l'action, nous purifions au moins l'intention; et ainsi nous corrigeons le vice du moyen par la pureté de la fin.' (id. p. 499)

After a good deal more in the same strain the Jesuit claims: 'Je crois vous avoir ouvert des moyens d'assurer son salut assez faciles, assez sûrs et en assez grand nombre.' (*Lettre* IX, p. 526)

The claims for the Jesuit method verbally recall those made in the *Discours*, but as we have seen, here the prize is salvation instead of mere certainty.

Various other doctrines are discussed, including those socially invaluable techniques of equivocation and mental restriction in the face of a truth which embarrasses. Finally comes the charge to which all the rest has been leading: 'Je vois bien, répondit le Père, . . . que vous avez besoin de savoir la doctrine de nos Pères touchant l'amour de Dieu. C'est le dernier trait de leur morale, et le plus important de tous.' (*Lettre* X, p. 546)

A long series of quotations from Jesuit authors is summed up:

> C'est ainsi que nos Pères ont déchargé les hommes de l'obligation *pénible* d'aimer Dieu actuellement. . . . Vous y verrez donc que cette dispense de l'obligation *fâcheuse* d'aimer Dieu est le privilège de la loi évangélique par-dessus la judaïque. (id. 547)

This is too much for the writer of the letter, and he pays no more visits to the Jesuits. As he says, confusion has wrought its masterpiece when the merits of Our Lord can be invoked by the Society which bears his name to absolve men from the painful duty of obeying the first and greatest commandment, on which all the rest depend. What so incenses Pascal is not just the impertinent blasphemy of which he accuses the Jesuits, but the effect it will have on their penitents, and in general on those to whom the line of least resistance will always appeal.

Mention was made earlier of the Pelagian tendencies of the Jesuits, a charge often recurring in Jansenist authors, but the doctrine attacked in the *Provinciales* goes far beyond Pelagianism in its pernicious implications. The Pelagian heresy was based on an optimistic view of human nature, and led to a gradual squeezing out of the need for the Cross by an emphasis on human merit, in itself claimed as sufficient for redemption. One thing that can be said for Pelagius and his followers, however, is that they may have been foolishly arrogant and they may have attached excessively small importance to Christ's redemptive role, but they did at least claim that virtue would secure man's eternal reward and they were 'against sin'. The successive arguments discussed in this chapter eliminate sin and ignore virtue; salvation through individual human merit is transformed into salvation through a confessor's skill. The Pelagian may love man too much and Christ too little, but it cannot be said that he avoids the obligation of loving God. For any Christian, salvation means in some sense eternal life with God, damnation eternal separation from God, and most people admit some connexion, ranging from causal to symptomatic, between our earthly life and future abode. The doctrines advanced by the Jesuits of the *Provinciales* reduce the whole economy of salvation to something like a Welfare State, whose benefits are available to anyone filling up the appropriate form.

Grâce actuelle removes all guilt from thoughtless acts, deriving from an undisciplined or wilfully ignorant way of life; Probabilism encourages detailed attempts at self-justification on the flimsiest grounds, and adds a deliberate element to the picture; direction of the intention absolves the penitent from the last vestigial obligations of personal responsibility, and invites him to silence his conscience in favour of a referee who knows the book of rules. The final dispensation from the need to love God removes all pretence, and reveals the whole purpose of the exercise as the gratification of amour-propre. The extra details of equivocation, mental restrictions, ignoring fasts, exploiting underlings, all add up to a comprehensive endorsement of contemporary social life as lived by the privileged classes. The only intolerable evil is inconvenience or a threat to personal indulgence. There is almost no aberration in Corneille or Retz which could not be justified by such arguments as those quoted in the *Provinciales*. The relevance of such teachings may be judged from the following which might equally well have come from the *Examen* to *le Cid*:

> Il est permis de tuer celui qui nous veut donner un soufflet. . . . N'est-il pas véritable, dit Escobar, que tandis qu'un homme laisse vivre celui qui lui a donné un soufflet, il demeure sans honneur?—Oui, mes Pères, sans cet honneur que le diable a transmis de son esprit superbe en celui de ses superbes enfants. C'est cet honneur qui a toujours été l'idole des hommes, possédés par l'esprit du monde. (*Lettre* XIV, p. 603)

The final comment applies to much of what has been discussed in earlier chapters.

Salvation which depends on such theological concessions to amour-propre is now seen to be only an extension to earthly life, and the God with whom such penitents are to spend eternity is only the apotheosis of self. Thus the Jesuits are accused of undermining the moral order and the truth of religion, all for the furtherance of their own ambitions. They have chosen to *faire le mal par dessein*, but in a manner infinitely more blameworthy than Retz, who while prepared to damn himself, resolved to do what he could to lead others to salvation.

This is not the place for assessing how far the situation denounced in the *Provinciales* was actually brought about by the Jesuits, but certain historical facts should be added in conclusion lest this whole discussion should appear unnecessarily artificial. Rightly or wrongly, Molinism triumphed over Jansenism, and can to this day be professed by Catholic theologians, while Jansenism is a heresy. For the sake of the seventeenth-century controversy, both sides were led to attribute extreme views to their opponents and, at the same time, to adopt somewhat exaggerated versions of their own position. The Jansenist insistence on man's corrupt and helpless nature inevitably provoked a reaction in extravagantly contrary terms; the Molinism attacked by Pascal is this polemical presentation, rather than the basic doctrine. Probabilism, too, after a chequered career is now accepted by the Catholic Church, in preference to Probabiliorism or Tutiorism, both of which, as their names suggest, were weighted on the side of caution and rigidity. Here again the needs of controversy sharpened distinctions, and for a seventeenth-century penitent the confessor least likely to be difficult was the one who accepted Probabilism. The fact that the dispute was so bitter tended to obscure the purpose of confession and the position of the penitent, who might be expected to take the line of least resistance when the experts disagreed. Another doctrine which did nothing to clarify moral problems was Laxism, propounded by certain Jesuit writers and condemned by the Pope in 1659. The fact that members of a highly disciplined and centralized order could go so far as to embody the practices of *morale relâchée* into a doctrine warranting papal intervention strikingly justifies Pascal's misgivings, for it must not be forgotten that Laxism, though a perversion, has natural affinities with Molinism and Probabilism, but could not conceivably be reconciled with a position of even moderate rigour. It is interesting, for example, to find Bossuet writing to Rancé much later, in 1682, of 'les relâchements honteux et les ordures des casuistes.'[1]

Finally there is the abundant evidence of the way society behaved at Versailles and elsewhere, especially in the decades following Pascal's death, to show that nothing was done to stop the moral rot. What was worse, the *dévots*, or *faux dévots*, became a major element in social life. The superficial practice of religion by those whose lives were notoriously scandalous and the abuse of religion by hypocritical opportunists, lay and clerical, are phenomena familiar to any student of Louis's reign. Much responsibility for this state of affairs must rest on those who administered the sacrament of penance. They were not all Jesuits and all Jesuits were not like that, but it is hard to dissociate these historically verifiable effects from some such causes as those

[1] *Œuvres*, (1875) vol. xxvi, p. 302.

denounced in the *Provinciales*. Too many confessors treated hell-fire frivolously and unscrupulously, echoing in a different sense Jason's 'J'accommode ma flamme au bien de mes affaires.' It is hardly going too far to say that this habit of treating absolution as a defence brief eventually became a game like the rest of the social round. Religion ended, as we can read in La Bruyère, as a senior branch of lifemanship.

This is not how the 'moi' will find its axis again, and Port Royal, as well as many who stopped well short of Jansenism, were both indignant and alarmed at this influential debasement of the spiritual currency. For a fuller diagnosis of the malady and its cure we must go to the *Pensées*. The present chapter is the religious counterpart of those which precede it; the wit and philosopher of the salons, the theatre-goer, the frondeur, found too in pulpit and confessional a religion tailored to his needs, with the triple motto *certitude*, *gloire*, *salut* covering this world and the next.

Among those who shared Pascal's view is La Rochefoucauld, who puts things in perspective when he asks Mademoiselle de Sillery to answer his letter on pain of incurring: '. . . de la fumée en hiver, des punaises en été, des fermiers qui paient mal, des procès en défendant, des valets qui vous volent, un confesseur moliniste . . .'

[1] La Rochefoucauld, *Œuvres*, p. 493.

7: PASCAL—METHOD

ADMIRERS of the great men of literature and philosophy are often surprised to find that the scientific activity of their heroes, to which biographers give so much weight, passes unnoticed by modern scientists. Rabelais's renown in medicine, Descartes's work in physics and optics—and, dare one add, Valéry's mathematics—are more highly prized by their literary followers than by the specialists concerned in these particular fields. This is not the case with Pascal; while Torricelli rightly takes precedence over him in his work on the vacuum, Pascal's own experiments, and his presentation of their results, are still acknowledged as models of scientific method; Fermat, whom he modestly addressed as the greatest geometer in Europe, is today put on the same level by mathematicians as Pascal, whose work on probability and conic sections is still classic; the omnibus service inaugurated by Pascal testifies even more strikingly to his practical gifts, though few of the millions who use it know to whom they owe the debt. While remaining well on this side idolatry, one may reasonably disagree with all Pascal himself claimed to stand for and continue to admire him as a person of extraordinary gifts. Though there is less support than formerly for the view that Pascal came to his last religious phase as a sort of fanatical renegade from science and mathematics, there is no doubt that it was in these fields that certain thought patterns and methods had become firmly established in his mind before he began to apply them to religious problems. It may be helpful to study these separately before going on to the *Pensées*.

Two characteristic ideas are already to be found in most of his work, whether mathematical, scientific, or psychological, before they reach their fullest development in the *Pensées*, and even if Pascal may not be their inventor, he is their clearest exponent. In their many different forms these ideas may be summed up as the theory of orders and the theory of intellectual approach. In the *Traité du vide*, *Entretien avec M. De Saci*, *De l'Esprit géométrique*, as well as in the *Provinciales* and *Pensées*, these two ideas are either explicitly discussed or else embedded in the heart of the argument.

Just as it is almost impossible to do justice to Cartesian method without reference to Montaigne, so much of Pascal can only be seen in its proper perspective by referring to Descartes (and through him back to Montaigne). In his treatise *De l'Esprit géométrique* Pascal explicitly states what is implied in many other places, that he regards his own approach as essentially different from that of Descartes, but in an important sense also complementary. By the time Descartes had formulated his system in published works it appeared as a linear argument, proceeding with rigorous logic from step to step, all ultimately derived from the *Cogito*, which gave at once an irreducible first principle and an existential reference, in which a universal criterion of truth is found to be included. It is only as if by accident, and in a comparatively obscure place, that he comes to state his axioms, definitions and postulates (in the *Secondes Réponses*), which throw a very different light on the apparent immediacy of Cartesian first principles. The reasons for this development are probably very complex, and cannot be discussed here, but the interesting point is that we now know what his contemporaries generally did not, that in an earlier, and incomplete work, the *Règles*, Descartes had started from a much less rigorous point of view, and in place of the uniquely privileged *Cogito* had derived true knowledge from an act (or process, or what you will) which he calls 'intuition', a word he subsequently abandoned. Even more interesting, while he derived knowledge in the main from a rigorously logical chain of deduction from such intuitive first principles, he did seem ready at this early stage of his thought to admit the value of *induction*. Perhaps the shortest explanation of why Descartes gave up this promising approach for his rigid and disastrous *a priori* derivation of physics from metaphysics is his growing and excessive self-confidence and a passion for simplification, leading, in fact, to inextricable complications. The point of mentioning these facts here is to show that two equally gifted men, living in the same age, confronted just the same problems but parted in opposite directions for reasons which can in the last analysis only be called temperamental.

The arguments of this treatise are most conveniently summed up in the corresponding part of the *Pensées*, those fragments which introduce the Brunschvicg edition:

> Il y a donc deux sortes d'esprits: l'une, de pénétrer vivement et profondément les conséquences des principes, et c'est là l'esprit de justesse; l'autre, de comprendre un grand nombre de principes sans les confondre, et c'est là l'esprit de géométrie. L'un est force et droiture d'esprit, l'autre est amplitude d'esprit. Or, l'un peut bien être sans l'autre, l'esprit pouvant être fort et étroit, et pouvant être aussi ample et faible. (P. 22/2)
>
> Ceux qui sont accoutumés à juger par le sentiment ne comprennent rien aux choses de raisonnement, car ils veulent d'abord pénétrer d'une vue et ne sont point accoutumés à chercher les principes. Et les autres, au contraire, qui sont accoutumés à raisonner par principes, ne comprennent rien aux choses de sentiment, y cherchant des principes, et ne pouvant voir d'une vue. (P. 23/3)

In the terms of this definition, Descartes is the very type of 'esprit géométrique', with all the faults and virtues that implies:

> *Descartes*: Il faut dire en gros; 'Cela se fait par figure et mouvement'; car cela est vrai. Mais de dire quels, et composer la machine, cela est ridicule; car cela est inutile, et incertain, et pénible. Et quand cela serait vrai, nous n'estimons pas que toute la philosophie vaille une heure de peine. (P. 192/79)

That part of the *Discours de la méthode* devoted to the physical world follows directly upon the section setting out Descartes's metaphysics, and is introduced by the statement that the universe is run according to 'les lois que Dieu a imprimées en nos âmes', that is the knowledge of such divine perfections as immutability and stability, whence are directly derived, and eternally guaranteed, the laws of inertia, linear motion and the rest. Such a solid beginning is unfortunately marred by the main part of the section, proving irrefutably that the heart is a heat engine, fanned by the lungs, dealing with the blood in a way quite different from that described by the misguidedly empirical Harvey.

This typical example of *a priori* reasoning is based on a misapplication of the Cartesian method to a strictly scientific field where an inspired guess, confirmed by observation, is worth more than legislation claiming divine sanction. It is, however, less serious than the absolutely fundamental Cartesian identification of matter and extension. Here in its clearest form is illustrated the difference between Descartes and Pascal. In the *Fragment d'un traité du vide*, Pascal outlines his successive targets; he denies the impossibility of a vacuum, for which Cartesianism left no place, he denies the medieval and Aristotelian dogma 'Natura abhorrat vacuum', and claims finally that a vacuum is readily created and sustained in Nature. The details and findings of the great experiment, in itself a considerable feat of practical organization and efficiency, are familiar in their broad lines to all those who have studied the history of work on barometric pressure, weather conditions and hydraulic power. What is of supreme importance is Pascal's declaration of faith; 'soumission aux faits', obeying not *a priori* principles but the evidence of observed fact.

Addressing the reader, Pascal speaks of his reactions as he contemplates the ruin of traditionally accepted doctrine:

> Ce n'est pas toutefois sans regret, que je me départs de ces opinions si généralement reçues; je ne le fais qu'en cédant à la force de la vérité qui m'y contraint . . . Mais, enfin, l'évidence des expériences me force de quitter les opinions où le respect de l'antiquité m'avait retenu. (p. 176)

It is not enough to be strong and single-minded in the face of challenge; all men may err. The *esprit fin* is not committed in advance to principles based on abstract thought, and has thus opened the way to modern scientific progress, of which an essential ingredient has always been surprise.

In *De l'Esprit géométrique* this is put in a general way;

> C'est une maladie naturelle à l'homme de croire qu'il possède la vérité directement; et de là vient qu'il est toujours disposé à nier tout ce qui lui est incompréhensible; au lieu qu'en effet il ne connaît naturellement que le mensonge, et qu'il ne doit prendre pour véritables que les choses dont le contraire lui paraît faux. (p. 369)

As a final note on the distinction between these two types, there is an unexpected application to the realm of psychology in the *Discours sur les passions de l'amour*. Though the authenticity of the work can no longer be maintained, the Pascalian imprint of some passages cannot be mistaken:

Il y a deux sortes d'esprits, l'un géométrique, et l'autre que l'on peut appeler de finesse. Le premier a des vues lentes, dures et inflexibles; mais le dernier a une souplesse de pensée qui l'applique en même temps aux diverses parties aimables de ce qu'il aime. Des yeux il va jusqu'au cœur, et par le mouvement du dehors il connaît ce qui se passe au dedans.

Quand on a l'un et l'autre esprit tout ensemble, que l'amour donne de plaisir! Car on possède à la fois la force et la flexibilité de l'esprit, qui est très nécessaire pour l'éloquence de deux personnes. (p. 314)

Though little more is said in this work on this particular point, one paragraph farther on there is such a faithful echo of a major argument, later to be discussed in connexion with the *Pensées*, that it deserves quotation:

L'homme n'aime pas demeurer avec soi; cependant il aime; il faut donc qu'il cherche ailleurs de quoi aimer. Il ne le peut trouver que dans la beauté; mais comme il est lui-même la plus belle créature que Dieu ait jamais formée, il faut qu'il trouve dans soi-même le modèle de cette beauté qu'il cherche au-dehors . . . Cependant, quoique l'homme cherche de quoi remplir le grand vide qu'il a fait en sortant de soi-même, néanmoins il ne peut pas se satisfaire pour toutes sortes d'objets. Il a le cœur trop vaste; il faut au moins que ce soit quelque chose qui lui ressemble, et qui en approche le plus près. (p. 315)

Here is the consequence on the purely psychological plane of a distinction originally made in methodology, and subsequently applied to religion. Once again in a purely human context there is a phrase in this work which parallels the religious thought of the *Pensées* as regards the human condition: 'Ce qui fait que l'on va si loin dans l'amour, c'est qu'on ne songe pas qu'on aura besoin d'autre chose que de ce que l'on aime; l'esprit est plein; il n'y a plus de place pour le soin ni pour l'inquiétude.' (p. 320)

In pursuing this particular line, for a moment apparently irrelevant, one unconsciously follows Pascal's own declared method, from which it is hard to escape when dealing with him or even his imitators. Intimately connected with the idea of *esprits fins et géométriques* is the other essential pattern in Pascal's thought: the theory of the three orders. A capital text here shows how much is at stake, and how each aspect of Pascal's thought suddenly receives unexpected illumination from some other, at first sight distant, quarter:

L'ordre. Contre l'objection que l'Ecriture n'a pas d'ordre:—Le cœur a son ordre; l'esprit a le sien, qui est par principe et démonstration, le cœur en a un autre. On ne prouve pas qu'on doit être aimé en exposant d'ordre les causes de l'amour; cela serait ridicule.

Jésus-Christ, saint Paul ont l'ordre de la charité, non de l'esprit; car ils voulaient échauffer, non instruire. Saint Augustin de même. Cet ordre consiste principalement à la digression sur chaque point qu'on rapporte à la fin, pour la montrer toujours. (P. 72/283)

This quotation in itself shows the peculiar problems entailed in presenting Pascal's thought. It is not that there are contradictions, or irreconcilable dualisms, simply that his thought is so dense that each idea has a number of connotations extending over a very wide range. To start at the end, the actual context is that of Scripture, and the end on which all arguments are to converge is that central truth 'Jésus-Christ est le centre de tout'. In a quite secular context this is equally a statement of Pascal's methodology, which rejects linear argument in favour of converging testimony, and, to take another step back, is connected with Pascal's views on probability in evidence, where he accepts, for instance, the cumulative testimony of independent witnesses, none individually conclusive, to have no less the force of proof, than the clear and distinct ideas required by Cartesian method. The first part of the fragment clearly associates 'cœur' with 'esprit fin', 'esprit' with 'esprit géométrique', and is closely related in its references to love with the views just quoted from the treatise on that subject. Passages with a similar wealth of allusion are frequent in Pascal's work, and in exposition one has no alternative but to concentrate on one aspect rather than others.

Even so the full statement of Pascal's thought on this subject must be sought elsewhere. First there is a specific and concrete application in the *Provinciales*, which links scientific and religious views. Towards the end of the Eighteenth Letter, in which he examines the question *de fait* (i.e. whether the censured Propositions actually do occur in Jansenius), Pascal writes: 'D'où apprendrons-nous donc la vérité des faits? Ce sera des yeux, mon Père, qui en sont les légitimes juges, comme la raison l'est des choses naturelles et intelligibles, et la foi des choses surnaturelles et révélées.' (p. 670)

Here is exactly that experimental method, 'soumission aux faits', expounded and indicated by the *Traité du Vide*. The phenomena can only be recorded by the senses, analysed by the reason, answering the question 'how', and, if appropriate, explained by faith (which in that scientific context means faith in the antiquity of tradition, in authority as such), answering the question 'why'. Literal application of the apparently geocentric assumptions of revealed Scripture is as inadequate an answer to Galileo as is *a priori* reasoning from metaphysics to the observable facts of the existence of a true vacuum in nature.

This same triple arrangement recurs several times in the *Pensées*. A good example is this justification of Christianity:

> Il y a trois moyens de croire; la raison, la coutume, l'inspiration. La religion chrétienne, qui seule a la raison, n'admet pas pour ses vrais enfants ceux qui croient sans inspiration; ce n'est pas qu'elle exclue la raison et la coutume, au contraire; mais il faut ouvrir son esprit aux preuves, s'y confirmer par la coutume, mais s'offrir par les humiliations aux inspirations, qui seules peuvent faire le vrai et salutaire effet: *Ne evacuetur crux Christi.* (P. 482/245)

'Coutume' in this fragment corresponds to 'machine' in others, and both come under the more general heading of 'corps'. Pascalian terminology needs some sorting out, because he uses a number of different words to convey the same ideas, but the difference remains purely verbal. When, in the argument immediately following the *Pari*, he speaks of 'plier la machine' and 'cela vous abêtira' he is using expressions already made familiar by Descartes with his *bêtes-machines*. In effect Pascal takes the Cartesian pair *corps-esprit* and adds to them *cœur*, but the consistency and range of his thought necessitates some rephrasing according to whether the arrangement is applied to scientific, philosophical or religious contexts.

Broadly speaking the picture which can be reconstructed from the totality of Pascal's writings is as follows: There is first the material order, that of *corps*, of which the channel of knowledge is through the senses, and which extends into that part of psychology and conduct properly described as 'machine', that is unthinking habit, mechanical reliance on memory, custom and the like. In the religious sphere an outlook limited to the material order is described as 'charnel', and arouses 'concupiscence', akin to materialism in a modern sense. Next comes the order of *esprit*, operating through *raison*, *entendement*, and represented by *l'esprit géométrique*, 'par principe et démonstration'. It includes all intellectual activity, discursive reason, logic, abstraction, and may lead in religion, if exaggerated, to 'la superbe des philosophes', intellectual arrogance. Last comes the order of *charité* or *cœur*, operating through *volonté* to produce intellectual assent and physical compliance as appropriate. The *esprit fin* is proper to this order, which covers also *foi* and *inspiration* in a religious sense, *sentiment* (as opposed to *raisonnement*) in a psychological sense and, most characteristic of Pascal, *intuition* in the logical and mathematical sense in which Descartes originally used the word. First principles are thus known by *cœur* ('avant et au-delà de la raison', in the words of Mlle Russier), dealing alike with pre-rational instincts (but not mere physiological reflexes) and supra-rational inspirations:

> Nous connaissons la vérité, non seulement par la raison, mais encore par le cœur; c'est de cette dernière sorte que nous connaissons les premiers principes, et c'est en vain que le raisonnement, qui n'y a point de part, essaye de les combattre . . .
>
> Et c'est sur ses connaissances du cœur et de l'instinct qu'il faut que la raison s'appuie, et qu'elle y fonde tout son discours. (Le cœur sent qu'il y a trois dimensions dans l'espace, et que les nombres sont infinis; et la raison démontre ensuite qu'il n'y a point deux nombres carrés dont l'un soit double de l'autre. Les principes se sentent, les propositions se concluent; et le tout avec certitude, quoique par différentes voies.) (P. 479/282)

This essential text should be accompanied by two brief remarks on miracles, which show that Pascal constantly had the whole man in mind: 'Les miracles et la vérité sont nécessaires, à cause qu'il faut convaincre l'homme entier, en corps et en âme.' (P. 746/806) 'Les miracles prouvent le pouvoir que Dieu a sur les cœurs, par celui qu'il exerce sur les corps. (P. 747/851)

The example of the miracle of the Holy Thorn illustrates most of these ideas in action; first the cure (of Pascal's niece) had to be *seen*, then *examined* by doctors, who found no rational explanation, and only then *accepted* as an act of divine intervention. Pascal's attitude to exegesis is another example of the same kind.

For the theory of orders to be fully intelligible it is necessary to recall its origins in the development of Pascal's thought, and to see how he conceived the relationship between the orders. This is best seen in a fragment which, by its form of words, invites comparison with a very similar argument in *De l'esprit géométrique*, where Pascal points out that indivisibles, such as geometrical points, can never add up to extension, since they are of a different genre, just as squares cannot be added to cubes. The fragment begins: 'La distance infinie des corps aux esprits figure la distance infiniment plus infinie des esprits à la charité; car elle est surnaturelle.' (P. 829/793)

The fragment continues at some length with a consideration of types of greatness within the different orders, showing how one has no 'rapport' with the others, and concludes on a lyrical note:

Tous les corps, le firmament, les étoiles, la terre, et ses royaumes ne valent pas le moindre des esprits; car il connaît tout cela, et soi; et les corps, rien.

Tous les corps ensemble, et tous les esprits ensemble, et toutes leurs productions, ne valent pas le moindre mouvement de charité. Cela est d'un ordre infiniment plus élevé. De tous les corps ensemble, on ne saurait en faire réussir une petite pensée: cela est impossible et d'un autre ordre. De tous les corps et esprits, on n'en saurait tirer un mouvement de vraie charité: cela est impossible, d'un autre ordre, surnaturel.

There is no need to point out here the many ideas already met elsewhere, but leaving aside the finalism of this pattern, it is evidently that of the mathematician applying on a cosmic scale the notion of powers or orders.

Once again an inquiry into the theory of orders leads in turn to mathematics and religion, always converging on the same central truth. There can be no question of de-Christianizing Pascal's thought, that would be a contradiction in terms, but it would be false to suppose that his method is only applicable to religious questions, or nullified by rejection of his religious premisses. If the 'why' can only be answered by reference to Christianity, it is none the less true that the question is simply inappropriate or premature in a great number of cases. On the methodological and human plane there is a preliminary truth of primary importance to Pascal's thought, forming the indispensable threshold to a realization of the final truth of the Christian revelation. This truth derives from the two fundamental ideas discussed in this chapter, and consists in a recognition of the essential unity in diversity of human nature and of the paramount claims of each of its three components within their respective orders. It would be misleading to speak without qualification of a hierarchy of orders (except in a religious context, where it is just that), since none can be supplanted or invalidated by the other. Indeed *cœur* in its polar aspects embraces natural and supernatural alike on either side of reason, and it would be absolutely wrong to suggest any conflict between the orders when properly observed. Such a view of man amounts to a rehabilitation of his animal nature, a revaluation of the excessive claims of the intellect, a reconciliation between the divergent tendencies of reason and faith, reason and instinct, reason and feeling; in a word the reintegration of the human person, making man whole again. The 'moi' finds equilibrium, and is then free to seek its new axis. The dignity of matter and the modesty of mind are coupled with respect for the heart, so that balance succeeds conflict.

Some of the effects of such an outlook have already been illustrated; intellectual humility and flexibility in the face of awkward phenomena, with proper regard for inspiration (in the sense of guesswork) has proved its worth in the furtherance of scientific knowledge, and incidentally explains why Pascal never attempted a system like most thinkers before him; the acceptance of man's complex but total nature has been equally fruitful in the fields of art and, more recently, psychology; in religion it is unnecessary to consider the extraordinary influence of Pascal, now perhaps more than ever, on those troubled in mind. It is particularly ironic that so many critics refuse to apply Pascal's own many-sided method to their interpretation of his work: 'Le cœur a ses raisons que la raison ne connaît point.' (P. 477/277)

The undeniably polemic nature of the *Provinciales* and the inevitably restricted approach of the *Pensées* cannot be adduced as evidence of Pascal's preference for extremes, not even at the period in question. Indeed in his fragments on heresy he clearly shows the way to a sound understanding of his own position:

> Il y a donc un grand nombre de vérités, et de foi et de morale, qui semblent répugnantes, et qui subsistent toutes dans un ordre admirable . . . La source de toutes les hérésies est l'exclusion de quelques unes de ces vérités. (P. 788/862)
>
> Les deux raisons contraires.—Il faut commencer par là: sans cela on n'entend rien, et tout est hérétique; et même, à la fin de chaque vérité, il faut ajouter qu'on se souvient de la vérité opposée. (P. 791/567)

Pascal's method is not an either–or, but a both–and. To attribute to him the extreme exclusivism of Port Royal is thus to ignore his own frequently reiterated method. When one goes on through the seventeenth and into the eighteenth century one can see how now the cult of science and reason, now that of feelings and emotions, now that of pure sensuality or modified sensuality parading as naturalism, variously offer a solution to the 'moi désaxé', but one looks in vain for a view as balanced and comprehensive as that of Pascal. Even his bitterest opponents, like Voltaire, are in fact much more one-sided. It is of course true that the mere passage of time lessened the intensity of the strain on the 'moi', and palliatives were proposed and practised not wholly without success. In the authors still to be considered the inexorable social pressure of the age of Versailles is the determining factor in producing solutions which vary according to each man's occupation and temperament. In order to survive one had to please, and each encountered the problem posed in the *Art de persuader*, perhaps without finding any better answer than Pascal:

> Ce n'est pas que je ne croie qu'il y ait des règles aussi sûres pour plaire que pour démontrer, et que qui les saurait parfaitement connaître et pratiquer ne réussît aussi sûrement à se faire aimer des rois et de toutes sortes de personnes, qu'à démontrer les éléments de la géométrie à ceux qui ont assez d'imagination pour en comprendre les hypothèses. Mais j'estime, et c'est peut-être ma faibless qui me le fait croire, qu'il est impossible d'y arriver. (p. 378)

8: PASCAL—*PENSÉES*

THE *Provinciales* show Pascal's reactions to certain moral and religious aspects of his age, and stirred up enough controversy to bring these questions into the forefront of public discussion. Their context is essentially polemical and topical, but the brilliance of their style has ensured their survival, while the abundant contributions of other authors on both sides has been mercifully forgotten. As a commentary on religious trends the work must be taken very seriously, and La Bruyère, writing a generation later, shows how the problems remained, long after they had ceased to be exclusively associated with Jesuits or Jansenists. Whatever claim may be made for the *Provinciales*, however, they cannot be said to have made in the long run a positive contribution to the cause of Christianity. In the sense that they represent in some detail the negative side of an argument which is never properly balanced by its positive side they may be compared with the *Maximes*, also composed in the atmosphere of Port Royal. The comparison with the *Maximes* cannot be pushed too far, for despite obvious similarities of outlook and intention, Pascal and La Rochefoucauld finished their work in very different moods. Many of the faults castigated by La Rochefoucauld in his picture of a society dominated by amour-propre had recognizably been his own before he came under the influence of Port Royal, but with the enthusiasm of a convert he brought to his punitive task a spirit not visibly informed by charity. Given the systematically non-religious treatment of the work this may not seem too serious, and there is no evidence that La Rochefoucauld had any misgivings in this direction. The last few *Provinciales* tell a very different tale. Carried away at first by zeal for his unjustly persecuted friends, Pascal waged total war on the Jesuits, with startling success. As the battle wore on, he came to realize that however pure his original motives this public exchange of insults between Catholics could do no good to a Church, which already for a century had been in a state of war with heretics, who still clung to the name of Christian. The enemies of Christ had been sufficiently cheered by the major split within Christendom, now they were being offered fresh aid and comfort by the champions of orthodoxy turning on each other. There can be little doubt that the *Provinciales* did substantial damage, not only to the Jesuits, who are never likely to forget the lesson in tactics, and to the Jansenists, whose unexpectedly effective opposition was a principal cause of their own ultimate downfall, but to the Catholic Church and the Christian cause in general. It was with some such consideration in mind that Pascal belatedly changed his tone in the last *Lettres*.

His reparation went much further than the epilogue of the *Provinciales*, and next time he came to write on religion he left partisan skirmishes aside in order to undertake that general defence of the Christian religion which survives unfinished in the *Pensées*. Unfortunately the *Pensées* were interrupted by death, and the circumstances of their posthumous publication by overcautious friends at Port Royal diminished their contemporary impact. For these reasons they cannot be said to have undone the harm caused by the *Provinciales*, but on the other hand the full influence of the *Pensées* is still actual, and it could be claimed that the need they were intended to meet has never been more real. The preceding chapters have attempted to clear the way for a discussion of the *Pensées* by showing in turn the main objects of Pascal's dislike and the methods he followed in all his work, whether scientific or not. Integration is the watchword, the aim is to provide an axis. Thus all exclusivist tendencies are rejected and denounced, whether it be the *a priori* science of Descartes or the excessively legalistic casuistry of the Jesuits, a dualism which splits man in two or a form of spiritual direction which deflects him from his duty to God and neighbour. As well as the main moral, philosophical, religious and even scientific ideas to be found dispersed in his other work, Pascal includes in the *Pensées* the positive side of what is elsewhere negative criticism, and puts into perspective the other interests and activities with which he has been concerned.

One of the consequences of Pascal's concern for integration and of his method is that his book appeals to a far wider audience than most of those so far discussed. It is ostensibly directed at the same *honnêtes gens* as were the *Discours*, or the posthumous *Recherche*, of Descartes, the plays of Corneille and the *Maximes* of La Rochefoucauld. To that extent the picture of man represented in the *Pensées* is primarily that of the *salons* and *haute bourgeoisie* to whom the book was originally addressed, and indeed the argument *ad hominem* frequently introduces a portrait of Miton, or some other member of his specific and limited class. But beneath the specific examples drawn from a limited social range, Pascal so accurately discerns the essential man that the limitations are transcended. When he describes current social behaviour he is no more universal than La Rochefoucauld, whose psychology ignored all but the upper classes, but as soon as he comes on to the human condition he paints on a canvas wide enough to carry a panorama of all sorts and conditions of men in all ages. There is certainly some generalization from the particular, but in the terms of Pascal's method this is intentional, and in any terms is not necessarily invalid. It has to be admitted that an attempt to isolate single aspects of Pascal's thought is even more artificial than would be the case with most other writers, but the excuse may be offered that he himself invited the isolation, at least temporarily, and that inspection of vital organs is a necessary preliminary to comprehension of the whole body. What follows is not intended as a substitute for the whole, but rather as a method of approaching it.

It is notoriously easy to read the *Maximes* as a cynical expression of pessimism from a man whose whole life had been largely a failure. When one learns subsequently something of the author's intentions and the circumstances of the work's composition, one may well be surprised, and a new interpretation will probably be necessary. This is far from the case with the *Pensées*, which though covering much the same ground at first, never leave the reader in doubt as to the main line of the argument. Had nothing survived but the section 'Misère de l'homme sans Dieu' as far as the *Pari*, Pascal's aims would still have been clear and, some may think, more nearly achieved than in what follows. He himself divides the apology into two separate and successive stages: 'Que la nature est corrompue, par la nature même; Qu'il y a un réparateur, par l'Ecriture.' (P. 73/60)

Another formulation of the two stages is more succinct, but in its theological expression can be misleading: 'Misère de l'homme sans Dieu; Félicité de l'homme avec Dieu. (id.)

Whichever version one may prefer, the first stage in each case demands that God should not be brought into the argument, which is solely concerned with proving man's wretchedness, before going on to consider God's existence.

Although it adds to the difficulties of the present exposition, it would be betraying Pascal's method to omit at this stage the crucial text, whose sense permeates the whole work and which could be inserted at almost any, and every, point within it. 'Jésus-Christ est l'objet de tout, et le centre où tout tend.' (P. 603/556)

To the extent that Pascal never lets this central truth out of his sight, there is inevitably an element of circularity implicit in the argument, though it would be more accurate to describe it as convergent. His own position makes him more acutely conscious of that which he has abandoned, and leads him to an analysis more penetrating than would be possible for an uncommitted observer. This circularity can be exaggerated, and often is, by Pascal's critics, and the argument needs to be studied as it is actually presented before its validity can properly be estimated. Circularity, after all, is not peculiar to Christian apologists, and a distrust of the theological conclusions sometimes inspires critics to reject the psychological working. It may be noted incidentally that more than one academic syllabus has cautiously stopped short of the theological argument of the *Pensées* in defiance of Pascal's method.

In the light of Pascal's method it is possible to divide the subject-matter of the *Pensées* into three distinct questions, each dependent on that which precedes. There are first the symptoms, as he sees them, that is, the facts of human behaviour, private and public, individual and collective; then there is the diagnosis of the malady, based on natural (i.e. psychological) grounds, and deduced from the observed symptoms; finally there is the prescription of the remedy, again initially psychological. To continue the clinical analogy, the second part of the apology, that based on Scripture, attempts to identify the remedy prescribed with that which Christian teaching specifically makes available, but does not as such concern the present study in any detail. As far as the validity of the argument is concerned, Pascal's selection and description of symptoms is the first premiss, and can readily be checked against independent contemporary evidence, with certain qualifications which will not be ignored. The diagnosis is more controversial, but still amenable to some degree of rational inquiry, and it is only when we come to the remedy that the argument can no longer proceed without the introduction of elements going beyond rational proof. An apology for religion must necessarily appeal to reason, even if this is only a preliminary to touching the heart (in Pascal's sense of the word), but it is a matter of common experience that arguments from Scripture, even with exegesis brought up to date, do not have for the unbeliever the same cogency as the preceding arguments from Nature.

It should be emphasized at this stage that apart from Pascal's special gifts of psychological insight, the theological conclusion to which his argument was committed, namely the salvation of mankind, obliged him to select as far as possible symptoms of universal relevance, while making his immediate appeal to a given class at a given time. It is also, of course, true that he was writing for readers who were all conversant with Christian terminology and doctrine, who belonged to a nominally Christian society and whose psychology had been deeply conditioned by centuries of Christian reactions; this fact may reinforce the impression of circularity but is historically inevitable. An apology addressed to Hurons or Hottentots, Turks or Tibetans would obviously have been conceived in very different terms.

The first problem is to identify and define the patient, before beginning to discuss his symptoms. Telescope and microscope offer equally inconclusive answers:

> Car enfin qu'est-ce que l'homme dans la nature? Un néant à l'égard de l'infini, un tout à l'égard du néant, un milieu entre rien et tout.

Infiniment éloigné de comprendre les extrêmes, la fin des choses et leur principe sont pour lui invinciblement cachés dans un secret impénétrable, également incapable de voir le néant d'où il est tiré, et l'infini où il est englouti. (P. 84/72)

A little later in the same fragment man's position is summarized: 'Connaissons donc notre portée: nous sommes quelque chose, et ne sommes pas tout; ce que nous avons d'être nous dérobe la connaissance des premiers principes, qui naissent du néant; et le peu que nous avons d'être nous cache la vue de l'infini.' (id.)

Here is a statement of man's existence vastly different from the *Cogito*; a new *Dubito*, indeed, but offering in its vertiginous solitude no foothold for the 'principes de la philosophie' mocked a few lines earlier. Reason is not this time to be the lifeline, and Pascal echoes Montaigne in finding it an unreliable aid: 'Ne cherchons donc point d'assurance et de fermeté. Notre raison est toujours déçue par l'inconstance des apparences; rien ne peut fixer le fini entre les deux infinis qui l'enferment et le fuient.' (id.)

The end of this long fragment, which has earned Pascal the title of the French Hamlet, aims directly at the *Cogito* and the stage immediately following it: 'L'homme est à lui-même le plus prodigieux objet de la nature; car il ne peut concevoir ce que c'est que corps, et encore moins ce que c'est qu'esprit, et moins qu'aucune chose comme un corps peut être uni avec un esprit.' (id.)

The reference to Descartes is unmistakable. Here again are his own words; having established 'je pense donc je suis' as 'le premier principe de la philosophie', he goes on: 'Ce moi, c'est-à-dire l'âme par laquelle je suis ce que je suis, est entièrement distincte du corps, et même (qu'elle est) plus aisée à connaître que lui . . .'[1]

The fact that body and mind are distinct may be accepted as a matter of proof or simply blind faith, but the development of the science of psychology has done nothing to encourage acceptance of the latter part of Descartes's phrase.

[1] *Discours*, p. 114.

What a piece of work is a man! How noble in reason! how infinite in faculty! in form, in moving, how express and admirable! in action how like an angel! in apprehension how like a god! the beauty of the world! the paragon of animals! And yet, to me, what is this quintessence of dust? man delights not me. (*Hamlet*, Act II, sc. ii)

It is almost uncanny to read this prophetic parody of Cartesian claims (including the alleged angelism), followed by the same dusty answer as Pascal gave.

This giddy feeling of insecurity wrings from Pascal's interlocutor the famous cry: 'Le silence éternel de ces espaces infinis m'effraie.' (P. 91/206) The cosmos offers no refuge, and no answer to man's questions about himself; such truths as there may be can come only from within.

This cosmic introduction forms part of the general argument 'que la nature est corrompue . . .' and is followed by a description of man's nature under specific headings. Two formulae, found side by side in the original MS. (and similarly classified by Brunschvicg) afford a good starting-point. 'Description de l'homme: dépendance, désir d'indépendance, besoin.' (P. 160/126) 'Condition de l'homme: inconstance, ennui, inquiétude.' (P. 199/127)

Like Descartes and Montaigne before him, Pascal begins with demolition before attempting to build, and the ruins turn out to be rather the same in each case. One of the first casualties, as always, is the outside world as revealed by the senses, but Pascal's plan of attack brings him much nearer the Montaigne of the *Apologie pour Raimond Sebond* than to the Descartes, even of the *Méditations*:

L'homme n'est qu'un sujet plein d'erreur, naturelle et ineffaçable sans la grâce. Rien ne lui montre la vérité. Tout l'abuse. Ces deux principes de vérités, la raison et les sens, outre qu'ils manquent chacun de sincérité, s'abusent réciproquement l'un l'autre. Les sens abusent la raison par de fausses apparences; et cette même piperie qu'ils apportent à la raison, ils la reçoivent d'elle à leur tour: elle s'en revanche. Les passions de l'âme troublent les sens, et leur font des impressions fausses. Ils mentent et se trompent à l'envi. (P. 92/83)

This is bad enough, and Pascal recalls, like Montaigne, how easily man is distracted in the exercise of his reason, that sovereign faculty which a mere sneeze may suspend. Even if some working formula can be devised for keeping the senses and their data in order, there is an inner defect no less dangerous: 'La mémoire est nécessaire pour toutes les opérations de la raison.' (P. 97/369)

It was precisely because Descartes was honest enough to recognize this critical truth that he went to such lengths to find a guarantee for time and memory, and in so doing inadvertently tied himself up in the Cartesian circle.

Even this is not all, and to the fallibility of senses and memory Pascal adds a weakness, corresponding to Descartes's 'prévention', that may compromise right thinking still more:

> *Imagination.*—C'est cette partie décevante dans l'homme, cette maîtresse d'erreur et de fausseté, et d'autant plus fourbe qu'elle ne l'est pas toujours; car elle serait règle infaillible de vérité, si elle l'était infaillible du mensonge . . . Cette superbe puissance, ennemie de la raison, qui se plaît à la contrôler et à la dominer, pour montrer combien elle peut en toutes choses, a établi dans l'homme une seconde nature. . . . Qui dispense la réputation? qui donne le respect et la vénération aux personnes, aux ouvrages, aux lois, aux grands, sinon cette faculté imaginante? (P. 104/82)

This very long fragment ends with a note on another source of error, to be dealt with later at much greater length, and on a tone of relativism very reminiscent of Montaigne:

> Notre propre intérêt est encore un merveilleux instrument pour nous crever les yeux agréablement . . . La justice et la vérité sont deux pointes si subtiles, que nos instruments sont trop mousses pour y toucher exactement. S'ils y arrivent, ils en écachent la pointe, et appuient tout autour, plus sur le faux que sur le vrai. (id.)

The maxim of Conformism is given its proper commentary. If men live according to custom and usage it is because such conduct has become habitual, not because of any inherent justice or virtue in the customs. 'Montaigne a tort: la coutume ne doit être suivie que parce qu'elle est coutume, et non parce qu'elle soit raisonnable et juste; mais le peuple la suit par cette seule raison qu'il la croit juste.' (P. 287/325)

An example of a custom generally accepted, but which defies all normal arguments of reason and justice, is the right of primogeniture: 'Qu'y a-t-il de moins raisonnable que de choisir, pour gouverner un État, le premier fils d'une reine? On ne choisit pas pour gouverner un vaisseau celui des voyageurs qui est de la meilleure maison: cette loi serait ridicule et injuste.'

But what is the alternative? The virtue and ability which should decide high office at once give rise to endless controversy: '. . . chacun prétend être ce plus vertueux et ce plus habile. Attachons donc cette qualité à quelque chose d'incontestable. C'est le fils aîné du roi; cela est net, il n'y a point de dispute. La raison ne peut mieux faire, car la guerre civile est le plus grand des maux.' (P. 296/320)

It is reason itself, *bon sens*, that tells us to abjure rational arguments in favour of tradition; just the same argument occurs in the *Morale Provisoire* when Descartes disclaims all desire to apply the findings of his philosophy, however certain, to the body politic. Recent experience had been bitter enough to guarantee the sincerity of the disclaimer, and to justify this reasonable abdication of reason. Thinking back on the tragedy of the Wars of Religion, terminated only by the providentially (and remotely) legitimate succession of Henri IV, or to the farce of the Fronde, which could easily have been tragic but for the visible presence of a king, however young and weak, no one would have wished to set his own, or anyone else's, reason above a tradition which might be arbitrary but did avoid anarchy. So much for divine right, so much for higher law and just cause.

The abdication of individual reason may not seem too heavy a price to pay for political stability, but it would be asking too much of men that they should consent to the same sacrifice when lesser issues are at stake. If human laws and customs could plausibly appeal to true reason and justice, all would be well, but they cannot, and so the only alternative is continual debate and dissension, with every man a law unto himself, varying with the state of the weather or his digestion. Inconstancy is thus the first element of the human condition to be established. In this Pascal again follows Montaigne, and all that need be added is that this inconstancy is purely negative, very different from that divine discontent to which the alternative is stagnation and complacency.

The next stage of the argument puts inconstancy in a sharper focus by showing its link with *ennui*.

The medieval thinkers had always had their sights firmly fixed on eternal values, and therefore saw no inconvenience in making matter the realm of the contingent. Descartes was impatient with any threat to the autonomy of the thinking self, and despite the determinism of his physics, took great pains in metaphysics and psychology to bring the potentially unruly forces of matter, *corps*, under the right rule of *esprit*, that is, reason guiding will. Theoretically he admitted no limits to the controlling power of the 'esprit pur et attentif', particularly in coping with the physiologically inspired mutiny of the passions. For La Rochefoucauld the passions were equally physiological in origin, and much more likely than in Descartes to hamper the use of reason. Indeed, control is in the *Maximes* shown to be exercised only when amour-propre succeeds in dominating the other passions. Pascal's analysis of human reason goes much further, and he sees it not merely threatened by passions, but of its very nature an inadequate instrument for guiding man to truth and virtue. This is very different from the concessions made by, for example, La Rochefoucauld, who is prepared to admit the existence of a few exceptional men who are virtuous and reasonable; to such unaided human reason (and there is nothing in the *Maximes* to suggest a source of aid) Pascal makes no such concessions, and he sees man as perpetually subject to the contingent, which he cannot bring under his control. This is not just scepticism, but rather an insistence on the limitations of a faculty universally admitted to be finite. It follows from this that inconstancy is a state imposed on man, and *ennui* is the psychological reaction to a state of uncertainty from which he cannot escape. *Inconstance* and *ennui* are thus seen to be causally linked, and not separate symptoms of the complex human malady.

Pascal distinguishes between two types of instability; the one just discussed, which is passive and an abiding factor in human nature, the other, which is active, and represents man's efforts to deceive himself into thinking that he can change his occupation at will: this he calls *divertissement*. It originates in an attempt to cure *ennui*, but can have no other effect sooner or later than to leave man more exposed to *ennui* than before.

The key to the long section on *divertissement* is this:

> *Ennui.*—Rien n'est si insupportable à l'homme que d'être dans un plein repos, sans passions, sans affaire, sans divertissement, sans application. Il sent alors son néant, son abandon, son insuffisance, sa dépendance, son impuissance, son vide. Incontinent il sortira du fond de son âme l'ennui, la noirceur, la tristesse, le chagrin, le dépit, le désespoir. (P. 201/131)

Elsewhere he explains why rest is so disagreeable:

> . . . j'ai découvert que tout le malheur des hommes vient d'une seule chose, qui est de ne savoir pas demeurer en repos, dans une chambre. . . . Mais quand j'ai pensé de plus près, et qu'après avoir trouvé la cause de tous nos malheurs, j'ai voulu en découvrir la raison, j'ai trouvé qu'il y en a une bien effective, qui consiste dans le malheur naturel de notre condition faible et mortelle, et si misérable, que rien ne peut nous consoler, lorsque nous y pensons de près.

Hence the delight of the hunt, and similar pastimes: '(les hommes) ne recherchent en cela qu'une occupation violente et impétueuse qui les détourne de penser à soi.' (P. 205/139)

The ostensible prize, whether in hunting, games, gambling, is of no importance. All that is required is that it should elude man's grasp for as long as possible, over as stiff a course as possible, but nothing can prevent the ultimate recognition that: 'la chasse vaut plus que la prise.'

The long section on *divertissement* all amounts to this; any pursuit or occupation sufficiently absorbing to distract man from thinking about himself is preferable to the repose and solitude which will eventually force such thoughts upon him. *Ennui* in this context means fear and dislike of thought, as the consequence of inactivity, not the boredom of inactivity in itself. There could be no greater contrast to the *Cogito*; Cartesian man first finds his true self in solitary reflection, and is reassured by what he finds against the assaults of the *malin génie*, Pascal's man finds himself and recoils from the terrors of isolation. To use Descartes's own metaphor, the one supports and moves the world on the Archimedean lever of pure thought, the other finds himself like Atlas with the world on his shoulders, forced to walk the tightrope over a spiritual abyss.

> Could man be drunk for ever
> With liquor, love and fights,
> Lief should I rise at morning
> And lief lie down of nights.
> But men at whiles are sober
> And think by fits and starts,
> And if they think, they fasten
> Their hands upon their hearts.
>
> (A. E. HOUSMAN, *Last Poems*)

The third symptom, *inquiétude*, turns out to be intimately related to the other two. Incessantly shifting, and shiftless, man feels angry and humiliated at his lack of stability, but should circumstances temporarily force him to remain inactive or alone, he is filled with terror and disgust at his own company. *Ennui* persists until some fresh frivolity comes along to distract him, but all the time he knows that *inquiétude* lies in wait for him, whatever he may be doing. These feelings are implicit in the facts of human existence, revealed first in precarious balance between the two infinites, then deprived successively of the false props of reason, custom and justice. Until or unless man is willing and able to diagnose his true malady, the only remedy is a series of palliatives, whether stimulant or sedative, which are all equally useless when the day of mortal reckoning draws near.

Here is the crux. For the first time *timor mortis conturbat me* comes into the discussion. Descartes is concerned with life, to prolong it if possible; Corneille's heroes set the seal on their 'gloire' by a noble, and often welcome, death; Retz and La Rochefoucauld were personally unafraid, and speak of death only as of something of which cowards are frightened. Pascal like Hamlet dwells on man's fears of the unknown, and puts the pretentions of human vanity to the ultimate test. Long before there can be any talk of salvation, or an afterlife, man wants to know *why* all paths lead to the grave. At the same time he wants to know why it is his nature to be full of *inconstance*, *ennui*, *inquiétude*. Only when he knows why he is as he is can he do anything about it. *Angst* is the permanent state of the person unable, or afraid, to think out the why for himself, and equally unable to rid himself of the obsessive existence of the problem. This failure to solve the problem explains the elaborate defence mechanisms devised to deceive others, as in the performance of motions universally recognized as meaningless, or to deceive ourselves, thus promoting insincerity and psychological instability.

Happily this is no dead end; at the height of suffering, when *Angst* is at its worst, man is never without his lifeline, if he will only use it properly: 'L'homme est visiblement fait pour penser; c'est toute sa dignité et tout son mérite, et tout son devoir est de penser comme il faut. Or l'ordre de la pensée est de commencer par soi, et par son auteur et sa fin.' (P. 210/146)

The key to Pascal's whole conception of the human predicament lies in these last half-dozen words, typically arranged so as to span the immediate problem. Cut the sentence off at the word *soi* and it faithfully reflects the views of Descartes, Corneille and their friends; add the final words and the reason for Pascal's attack on *la superbe des philosophes*, as well as on the Jesuits of the *Provinciales*, becomes apparent. For the key is not just thought. Everyone knows the phrase: 'L'homme n'est qu'un roseau, le plus faible de la nature; mais c'est un roseau pensant.' (P. 264/347)

This insistence on thought as man's most worthy possession is frequent in the *Pensées*, but must not be confused with similar insistence in other writers. This famous sentence is followed by others, less often cited: 'Mais, quand l'univers l'écraserait, l'homme serait encore plus noble que ce qui le tue, parce qu'il sait qu'il meurt, et l'avantage que l'univers a sur lui; l'univers n'en sait rien.' (id.)

True greatness comes from self-knowledge, not self-conceit: 'La grandeur de l'homme est grande en ce qu'il se connaît misérable. Un arbre ne se connaît pas misérable.' (P. 255/397)

There may seem to be a paradox in such statements, seen in relation to the analysis of man perpetually shrinking from his own thoughts, but Pascal's method of both–and reconciles the paradox. The order of thought must not stop at self, but go on to *son auteur et sa fin*. If arrogant denial of weakness is false, defeatist surrender to weakness is fatal. Man's true strength lies in admitting his weakness; the cure for his ills lies in steadfast combat with the feeble arms at his command. If one looks only inward to rejoice in omnipotent self, and sees the cosmos as ripe for exploitation by a human reason for whom it holds no mysteries, one must be *plus que homme* to avoid disaster. Self-knowledge as a goal in itself is too near self-interest to be without perils, hence Pascal's triple order of thought.

There is a capital text on amour-propre, which offers an excellent commentary on some of the problems raised by authors studied already, as well as by Pascal himself.

> *Amour-propre.*—La nature de l'amour-propre et de ce *moi* humain est de n'aimer que soi et de ne considérer que soi. Mais que fera-t-il? Il ne saurait empêcher que cet objet qu'il aime ne soit plein de défauts et de misères: il veut être grand, et il se voit petit; il veut être heureux, et il se voit misérable; il veut être parfait, et il se voit plein d'imperfections; il veut être l'objet de l'amour et de l'estime des hommes, et il voit que ses défauts ne méritent que leur aversion et leur mépris. Cet embarras où il se trouve produit en lui la plus injuste et la plus criminelle passion qu'il soit possible de s'imaginer; car il conçoit une haine mortelle contre cette vérité qui le reprend, et qui le convainc de ses défauts. Il désirerait de l'anéantir, et, ne pouvant la détruire en elle-même, il la détruit, autant qu'il peut, dans sa connaissance et dans celle des autres, c'est-à-dire qu'il met tout son soin à couvrir ses défauts et aux autres et à soi-même, et qu'il ne peut souffrir qu'on les lui fasse voir, ni qu'on les voie. (P. 130/100)

It is instructive to recall how Descartes dealt with the question of his own weakness. Having at an early stage in his argument realized that the *moi pensant* lacks certain desirable qualities, such as infinity, perfection, omniscience, he deduces from the fact of his own imperfection the existence of a perfect being, adequate to produce in his mind the ideas of those qualities which he knows himself to lack. This perfect being he calls God whose veracity (one of the required perfections) then provides the guarantees of memory, senses and so on, enabling Descartes to pursue his method. Descartes never doubts for a moment that, once he has proved the existence of God, he has earned that immunity from deception which God alone can provide. It is significant in the present context that this is a purely personal transaction between Descartes and God with no third parties, and imposes no obligations with regard to other people. Amour-propre is thus powerfully reinforced. One result is that ethics, just as much as physics, remain self-centred, and while the teaching in the *Discours* and elsewhere need be neither anti-social or in any way objectionable in practice, it remains based on self.

Another famous fragment, directly addressed to Miton, begins with the words 'le *moi* est haïssable', and ends with a paragraph which sums up the views on social behaviour of both Pascal and La Rochefoucauld:

> En un mot, le *moi* a deux qualités: il est injuste en soi, en ce qu'il se fait centre de tout; il est incommode aux autres, en ce qu'il les veut asservir: car chaque *moi* est l'ennemi et voudrait être le tyran de tous les autres. Vous en ôtez l'incommodité, mais non pas l'injustice; et ainsi vous ne le rendez pas aimable à ceux qui en haïssent l'injustice: vous ne le rendez aimable qu'aux injustes, qui n'y trouvent plus leur ennemi, et ainsi vous demeurez injuste et ne pouvez plaire qu'aux injustes. (P. 136/455)

This is the answer to those *honnêtes gens* who are content to avoid social friction, while leaving self-interest at the centre of their moral system. This is why Pascal speaks so severely at the end of the long section just quoted on amour-propre:

> L'homme n'est donc que déguisement, que mensonge et hypocrisie, et en soi-même et à l'égard des autres. Il ne veut pas qu'on lui dise la vérité, il évite de la dire aux autres; et toutes ces dispositions, si éloignées de la justice et de la raison, ont une racine naturelle dans son cœur. (P. 130/100)

These extensive quotations cover Pascal's view of how man stands with relation to the cosmos, to his fellow-men and to himself; his relations with God are not yet in question. As a classic and accurate description of familiar psychological patterns of *Angst*, frustration, instability, no one would dispute Pascal's account of the symptoms. To some extent too such symptoms must indicate a morbid condition, which *la nature corrompue* may reasonably be taken to translate. Man in the cosmos is a feeble creature, man in society is frivolous and insincere, man abandoned to his own thoughts is more often melancholy than not; all these observations can be made as pertinently today as in the seventeenth century. Yet even if these things are largely true, they are not always or necessarily true. The appropriate response to the worlds revealed by telescope and microscope may not be terror at all, but the thrill of exploration, in some cases an unshakable confidence in man's ability to master any world revealed to his reason. The Stoics offer an example of a non-Christian social code both stable and serious. The self-analysis of a Socrates can be calm and fruitful. Such objections as these are based mainly on exceptions, since they belong to the same Western cultural tradition as Pascal and his readers. A more serious objection is that such a picture of man would mean nothing to a Moslem or a Buddhist. None the less, one should not be too hasty in rejecting Pascal's reading of the human condition. *Angst* frequently appears as a product of Christianity, but given appropriate circumstances is equally found in societies untouched by Christian tradition. It may well be that any attempt to define man, or the human condition, in general is directed at a pseudo-problem, that human nature is not amenable to universal laws, but, being lodged in each of the individuals of the human race, may at best reveal statistical trends. In the context of this study these considerations are of secondary importance, because it is the applicability of the picture to the seventeenth century which is of immediate concern, but in any serious assessment of Pascal's place in the history of thought they cannot be ignored.

There is another point which cannot be passed over, although it raises difficulties of exposition; the *Pensées* are an apology for the Christian religion, of which the Fall is an integral doctrine. Catholics in the seventeenth and every other century accept it as an article of faith, to which an obvious alternative would be belief in pagan virtue. It must therefore be admitted once again that, in the last analysis, Pascal had no choice but to select symptoms of a spiritual disease which he believed inherent in man, and which a convert would also have to accept as such. In the historical context this is no weakness; the society from which his examples are drawn was recently or vestigially Christian, and could thus not fail to exhibit the symptoms in question. In addressing his apology to the minority of unbelievers in such a society, he could rely on the weight of numbers to support his picture of human weakness, and could also no doubt appeal both to normal suggestibility and the desire to conform socially in order to induce in his victims feelings similar to those of the majority. While it remains ultimately a matter of personal conviction whether Pascal's picture is universally true, given all the known facts, there is every reason to assume that his contemporaries in France acted, and even felt, as he says they did in significant numbers.

Passing from the symptoms to the diagnosis one sees at once that amour-propre, some of the social results of which have already been discussed as symptoms, is in fact the disease. When the whole of Pascal's argument has been unfolded amour-propre is clearly seen in the key role, usurping the central place properly assigned to God and Christ, but even at the psychological stage its centrality is unmistakable. The alternatives before man are either to obey some external set of values or to follow self-interest. In each case weakness in following the chosen course will lead to the symptoms described, and is therefore in itself bad; a lukewarm Christian will display at his weakest no less *inconstance*, *ennui*, *inquiétude* than the unbeliever who feels depressed at his own inadequacy. This is obviously an argument in favour of will; though total self-sufficiency is rare, it is not unattainable, and eliminates most of the psychological ailments described, but only at the price of what Pascal calls justice. In his view the most benevolent Stoic is still adding to the store of human misery. For one thing he is practising a remedy which is only accessible to an *élite*; for another even the most enlightened self-interest, when it conflicts with others no less enlightened, works to the eventual detriment of all. Ideally the ego should have an axis round which to revolve, this must be adjusted to meet the needs of other egos, and also geared to whatever external values may be accepted. The most economical solution is evidently to make the axis transcendental, so that the relationship of one ego with others will be found in their common axis. Put in this way the situation denounced in the fragments on amour-propre amounts to this; the ego not only usurps the place of a transcendental, and becomes its own axis, but imposes this same axis on others, whether they realize it or not.

Taking this line of argument to its logical conclusion, it can be said that at best a purely social 'honnêteté', divorced from religious or moral standards, leads each individual to recognize that others have desires analogous to his own. In practice these desires are not resisted, so long as mutual respect and non-interference are not interpreted as signs of weakness, inviting exploitation and eventually the domination of the many, who are complaisant, by the one, who is not. Such multilateral non-aggression pacts form the basis of *politesse mondaine*, and are a constant feature of daily life in any settled society, but this solves no long-term problems. On the level of action and expediency a 'do-as-you-would-be-done-by' ethic may work well enough, but if it rests on no better foundation than the instinct for self-preservation just ignores moral problems; 'an eye for an eye' easily becomes 'might is right.'

There is then an impasse, with all roads to a solution blocked by the ubiquitous 'moi'. Faced with the two cosmic infinites, man is too puny to support the weight alone, and yet puts himself at the centre of the world; in his relations with others, from whom he might otherwise derive aid and strength, he again puts himself in the centre, with the results just seen; left to himself he has the precious gift of thought, but while it is imprisoned in the circle of himself and his woes, thought can only add to his despair. This is the diagnosis, based on the symptoms, and invoking no argument which goes beyond psychological observation; *que la nature est corrompue*, *par la nature même*.

It might seem logical after discussing Pascal's criticism of contemporary 'honnêteté' to go on to his positive views on that subject, but to do so would be to ignore his own declared method and intention. At this stage the next thing to do is to prescribe the remedy, and now the arguments from nature must be supplemented by others. There is no piecemeal remedy for social ills for Pascal, and he aims to cure the whole man or nothing. Once the remedy has been prescribed and taken, 'honnêteté' will be as much a symptom of new health as the disappearance of *inconstance*, *ennui*, *inquiétude*. Given the facts of the case, as described in physical and psychological terms, it remains to translate them into a language which will permit a new approach. It is largely a matter of vocabulary and context whether one speaks of corrupt nature or the Fall, of cure or Redemption, but in translating the central problem, the fulcrum of the antithesis, there can be no ambiguity. What is required is a solution which will put man in a new relationship to the physical world, to his fellow-men and to himself, an axis which will reconcile *misère-grandeur*, making sense of both. An essential part of the requirement is that man by thought should be able to see within himself the seeds alike of corruption and redemption, so that the axis should be both outside him and intimately linked to him. Pascal has already said that 'le centre de tout' must be Christ, but for the purposes of his demonstration he must so define the type of remedy needed that the natural terms appropriate to the first stage of the argument should provide an easy transition into the second. Philosophy can offer partial solutions; thus God (on Cartesian lines) would meet the transcendental requirement, but would leave the gap to be bridged between Creator and creature; some ideal of human brotherhood (e.g. the Stoics) would solve some moral and social problems for a time, but not those of man's position in the universe, and so on. If among other working hypotheses Christianity is tried, one finds that Christ in the central position links God and man, Creator and creature, in the Incarnation, links man and man in the Redemption and in the Resurrection reconciles physical mortality and spiritual survival, without undoing the sanctification of matter achieved at the Incarnation. This does not, of course, prove the truth of Christianity, but it is intended to show that some such solution would work better than any other so far devised, satisfying all the requirements specified, so that if Christianity did not already exist, something very like it would have to be invented. As for its truth, the revelation contained in the Bible is on many points open to objective corroboration, on historical grounds, and it is this detailed examination of the credentials of Christianity that occupies the latter part of the apology. It is not the least of Pascal's merits that he accepts that the Bible is an integral part of the truth of which he has to convince the unbeliever.

It remains to examine in more detail some of the passages which link the argument from nature with the Christian hypothesis, and then to Scriptural evidence. The outstanding feature of the apology is that it is directed from the first at Christianity, and does not proceed from proofs of the existence of God, in a deistic sense, to elaboration in a Christian sense. This, like the attitude to the Bible, is Pascal's great strength, for anyone converted by his argument is specifically converted to Christianity, and not to some vague form of deism, with the hope of more light later.

In one of his longest fragments Pascal writes: 'Car la foi chrétienne ne va presque qu'à etablir ces deux choses: la corruption de la nature et la rédemption de Jésus-Christ.' (P. 335/194) This at once establishes the pattern for what is to follow, with its emphasis not on irreconcilable dualism but on balanced antithesis. As the chapter on *Method* has tried to show, this is Pascal's favourite formula, with a fulcrum normally supplied to link and balance the two apparent opposites; in this case, it is implicitly the Incarnation. This may be an appropriate moment to stress that whatever Pascal's connexions with Port Royal, and whatever his tendency in other works to exaggerate or distort the doctrine, he is here speaking of the Fall as any other Christian would. Augustinian influence on Pascal is so obvious as to need no comment, but in the *Pensées* his use of terms like Fall, sin, corruption should not be taken here in any restrictive or partisan sense, and this part of the argument at any rate is as inter-denominational as one could wish.

A series of apparent paradoxes leads up to the threshold of the mystery, before the link is revealed:

'Levez vos yeux vers Dieu, disent les uns; voyez celui auquel vous ressemblez, et qui vous a fait pour l'adorer. Vous pouvez vous rendre semblable à lui; la sagesse vous y égalera, si vous voulez le suivre.' 'Haussez le tête, hommes libres', dit Epictète. Et les autres lui disent: 'Baissez vos yeux vers la terre, chétif ver que vous êtes, et regardez les bêtes dont vous êtes le compagnon.'

Que deviendra donc l'homme? Sera-t-il égal à Dieu ou aux bêtes? Quelle effroyable distance! Que serons-nous donc? Qui ne voit par tout cela que l'homme est égaré, qu'il est tombé de sa place, qu'il la cherche avec inquiétude, qu'il ne la peut plus retrouver? Et qui l'y adressera donc? Les plus grands hommes ne l'ont pu. (P. 388/431)

There can be no solution which forces man to choose between God and beast; he is neither and he is both: 'Tous leurs principes sont vrais, des pyrrhoniens, des stoïques, des athées etc. Mais leurs conclusions sont fausses, parce que les principes opposés sont vrais aussi.' (P. 389/394)

If dualism is no answer, solipsism is worse: 'Nous sommes pleins de choses qui nous jettent au dehors. Notre instinct nous fait sentir qu'il faut chercher notre bonheur hors de nous.' (P. 390/464)

The Stoics are wrong to tell us to seek happiness within ourselves, so are those who urge us to seek it in distractions: 'Le bonheur n'est ni hors de nous, ni dans nous; il est en Dieu, et hors et dans nous.' (P. 391/465)

More in sorrow than in anger Pascal looks at those who remain heedless or ignorant of their plight, seeking at most palliatives instead of a remedy: '. . . j'admire comment on n'entre pas en désespoir d'un si misérable état.' (P. 393/693) Perhaps more than anything else in Pascal it is this emotional appeal that repels his critics. It is for this that Valéry, for example, delivered his saddening attack on his fellow-mathematician. Nor are all the critics self-sufficient intellectuals who quite understandably resent attempts to stampede them into a disquiet they genuinely do not feel. In his own day Pascal had to face opposition from those within the Catholic Church whom he doubtless regarded as fellow-travellers of Pelagius, and their descendants still find his pessimism exaggerated and ask what all the fuss is about. In the seventeenth-century context it is easy to see how real was the anguish felt by many who had lost, or never had, faith, and to them Pascal offered a remedy tried and proven by generations of unhappy people before them. It is easy, too, to see how the soft answers would no longer suffice for men of intellectual ability and personal integrity, who would not be fobbed off with some theological placebo; Pascal did not conceal the bitterness of the pill, but offered it as an effective cure for a disease which might otherwise destroy them. To those who do not seek he has nothing to offer beyond his sad astonishment, but it is not they who will want to read an apology. 'Console-toi, tu ne me chercherais pas si tu ne m'avais trouvé.' (P. 736/555)

Hamlet speaks again in a splendid passage from a long fragment in which Pascal begins by considering the Pyrrhonist position. This he approves, in that it puts reason in its place, but at the same time he finds it false, because instinct rebels against the logically irrefutable demand for limitless doubt:

> Quelle chimère est-ce donc que l'homme? Quelle nouveauté, quel monstre, quel chaos, quel sujet de contradiction, quel prodige! Juge de toutes chose, imbécile ver de terre; dépositaire du vrai, cloaque d'incertitude et d'erreur; gloire et rebut de l'univers. . . . Connaissez donc, superbe, quel paradoxe vous êtes à vous-même. Humiliez-vous raison impuissante; taisez-vous, nature imbécile: apprenez que l'homme passe infiniment l'homme, et entendez de votre maître votre condition véritable que vous ignorez. Écoutez Dieu. Car enfin, si l'homme n'avait jamais été corrompu, il jouirait dans son innocence et de la vérité et de la félicité avec assurance; et si l'homme n'avait jamais été que corrompu, il n'aurait aucune idée ni de la vérité ni de la béatitude. (P. 438/434)

The paradox is thus finally resolved, but only by a mystery surpassing our understanding: 'Chose étonnante, cependant, que le mystère le plus éloigné de notre connaissance, qui est celui de la transmission du péché, soit une chose sans laquelle nous ne pouvons avoir aucune connaissance de nous-mêmes!' (ibid)

The Fall, *damnosa hereditas*, original sin, can be psychologically explained as an attempt to fulfil literally the serpent's promise: 'Eritis sicut dei'. Man made of himself his own God, his own axis, and this overweening pride, amour-propre, remains his natural state. This is the crux, 'le nœud' as Pascal calls it, on which a multitude of human problems converge. If man's arrogance is horrifying, God's mercy in forgiving it is wonderful. The God of the philosophers is all-powerful, wise, just, but nowhere is there a hint of his gratuitous mercy, for nowhere is there a hint of the enormity of man's offence. Pascal shows how such a sin rightly inspires misery, but how greatly loved such a creature must be to earn such a pardon at such a price: 'La misère persuade le désespoir; l'orgueil persuade la présomption. L'Incarnation montre à l'homme la grandeur de sa misère, par la grandeur du remède qu'il a fallu.' (P. 677/526)

The dualism of the ghost in the machine is cancelled out by the Incarnation, which, for ever sanctifying matter, makes it no longer an object of Manichean loathing. Creator and creature come together in the fullness of creatural wretchedness; no aspect of man's abject state is repudiated and none untouched by divinity. This total integration of all the human faculties, the act by which *le roseau pensant* is confirmed in its privileges within the created world, here and hereafter, is the meaning of the Christian revelation as Pascal sees it. The Incarnation, though, is only the middle member of a triple truth, and must be seen in relation to the *felix culpa* and its reparation. Just as man's sin is timeless, so is God's will for man's redemption: 'ne evacuetur crux Christi'. The process historically begun with the Nativity continues for all time under the sign of the Cross. Here it is that men enter into a new relationship one with another, and it is through the Redemption that the true brotherhood of man arises.

The lesson Pascal draws from this is practical and concrete. If man must first find God by abandoning self-love, he can only fully practise the love of God by seeing in each one of his fellow-men an object no less worthy of God's love than himself. This may call for renunciation on the heroic scale: 'Jésus-Christ n'a fait autre chose qu'apprendre aux hommes qu'ils s'aimaient eux-mêmes . . . ; qu'il fallait qu'il les délivrât, eclairât, béatifiât et guerît; que cela se ferait en se haïssant soi-même, et en le suivant par la misère et la mort de la croix.' (P. 689/545)

But it also affects daily life: 'Il n'y a que la religion chrétienne qui rende l'homme *aimable* et *heureux* tout ensemble. Dans l'honnêteté, on ne peut être aimable et heureux ensemble.' (P. 695/542)

The importance Pascal attached to these practical consequences of Christianity may be judged from the fact that he concludes his long and controversial section on the *Pari* with what is evidently meant to be a decisive argument, showing that Christianity cannot fail to profit us here, even if the hereafter is in doubt:

Or, quel mal vous arrivera-t-il en prenant ce parti? Vous serez fidèle, honnête, humble, reconnaissant, bienfaisant, ami sincère, véritable. A la vérité, vous ne serez pas dans les plaisirs empestés, dans la gloire, dans les délices; mais n'en aurez-vous point d'autres? Je vous dis que vous y gagnerez en cette vie . . . (P. 451/233)

This is Pascal's answer to false 'honnêteté', and to 'gloire', which is always false. Christianity is not just theological, just spiritual, but practical too, and is incomplete if it is anything less. True 'honnêteté' as shown here is founded on disinterested service and fellowship, not just to man as man, but to men as members one of another in Christ. What would otherwise be as mortal as man thus endures, not indeed for ever, but to the end of the world.

More than once Pascal warns against the dangers of too close attachment to other people, mortal, like ourselves, which might weaken attachment to eternal values. Friendship, family love, is a consolation and a social good, but no substitute for the love of God, whose place it must never be allowed to usurp. Pascal asks of other men nothing for himself, and is ready to give of his own all that will not be robbing God. In this connexion it would be unrealistic to ignore Pascal's own temperament and experience, for it undoubtedly enabled him to follow his own precepts more easily than most men. It seems from his biographers that he had from his earliest youth some deep-seated psychological aversion to signs of affection, even between his own parents, and this persisted into later life, so that he resented such demonstrations of affection between his sister and her children. Some may feel that this only confirms their suspicions that Pascal's psychology was morbid, but, however that may be, it should be hardly necessary to point out that his views on the dangers of excessive human attachments find many echoes from men as orthodox as they are normal.

The broader social consequences of what has just been said shade off into politics. Society and the state are made up of individuals, and if each individual, or even a sizeable number, act according to the Christian principles proposed, laws and customs will insensibly become reformed. Ideally society should be as theocentric as the lives of the individuals composing it, but until (if so be God's will) it becomes so in the course of time, Pascal is willing to leave laws and customs as they are, on the clear understanding that they are as imperfect as all the other works of man; for the sake of peace we must bow the knee but not the heart.

Towards the end of the apology Pascal dwells at some length on the Church, and this account of his thought would be incomplete without a word on the subject. Once again, be it said, the *Pensées* do not represent propaganda for Port Royal, but an apology for Christianity addressed to all men of good will. Therefore it would be not only impolitic, but actually inconsistent with the whole preceding argument to stress the sense of election, the exclusivity of the chosen few. Instead Pascal insists on the continuity from Adam, through the Jewish people, to Christ, and thence through the Holy Spirit *in the Church* to the present day. The Protestants, who have set altar against altar, he condemns, preferring even the Jesuits, who with all their faults have not destroyed unity. Outside the Church there is no Christianity, and for Pascal the one true Church is that of Rome. To the authority of the Church we must bend heart and knee, for he sees this authority as vested by Christ himself. For obvious reasons, many critics have played down this section of the *Pensées*, but this is to do violence to Pascal's constant insistence on integration and unity. In an attempt to compensate for such an omission there is often emphasis on the role of personal experience in Pascal's religion, but this is again to distort his thought. He never denied that faith is a personal experience, that grace falls on individuals as it had fallen on him in the *nuit de feu*, but he does not conceive the doctrine and practice of Christianity apart from the Church, to which the most spiritually privileged 'moi' owes obedience.

This all comes back to the same point; amour-propre is always wrong, in whatever context or in whatever disguise, be it rebellion or conformism. If for the sake of peace at any price, amour-propre leads to socially acceptable conduct, that of the external 'honnête' *homme* or even the 'dévot', it is still wrong, and earns the illusory peace of the tomb, leading to the everlasting bonfire. True 'honnêteté', like true religion, demands inward and outward surrender, and springs from man's total integration in all his disparate elements, from his restoration to a proper axis.

There is a short text, preserved by Nicole, consisting of a paraphrase, or possibly the actual words, of Pascal, which may serve as epilogue to this study of his thought. It comes from the concluding paragraph of the third of the *Discours sur la condition des grands*, where Pascal addresses a noble youth, and recommends him to show benevolence to his future subjects:

Ce que je vous dis ne va pas bien loin; et si vous en demeurez là, vous ne laisserez pas de vous perdre; mais au moins vous vous perdrez en honnête homme. Il y a des gens qui se damnent si sottement, par l'avarice, par la brutalité, par les débauches, par la violence, par les emportements, par les blasphèmes! Le moyen que je vous ouvre est sans doute plus honnête; mais en vérité c'est toujours une grande folie que de se damner; et c'est pourquoi il n'en faut pas demeurer là. (p. 392)

9: MOLIÈRE

FOR all the excellence of the comedies with which Corneille first made his name, it is indisputably as a writer of tragedies that he occupies so eminent a position in the history of literature. Molière, too, had tried other paths before he found his highway to fulfilment, and though as a tragic author and writer of heroic comedies he knew more disappointments than success, this diversity of experience certainly contributed to the perfection of his comic masterpieces. It is this common variety of experience, as well as their common genius, which makes a comparison between the two at all possible; in fact, in so far as any generalizations are useful, it is more appropriate to consider Corneille with Molière than with Racine as the representative writers of their respective ages. At the height of their success they both enjoyed public as well as royal approval in the highest degree, and to that extent may be taken to reflect the point of view of a wide section of society. As for influence, this is harder to assess, but it was Molière's aim, as he says, to affect conduct by the portrayal of vices, and it is hard to believe that the message of his great comedies met with no response.

It is not just as an actor-author-manager with a sense of theatre second not even to Shakespeare's, but as a delineator of human problems that Molière continues to command respect and, above all, to entertain audiences. His farces, his Sganarelle and Scapin, may still raise a laugh, but it is those comedies which provoke thought which remain the most successful. All these, from his first great success *l'École des femmes*, to his last, *le Malade imaginaire* deal with monomaniacs and their impact on the society around them. Here, in a most forceful though perhaps unexpected way, the problem of the 'moi désaxé' is given the principal role, and in his treatment and solution of the problem Molière is as profound as any of the other authors studied. In comedy one would not look for metaphysical speculations of a formal kind, but none the less they are implicitly present in Molière's work, and a quite full and coherent picture of his views on life can be discerned in his major plays.

The plays to be discussed deal with a variety of situations, and entail a variety of solutions, but basically the problem is the same. In each case there is a monomaniac, normal in all respects save one, who knows that the rest of the world is against him but persists in believing himself to be the only one in step. The actual drama derives from a collision between the monomaniac and society, normally in the form of an action which will be irrevocable, marriage for example, and which will have the effect of annexing other individuals to the realm in which the maniac holds sway. The *dénouement* is produced by preventing in one way or another an issue on the point of being decided, and invariably has the effect of eliminating the danger to normal society of allowing an abnormal mind to impose its viewpoint on others. The exact mechanism varies according to the gravity of the mania, and produces *dénouements* ranging from the tragic end of Dom Juan to the genially comic one of M. Jourdain, but this basic pattern obtains throughout.

The first of Molière's great plays aroused a storm of protest, mainly inspired by jealousy at its success, but supposedly reflecting public indignation with features which were considered unseemly. The theme of *L'École des femmes* is not just *cocuage*, if it were the play would sound a very different note, nor is it the simple poetic justice to which Chrysalde refers early in the play:[1] 'Oui, mais qui rit d'autrui doit craindre qu'en revanche on rie aussi de lui.' (I/i)

There are in fact two themes, or rather one seen from two diametrically opposite standpoints: that of the title, the education of the perfect wife. In the eyes of everyone else Arnolphe is a kind of moral Canute, defying the tide of instinct, and callously sacrificing Agnès in doing so, but in his own eyes he is merely safeguarding his honour, his most treasured possession.

When, towards the end of the play, Chrysalde tries to make him see reason, his argument is turned by Arnolphe into a cynical

[1] All quotations have been taken from the 1932 edition of Molière, *Œuvres Complètes*, in *Bibl. de la Pléiade*. It should be noted that in some other editions the scenes are numbered differently.

approval of cuckoldry. All Chrysalde says is the evident truth:

> Être avare, brutal, fourbe, méchant et lâche,
> N'est rien, à votre avis, auprès de cette tache,
> Et de quelque façon qu'on puisse avoir vécu,
> On est homme d'honneur quand on n'est point cocu.
> (IV/viii)

His comment is the typical counsel of moderation found in most of Molière's comedies:

> Car pour se bien conduire en ces difficultés
> Il y faut, comme en tout, fuir les extrémités,
> (ibid.)

but he does not stop at this negative advice. Pointing out that marital good or bad fortune is an effect of fate (which is of course arguable, but by no means certain), he recommends a positive reaction to bad luck:

> Il faut jouer d'adresse, et, d'une âme réduite,
> Corriger le hasard par la bonne conduite.
> (ibid.)

Despite all that has happened and all this good advice, Arnolphe goes off to hasten the *dénouement*, as morally blind as ever:

> Moi, je le jure encore, or je vais de ce pas
> Contre cet accident trouver un bon remède.
> (ibid.)

This is obviously carrying the *point d'honneur* to the limits of absurdity, and in this sense Chrysalde's last words to Arnolphe offer the only possible answer to his monomania:

> Si n'être point cocu vous semble un si grand bien,
> Ne vous point marier en est le vrai moyen.
> (V/ix)

To this Arnolphe is too overcome by emotion to reply, but it seems more probable than not that he will prefer the pangs of secure celibacy to the vulnerable bliss of marriage. By choosing such a course he will at least assert his independence, even if this means moral isolation.

This Canute theme thus treated provides the basis for most of the comedy, but a further aspect of the same theme provides the element, so frequent in Molière, of potential tragedy. Arnolphe instructing Agnès in the duties of a wife is undoubtedly speaking for many serious-minded men, perhaps even the majority in his time, when he says:

> Votre sexe n'est là que pour la dépendance:
> Du côté de la barbe est la toute-puissance.
> Bien qu'on soit deux moitiés de la société,
> Ces deux moitiés pourtant n'ont point d'égalité:
> L'une est moitié suprême, et l'autre subalterne.

Despite the inequality, however, Agnès is to receive a powerful hostage:

> Songez qu'en vous faisant moitié de ma personne,
> C'est mon honneur, Agnès, que je vous abandonne.
> (III/ii)

These have been the commonplaces of anti-feminists for centuries; the Scholastics had given the Church's approval to such an attitude, and in Molière's audience there must have been many to whom it seemed a perfectly natural arrangement. If it were not for Arnolphe's long soliloquy immediately after Agnès has read the *Maximes du Mariage*, one could write him down as a domestic tyrant of perennial type. His opening words are the most significant:

> Je ne puis mieux que d'en faire ma femme.
> Ainsi que je voudrai, je tournerai cette âme:
> Comme un morceau de cire entre mes mains elle est,
> Et je lui puis donner la forme qui me plaît.
> (III/iii)

This is monomania in its ultimate form as a menace to others; so obsessed is Arnolphe by his fear of *cocuage*, and so confident of being able to avoid it, that he does not for one moment think that this inferior being, this girl, has any other rights than those which he, her creator, has allowed her. This surely is the supreme blasphemy of egoism; to take an infant of four and bring her up in seclusion to justify a theory at the price of her personality; in a word, to make a person into a thing.

Horace, in the next scene, does not know to whom he is speaking, but his comment is that of ordinary decency, outraged by conduct far exceeding anti-feminism in its denial of basic human rights.

> Malgré les soins maudits d'un injuste pouvoir,
> Un plus beau naturel peut-il se faire voir?
> Et n'est-ce pas sans doute un crime punissable
> De gâter méchamment ce fonds d'âme admirable,
> D'avoir dans l'ignorance et la stupidité
> Voulu de cet esprit étouffer la clarté?
> L'amour a commencé d'en déchirer le voile.
>
> (III/iv)

It is of course the last words which ensure the defeat of Arnolphe's project. As Horace had said just before, and as Agnès subsequently shows in her final interview with Arnolphe:

> Il le faut avouer, l'amour est un grand maître:
> Ce qu'on ne fut jamais, il nous enseigne à l'être.
>
> (ibid.)

And Agnès: '. . . dans l'âge où je suis/Je ne veux plus passer pour sotte, si je puis.' (v/iv)

The belief that Nature, expelled though she be by a pitchfork (here of solitary confinement) will return armed with invincible weapons is common in Molière's work. To that extent once Arnolphe leaves the realm of theory for that of practice his chance of success is negligible. At the same time, and this is what provides the drama, another hour or two would have seen a monstrous outrage legalized, and a personality permanently given into bondage. Any girl of less robust character than Agnès could hardly have survived the years of schooling (though the word is a parody of the fact) under Arnolphe's régime, and whatever natural instincts might eventually have found their way to the surface would have been repressed and punished, though sullen acquiescence would then inevitably take the place of ignorant docility.

If one agrees with Horace that Arnolphe's crime was deserving of punishment, it is fair to ask whether he is in fact adequately punished. Materially he has lost the outlay on Agnès from the age of four to the present, some dozen years, but is not physically punished in any other way. Psychologically his pride has been deeply wounded and there are signs that what he at least calls love has been awakened in the course of the play (e.g. 'Et cependant je l'aime après ce lâche tour,' (III/v) and the more suspect protestations of their final interview). What he admires in Agnès is above all her innocence, and ignorance; having planned his experiment when she was only four (and he is now forty-two) he had no reason to suspect her beauty, which impresses him when she grows up. Being struck by it, his reaction is to find it very desirable in itself, and, no less important, also an added tribute to his exceptional perspicacity and skill in managing marital problems. Love in any sense which implies respect or affection is not only unknown to him, but wholly incompatible with his monomania, which distorts his whole perspective and puts his honour in this single respect above and outside all other human obligations. The worst, then, that has happened to him is that he has been at the last moment deprived of what seemed a certain conquest. This must seem lenient punishment for a crime so nearly perpetrated, but psychologically Molière is undoubtedly justified. As a monomaniac Arnolphe is not fully responsible for his actions; as someone says in *La Critique* of this play 'Il n'est pas incompatible qu'une personne soit ridicule en de certaines choses et honnête homme en d'autres (Dorante, sc. vi). Now that his experiment, performed in virtual laboratory conditions, has failed it is most unlikely that Arnolphe will try again. He will be careful henceforth whom he mocks for wearing horns, he has at one stroke been rendered harmless. One can surely ask no more of justice than that. Morally this is no solution, unless the assertion of normal fallible social rules, including a quietly tolerant attitude to cuckoldry, be regarded as moral, but as a refusal to allow one aberrant ego to dominate any other it is wholly consistent with the preoccupations seen in previous writers.

The next two plays to be considered treat a far more serious problem, that of religion, and necessarily demand a more definite solution on a higher plane. *Tartuffe* and *Dom Juan* are by no means easy plays to interpret, and the latter in particular does not fit very readily into the general scheme of Molière's comedies. Despite the title it is not Tartuffe himself who is the monomaniac, but his patron Orgon—and to some extent Orgon's mother, Mme Pernelle, though senility has to be taken into account in her case. Orgon has been a good husband and father, respected and courageous:

> Nos troubles l'avaient mis sur le pied d'homme sage,
> Et pour servir son prince il montra du courage;
> Mais il est devenu comme un homme hébeté,
> Depuis que de Tartuffe on le voit entêté.
>
> (I/ii)

He seems to have been devout, since he went to church often enough to notice Tartuffe, then in extreme indigence, but loud and conspicuous in his devotions and pretence of piety. Tartuffe entered the house as 'un gueux qui n'avait pas de souliers/Et dont l'habit entier valait bien six deniers', (I/i) but now, well-dressed and overfed, enjoys an existence more privileged than anyone else in the household. Mme Pernelle, always censorious and puritanical, approved her son's association with Tartuffe in warm terms:

> Je vous dis que mon fils n'a rien fait de plus sage
> Qu'en recueillant chez soi ce dévot personnage;
> Que le Ciel au besoin l'a céans envoyé
> Pour redresser à tous votre esprit fourvoyé.
>
> (I/i)

but everyone else has seen immediately what sort of man he is, as Dorine tells her:

> Il passe pour un saint dans votre fantaisie,
> Tout son fait, croyez-moi, n'est rien qu'hypocrisie.
>
> (ibid.)

If there were no more at stake than the acceptance of an unscrupulous confidence trickster, as we have seen with *L'École des femmes* and *cocuage*, the comedy would have only limited implications. In itself this is bad enough; Orgon all but sacrifices his daughter's happiness and his wife's honour, his son's heritage and ultimately his own livelihood for the sake of his infatuation. The fact that religion is the cloak abused to conceal Tartuffe's iniquity (and of course the historical circumstances surrounding the play's production) demands a more striking *dénouement* than that of *L'École des femmes*. The sinister activities of so many *faux dévots* were a real social menace, and it was clearly essential that Molière should leave no room for doubt once he had introduced the theme of spiritual directors. Behind this general theme lies the special one, which makes Orgon not only a dupe but a monomaniac, and it is this which concerns the present study. Orgon, as already mentioned, had always been devout, but on meeting Tartuffe and taking him into his home he had acquired a quite new outlook:

> Qui suit bien ses leçons, goûte une paix profonde,
> Et comme du fumier regarde tout le monde.
> Oui, je deviens tout autre avec son entretien:
> Il m'enseigne à n'avoir affection pour rien,
> De toutes amitiés il détache mon âme,
> Et je verrais mourir frère, enfants, mère et femme,
> Que je ne m'en soucierais autant que de cela.
>
> (I/v)

A little later in the same conversation Orgon accuses his brother of libertinage, to which Cléante replies:

> [Vos pareils] Ils veulent que chacun soit aveugle comme eux.
> C'est être libertin que d'avoir de bons yeux,
> Et qui n'adore pas de vaines simagrées,
> N'a ni respect ni foi pour les choses sacrées.
>
> (ibid.)

This latter speech, together with Tartuffe's behaviour when he eventually appears, diverts attention from what Orgon has just said. Externals, it is true, represent the whole of religion as Tartuffe teaches it, but that does not explain his hold over Orgon, as do Orgon's words just quoted. Tartuffe is not a priest, has no institutional authority behind him, but he has converted Orgon to the belief that he, Orgon, is now saved but can only be sure of remaining among the elect while Tartuffe is there to guide him.

The monomania of Orgon, just like that of Molière's other monomaniacs, means that the fulfilment of his own desires becomes the overriding purpose in life to the exclusion of all others. He *must* remain elect, therefore he must obey Tartuffe. What is significant is that a man with his background could find it compatible to seek his own salvation, and believe he could ensure it, while professing total indifference towards those whom it was his Christian duty, and former habit, to love. There is no doubt that Molière is, through Orgon, attacking not only gullibility, but also a particular religious outlook, which he regarded as pernicious, quite apart from the way in which Tartuffe exploits it.

At the end, when Tartuffe's turpitude has been revealed, Orgon, now disabused, bursts out: 'C'en est fait, je renonce à tous les gens de bien,' (v/i) though his brother once again tries to make him see reason. Devout as he may have been, this violent reaction, following on his gullible acceptance of the improbable piety of Tartuffe, indicates religious convictions as unstable as they are shallow. Orgon is a spiritual hypochondriac, terrified of losing the source of his quack remedies. The proof that he is restored to health is his final resumption of paternal responsibilities. Neither God nor neighbour had come into Orgon's previous solipsist Paradise, where indeed Tartuffe usurped the place of each through his guardianship of the keys. Hellfire here plays the same role as *cocuage* in the earlier comedy, the difference being that it is an eternal calamity, and not so easily averted as Orgon thinks.

With *Dom Juan* this pattern is taken a stage farther, and it has often been argued that it is in fact taken too far to remain still within the bounds of comedy. The immediate association of Dom Juan is, of course, that of the sexual megalomaniac. As he says himself:

> J'ai sur ce sujet l'ambition des conquérants, qui volent perpétuellement de victoire en victoire et ne peuvent se résoudre à borner leurs souhaits . . . je me sens un cœur à aimer toute la terre; et, comme Alexandre, je souhaiterais qu'il y eût d'autres mondes, pour y pouvoir étendre mes conquêtes amoureuses. (I/ii)

It is at first in this sexual context that Dom Juan's disregard for higher laws is manifested; true, Sganarelle introduces his master at the beginning of the play as: '. . . le plus grand scélérat que la terre ait jamais porté, un enragé, un chien, un diable . . . qui ne croit ni Ciel, ni Enfer, ni loup-garou, qui passe cette vie en véritable bête brute' (I/i), and realizes some, if not all, of the implications: '. . . un grand seigneur méchant homme est une terrible chose'.

The first two acts add little to the familiar picture of the wholly unprincipled aristocrat, using any means to obtain the favours of the woman momentarily in view, and then brutally discarding her for the next. It is Act III which raises the wider issues and brings Dom Juan into line with the main problems under discussion.

Having mildly shocked Sganarelle by declaring his impiety to extend also to medicine—more a mystery than a science in the seventeenth century it is true—Dom Juan gives his famous confession of faith: 'Je crois que deux et deux sont quatre, et que quatre et quatre sont huit.' (III/i)

Sganarelle seems to assume that this point of view results from superior learning: 'Je n'ai point étudié comme vous; mais avec mon petit sens, mon petit jugement, je vois les choses mieux que tous les livres . . .' (ibid.)

He goes on with a conventional attempt to prove God's existence from His works, in this case the human machine, and concludes: 'Mon raisonnement est qu'il y a quelque chose d'admirable dans l'homme, quoi que vous puissiez dire, que tous les savants ne sauraient expliquer.'

It is noteworthy that here, as everywhere else, Dom Juan lets Sganarelle talk on until he is literally tripped up in his own reasoning, and never offers any amplification of his own radical impiety. Sganarelle's instinctive reaction against his master's superior tactics is a mistrust of learning and an affirmation of *la foi des simples*, but so far at least he is sufficiently moved by admiration to share the precarious life of Dom Juan, from whom human, let alone divine, retribution cannot be far distant.

There follow at once two scenes which explain how Dom Juan filled up the void which must otherwise result from limiting belief to mathematical certainty. Sganarelle says later on in the play: 'qui n'a point de loi vit en bête brute' (V/ii), and in these two scenes Dom Juan shows that his actions do in fact conform to an easily recognizable pattern: that, as one would expect, of self-interest. There is first the curious incident with the beggar, to whom Dom Juan gives alms 'pour l'amour de l'humanité'. In the context this means *not* for love of God, or any other higher law, and it is surely stretching a point too far to see in such a remark even the most embryonic faith in humanitarian principles. What Dom Juan loves, and this is genuine enough, is man's power, exercised through reason and will. It is in exercising this power himself, arbitrarily, but not as an *acte gratuit* (because it is specifically intended to demonstrate the independent power of man to one whose life is based on belief in divine assistance), that he invokes a love of humanity which the rest of his life proves to be hollow the moment it passes from amour-propre to some other object.

As if to underline this interpretation, a few moments later he explains why he has just risked his life to save that of an unknown, in the event the brother of his wronged Elvire: 'Notre propre honneur est intéressé dans de pareilles aventures'. (III/iii)

The meaning of 'honneur' is left in no doubt, since both Dom Carlos, before knowing the identity of his rescuer, and his brother, having recognized Dom Juan, have a lot to say about it. Dom Carlos explains his presence in these parts by: 'Une de ces fâcheuses affaires qui réduisent les gentilshommes à se sacrifier, eux et leur famille, à la séverité de leur honneur . . .' (ibid.) he finds: 'la condition d'un gentilhomme malheureuse, de ne pouvoir point s'assurer sur toute la prudence et toute l'honnêteté de sa conduite, d'être asservi par les lois de l'honneur au déréglement de la conduite d'autrui.'

His brother shares, though less reluctantly, just the same sentiments: 'L'honneur est infiniment plus précieux que la vie'. (III/iv)

It is interesting to find such agreement between three such different persons, and it is fairly clear from the context that 'honneur' is a purely external conception, 'good name', as it was for Arnolphe. There is, however, an important distinction to make between Dom Juan and all the others; for the brothers, honour is a family affair, as it was for Rodrigue and Chimène, a matter of vendetta (the scene is laid in Sicily, not France or Spain), and any nsult, whatever its nature, on one member had to be avenged by he others. Satisfaction was normally by feat of arms, and it is here and here alone, that Dom Juan joins them. Conduct in battle, the hinnest crust of chivalry, devoid of all content and significance, emains a law to be respected by all members of the former nightly class. Courage, in whatever cause, is an obligation which Dom Juan has never repudiated. But here his courage, just like his generosity a moment ago, is morally meaningless, if not actually immoral, since its sole motive and point of reference is amour-propre. None the less, the scene between Dom Juan and he two brothers is an excellent illustration of the force of a code, originally basic to noble conduct, and still no less binding despite ts divorce from all moral standards.

All this is more than enough to earn Dom Juan condign punishment at the hands of the society which he has so consistently outraged, but the sub-title, *Le Festin de Pierre*, is sufficient indication that even the stern civil penalties to be imposed on Tartuffe will not be enough for this far greater, because far more powerful, offender. The offences against Elvire and the peasant girls, reprehensible as they are, the mathematical credo, even the despicable contempt for his father's admonitions, all this is bad enough, but still on a human plane; to merit the extraordinary, and, for Molière, unique, intervention of the supernatural, Dom Juan has yet to commit his ultimate crime. This is his deliberate choice of hypocrisy as a cloak for new evildoing, a blasphemy from which even the hardened Sganarelle recoils.

The resolution to challenge Heaven by falsely parading under ts flag is thus expressed:

> C'est un dessein que j'ai formé par pure politique, un stratagème utile . . . l'hypocrisie est un vice à la mode, et tous les vices à la mode passent pour vertus. . . . C'est ainsi qu'il faut profiter des faiblesses des hommes, et qu'un sage esprit s'accommode aux vices de son siècle. (v/ii)

The resemblance with some of La Rochefoucauld's *Maximes* hardly needs stressing; what is more significant is the similarity, almost verbal, with the passage in Retz's *Mémoires* where he decides to 'faire le mal par dessein'. The reference to the *cabale* and the tone of the whole long speech on this theme are to be explained in the first instance in terms of the *Tartuffe* affair, but the abundance of contemporary references to *faux dévots* and hypocrites justifies taking this in the most general way.

Following so closely on the scenes in which Dom Juan first practises his new strategy on his father, then explains it to Sganarelle in the most cynical terms imaginable, only to outdo himself in the brief scene with Dom Alonse, his actual fate may seem solely due to his blasphemy, but it is in fact a little more complicated than that. A punishment on the purely human plane has clearly been an inadequate solution from the moment Dom Juan challenges Heaven, but once the punishment moves into divine hands, the question of mercy, irrelevant *ici-bas*, comes in. The precise mechanism of the *dénouement* is at first sight so crude that its real purpose may be obscured. After his father and Elvire have called him in vain to repent, Dom Juan is given a last chance in the very brief and rather unsatisfactory apparition which changes from a veiled woman to the figure of Time. Sganarelle implores him: 'Ah! Monsieur, rendez-vous à tant de preuves, et jetez-vous vite dans le repentir. DOM JUAN: Non, non! il ne sera pas dit, quoi qu'il arrive, que je sois capable de me repentir.' (V/V)

It is ironic that only a moment later the Statue takes him in its fatal grasp, and his very last words are his first and only genuine invocation: 'O ciel! que sens-je?'

To the last, honour and courage are the only laws Dom Juan respects, in other words he is himself the only judge and legislator to whom he pays attention. In all Molière's other plays, society either expels or neutralizes those whose tendencies, their monomania, threaten the common good. Dom Juan is popularly identified with sexual imperialism, but his monomania is far more serious; it is pride, at once satanic and solipsist, in its refusal to pay the slightest consideration to individuals, society or cosmic order. Pathological libertinage is the cause of Dom Juan's downfall. If his punishment is to be eternal it is because he has wagered in the full knowledge of the odds and stakes (to use Pascal's formula) and quite deliberately chosen damnation as the price for that freedom from constraint which his ego demands.

Of more general import than any of the previous plays is *Le Misanthrope*, perhaps Molière's best comedy, but the title should not be separated from the sub-title *L'Atrabilaire amoureux*. The whole situation is very much less serious in this play than in the other, and from the first it is clear that Alceste, and not society, stands to lose most. The point at issue is a very real and important one, and behind the comic treatment lies a problem, which engaged the attention of many who were no less misanthropic for being free of black bile.

Alceste's point of view is stated at the beginning of the play:

> Je veux qu'on soit sincère, et qu'en homme d'honneur
> On ne lâche aucun mot qui ne parte du cœur.
>
> (I/i)

These sentiments are admirable enough at first sight, though their social implications are clearly not without danger. Less attractive is another declaration:

> Je refuse d'un cœur la vaste complaisance
> Qui ne fait de mérite aucune différence;
> Je veux qu'on me distingue, et, pour le trancher net,
> L'ami du genre humain n'est point du tout mon fait.

Here speaks the authentic monomaniac, thanking Heaven that he is not as other men are, and wishing that more people would recognize the fact. Such an attitude robs the *homme d'honneur* of much of the sympathy which might otherwise be his. As a critic, then, of social insincerity Alceste loses much of his weight, though the facts speak for themselves. His friend Philinte is a much more interesting person, and perhaps the most distinctive of all the representatives of normal behaviour to be found in Molière's plays. His bile works well, and he sees what Alceste sees, but more clearly, and without drawing the same conclusions. His advice is that of Chrysalde:

> La parfaite raison fuit toute extrémité,
> . . . Et veut que l'on soit sage avec sobriété.
> Je prends tout doucement les hommes comme ils sont,
> J'accoutume mon âme à souffrir ce qu'ils font.
>
> (ibid.)

Despite the tolerance of the last lines, when he speaks his mind the verdict is as pessimistic as Alceste's:

> Oui, je vois ces défauts, dont votre âme murmure,
> Comme vices unis à l'humaine nature;
> Et mon esprit enfin n'est pas plus offensé
> De voir un homme fourbe, injuste, interéssé,
> Que de voir des vautours affamés de carnage,
> Des singes malfaisants et des loups pleins de rage.
> (ibid).

Philinte has come to terms with a society whose members he regards more in sorrow than in anger, he is accepted and respected by others, and he seeks by empirical means to live his own life with the minimum of friction. Alceste has not only failed to come to terms with society, but with himself. It is all very well to be prodigal with condemnations of insincerity and weakness, but logic requires that this global condemnation should not admit of exceptions recommended solely by considerations of passion. Having chosen Célimène as the object of his affections, he cannot reasonably protest when she lives up to the worst he had expected of a flighty and attractive widow; he says himself: 'Mais la raison n'est pas ce qui règle l'amour.' (ibid.) Nor, indeed, does it rule any of his conduct.

Unlike Philinte, his is an emotional misanthropy, compounded of humours and pride. Were it founded on virtue, a real love of morally admirable qualities, instead of amour-propre, the end would be not merely pathetic but tragic:

> Trahi de toutes parts, accablé d'injustices,
> Je vais sortir d'un gouffre où triomphent les vices,
> Et chercher sur la terre un endroit écarté,
> Où d'être homme d'honneur on ait la liberté.
> (v/iv)

Such a conception of solitary honour is at best impracticable, but as a comment on his previous conduct these words are ludicrous. In this play it is not the eminently sensible, if rather cynical, Philinte who provides the full answer to the monomaniac, but the rather inconspicuous Éliante. Here is a character of real worth, equally idealistic and practical:

> C'est ainsi qu'un amant dont l'ardeur est extrême
> Aime jusqu'aux défauts des personnes qu'il aime.
> (II/iv)

Particularly significant is Philinte's proposal to Éliante: how different from that of Alceste, made in pique as a reaction against Célimè. Éliante does not allow Alceste to make a fool of himself with her, though she would welcome a genuine proposal from his side, nor does she at first believe, or finally accept, Philinte, presumably in the hope that Alceste's desert sojourn will send him back with less bile and more sense. In his defence she says more than the spectator may be prepared to accept, and it reflects more on the goodness of her own character than on Alceste:

> Et la sincérité dont son âme se pique
> A quelque chose, en soi, de noble et d'héroïque.
> C'est une vertu rare au siècle d'aujourd'hui,
> Et je la voudrais voir partout comme chez lui.
> (IV/i)

Her constancy is almost gratuitous dramatically, but from the more general point of view puts the respective misanthropies of Philinte and Alceste in a truer perspective. Alceste is unstable, but obstinate like the other monomaniacs, and bound to return drastically changed from his retreat; Philinte is stable and pessimistic; Éliante is stable and optimistic. In that conformism does not satisfy her, she affords an exception to most of the good characters in Molière, and suggests that even the most artificial society may yet contain members unspoilt and unspoiling.

As far as the main comic theme goes, the play ends with Alceste's self-condemnation, rather than society's condemnation of him. His obstinate refusal to listen to his best friends may in this be compared with the equally self-destructive Dom Juan. The man who denies God and Heaven cannot expect to find a welcome after death, the man who condemns society and justice cannot expect friends or favour. Fortunately humours are less permanently corrosive than hellfire.

All four of these plays end with society reaffirming the normal order by the exclusion of the offending member or simply by the defeat of his monomania, which leaves him obliged to reform his life. The three other plays to be discussed show an important variation on the theme of re-establishment of the norm. None of them deals with a problem of quite such far-reaching implications as the earlier ones, but the mental states considered are in some ways more radically serious. Harpagon in *L'Avare* is deranged in a far more alarming way than Orgon or Arnolphe, let alone Alceste, and even as the comic effect reaches its height one has an uneasy feeling that the frontier between comedy and disaster (not to complicate the issue with talk of tragedy) may have been passed.

The pattern of *L'Avare* is the familiar one; the monomaniac, for whom money (and not what money can buy) is the only true good, chooses a girl, Marianne, who in her lack of wealth is as unsuitable a match for him as was Célimène for Alceste, quite apart from the dramatically decisive fact that his intended bride has already attracted the attentions of his own son. The play derives from the double match intended by this domestic tyrant, for whom a man of fifty, with wealth, is as admirable a match for his daughter as Marianne for himself, because Anselme will take her 'sans dot'. There is no need to analyse the familiar intrigue, recognition scenes and the rest, but two features of the play distinguish it. One does not actually see Arnolphe made *cocu*, but if the result of such a thing could be shown on the stage it might well produce a scene comparable to the last one of Act IV, when Harpagon sees that his treasure-chest, his only joy, has gone. To say that he is beside himself is no exaggeration; in his frenzy he accuses the audience (an audacious dramatic device), begs for their help in tracking down the thief, thinks he hears voices where there are none, and threatens suicide if his money is not recovered. All this, wild as it is, is almost an anti-climax to the initial moment of breakdown, when incoherence really reaches the point of insanity:

> N'est-il point la? N'est-il point ici? Qui est-ce? Arrête. Rends-moi mon argent, coquin . . . (*Il se prend lui-même le bras.*) Ah! C'est moi. Mon esprit est troublé, et j'ignore où je suis, qui je suis, et ce que je fais . . . tout est fini pour moi, et je n'ai plus que faire au monde. Sans toi, il m'est impossible de vivre. (IV/viii)

This is no more than the literal truth; he has lost with his money the centre of his world, his only *raison d'être*, his only point of reference, for moral or any other judgements. It is unique in Molière to find an object (rather than an idea) identified with the misplaced axis of the ego. This complete psychological breakdown results from the fact that unlike all the other monomaniacs, what rules Harpagon is not ordinary egoism but money, the physical object. Bereft of this he cannot even retire into his shell, he has no shell left, nothing to believe in now that he can see his loss.

Following from this is the second unusual point; the *dénouement*. Once Harpagon's derangement has been vividly demonstrated, it is clear that if the play is to remain within the limits of comedy he must be restored to the comparative sanity of his monomania. Since nothing but the physical handling of his *cassette* can reorientate him, and since nothing else matters to him but its restoration, all the personal complications which occupy the first four acts solve themselves. Orgon was never so indifferent to his family, surveyed from his position of elect eminence, as Harpagon, once his money is safely back in his hands. He sees Marianne married to his son, his daughter married ('sans dot') to the man she loves, but when Anselme rejoices in this happy ending, Harpagon has only one thought:

ANS.: Seigneur Harpagon, il faut lui pardonner cette imposture.
HARP.: Vous payerez donc le Commissaire?
ANS.: Soit. Allons vite faire part de notre joie à votre mère.
HARP.: Et moi, voir ma chère cassette.

The effect of this is to neutralize Harpagon as a menace to society, by removing from his shaky jurisdiction his two children, but his mania is respected and perpetuated by the return of the treasure. Psychologically this play amounts to saying that some pathological states can only be worsened, not cured. An ego fallen into such decadence as that of Harpagon is more frightening than comic, and the implications of the *dénouement* are anything but optimistic. Alceste is certainly no Timon of Athens, but Harpagon is equally no Shylock.

Both *Le Misanthrope* and *L'Avare* represent a triumph for Philinte's realistic acceptance of human faults, while at the same time they firmly assert the necessity for keeping eccentricity within bounds, above all not forcing it on others. This point of view, very different from that of *L'École des Femmes*, *Tartuffe* or *Dom Juan* is further illustrated by *Le Bourgeois Gentilhomme* and *Le Malade Imaginaire*. Snobbery and hypochondria (like pedantry in *Les Femmes Savantes*) are in themselves less dangerous than the type of monomania previously examined, though in the extreme form, which comedy lends them, these faults too threaten the stability of a home and disrupt the personality of the eponymous maniac. Neither M. Jourdain nor Argan will face reality, in their case agreeable enough. Jourdain is wealthy, a good business man, happy in his family, but like Orgon, taken in by a confidence-trickster who exploits his snobbery and manœuvres him into a position of absurdity; what salvation was for Orgon, ennoblement is to be for Jourdain, and if the price is to be the sacrifice of family and property, it is still worth while. Precisely the same situation obtains in the hypochondriac's household, only his ferociously rude health would have enabled Argan to survive so much medical attention, but he is determined at all costs to have bodily salvation on call, in the family, just like his *confrère* in folly, Orgon: 'Me voyant infirme et malade, comme je suis, je veux me faire un gendre et des alliés médecins.' (I/v) The two later plays, however, demand only a solution *ici-bas*: *Tartuffe* could only end with the punishment of the impostor, not the guaranteed salvation of the dupe. These two plays end with a fantasy which has the effect of making society (through its members on the stage) accomplices of the monomaniac. The simple device of handing back Harpagon's treasure-chest restores him to his fantasy-world, but implicates no one else. Here, on the contrary, the initiation of Jourdain into his Turkish dignity and Argan into his medical office is carried out with the co-operation of all. Instead of ending with punishment for evil done or with a solitary hangover in the desert, these plays end with the apparent fulfilment of a dream.

Harpagon is not cured, not curable, but the homœopathy

practised on Jourdain and Argan is enough to neutralize their monomania so that the other healthy elements in their psychology can play their proper part. Jourdain is no less anxious to be noble, but convinced of the authenticity of the *Turquerie* does not doubt that the miracle has been accomplished, and for him his wife's eventual acceptance of the situation marks fulfilment: 'Voilà tout le monde raisonnable!' (v/vi) For Argan health remains no less of an obsession, but his faith in doctors has been so shaken that he entrusts his precious life henceforth only to his own ministrations. This time it is Béralde who comments on the situation about to be created: 'L'on n'a qu'à parler avec une robe et un bonnet, tout galimatias devient savant, et toute sottise devient raison.' (III/xiv) Like Philinte, Béralde sees in conformism, custom and appearance, a sufficient justification for conduct. 'Raison' in these two plays is simply wishful thinking, granted official status, or fantasy, certified genuine.

It is perhaps not beside the point to recall Molière's lack of confidence in the medical profession and his realistic attitude towards the nobility, so that it could be argued that a man who believes himself noble or a physician is only at one, insignificant, step from the real thing, itself of no great substance. However that may be, *L'Avare* rather grimly and *Le Bourgeois* and *Le Malade* in festive mood admit madness into ordinary life. Mistaken identity is, however, a minor form of lunacy in the demands it makes on society, and can thus be treated more lightheartedly.

With the rather problematic exception of *Dom Juan*, these seven plays show the same conception of psychology, normal and abnormal, of society, as well as of comedy. The similarity of pattern throughout, and the two types of *dénouement*, corresponding to the abnormality to be corrected, form a coherent and comprehensive attitude. The general thesis advanced in all the plays is *fuir les extrémités*; nature is a better guide than abstract theory: 'La nature, d'elle-même, quand nous la laissons faire, se tire doucement du désordre où elle est tombée' (Béralde, *Le Malade*, III/iii); there is room in society for faults but tolerance must never become self-defeating by opening the door to tyranny. All this is familiar enough, and it would be strange if there were no more profound lesson to be drawn from Molière. On the psychological plane the outstanding fact is that Molière deals invariably not with people who are inherently comic, but with clinical cases of persons otherwise normal afflicted with a monomania. It is curious to see in the mechanism of the resultant comedy a parallel in exact reverse of Corneille's tragic psychology. Most of Corneille's tragic heroes begin, like Auguste, as 'maîtres de l'univers', endowed with immense material and physical power, but striving throughout the play in tragic conflict to arrive at that single-mindedness which Auguste is able at last to express: 'Je suis maître de moi comme de l'univers'. Molière's characters, as monomaniacs, are single-minded, pathologically so, from the start, and thus *maîtres de soi*, but the comic conflict derives precisely from their inability to extend their mastery to others, whether to individuals or to society as a whole. Harpagon, at a very low level, Dom Juan on the highest exemplify this equally well. For Molière there was no triumph of the will, egoism was permitted only within the private limits of one ego; for the rest public security, if need be reinforced by the Prince, remained the paramount consideration.

The strong emphasis on the family in most of the plays indicates the basis for social ethics; practical questions of family loyalty and discipline weigh heavier than theories about abstract virtue, even put forward by a worthy Éliante. Emphasis on the family, the basic unit of natural stability, goes with a strong emphasis on keeping one's place, doing one's job in society. These standards are bourgeois, not feudal, practical, not theoretical, social, not heroic, and they were those of Molière's time and class. Two quotations strike the balance between inner harmony and external conduct: the first, addressed by Béralde to Argan, applies equally well to Orgon and Jourdain: 'Songez que les principes de votre vie sont en vous-même' (III/vi); the other applies in the first instance to the playwright himself, but is also a summary of the views on social behaviour to be found in the plays: 'Je voudrais bien savoir si la grande règle de toutes les règles n'est pas de plaire.' (Dorante, *Critique de l'école des femmes*, sc. vi).

10: BOSSUET

FROM Molière to Bossuet is less of a jump than Bossuet for one might have wished to admit. In their totally opposite ways, they were both dealing with very much the same problem: that of making contemporary society see the truth about itself and profit thereby. To this end Molière used entertainment, Bossuet high seriousness, but each in his own way was equally concerned to instruct. Bossuet's ultimate aim was, of course, to bring men to God, but he belongs to the present series of studies because he devoted a good deal of time to dealing with the various obstacles put up by individuals and society against true religion, and particularly because not the least influential part of his teaching concerns relationships in this world. Alone of all the authors to be considered here Bossuet was a full member of the seventeenth-century Establishment. Retz and La Rochefoucauld, who were qualified by birth, were debarred through political adventure, and those who were accepted at Court, Corneille and Molière, were there only in a capacity limited by class and profession. The Church continued as always to offer a career genuinely open to all talents. Bossuet's position was in some ways an anomalous one; he was probably eclipsed as an orator by Bourdaloue, he was certainly not the leading historian or theologian of his age, episcopal preferment never carried him farther than the geographically convenient, but hierarchically inferior, see of Meaux, he was not confessor to either King or Queen, though for eleven years tutor to their son, and yet he acted on several occasions as spokesman for the Church in France and for much of his life enjoyed an influence unsurpassed by his ecclesiastical superiors. Perhaps most anomalous is the deep gulf between his private spiritual leanings and the public utterances to which his position committed him.

His significance in the picture of Louis XIV's reign derives from the uniquely privileged position he occupied for so many years at Court. Though his criticism of Court life was unsparing, and at times touched lightly on the King himself, his positive views on kingship and politics had as profound an effect in shaping society as did his criticism of abuses. Like many another courtier before and after him, he became the prisoner of his own *persona*, that which had originally won him the royal favour he must sometimes have regretted, and only at the end of his life, with his official course largely run and more modest pastoral cares to occupy him, did he find time and freedom to put the world in a truer perspective.

His life is eloquent of the tormented experience of his generation, which, spanning the middle years of the century, had seen the full development of all that has been discussed in these pages. Born in 1627, the year Retz was installed a boy-canon of Notre Dame, he had gone in his youth to see Corneille's plays with his then worldly friend Rancé, Richelieu's godson, who received deacon's orders from Retz and remained faithful to him in disgrace. By 1652, when he was ordained priest, the Fronde had collapsed, and he first came to royal notice while Mazarin was still in nominal control, rising to his summit when Louis was at his victorious height. His preaching covers the period from 1649, his first extant sermon, preached as sub-deacon at Metz, to 1687, when he returned to Court to honour the obsequies of Condé. Descartes and Pascal, Newton and Leibnitz, Corneille, Molière, Racine, all formed the background to his career, which saw too the whole Jansenist quarrel from start to finish, Quietism, Gallicanism, the Revocation of the Edict of Nantes, and both English Revolutions. It is sufficiently obvious that he represents almost ideally the end-product of so many conflicting tendencies. Though he made his influence felt in a variety of ways, there can be no doubt that he originally won his position and subsequently established his reputation in the pulpit. If one were studying Bossuet for himself it would be necessary to take the great mass of his other work into account, but for the present purpose the sermons give a better idea than anything else of how he found and how he affected the world around him. What Molière was to the Court at play, he had to try to be for the Court at prayer; the resultant presentation of religion is an integral part of the *grand siècle*.

Out of some 200 surviving sermons, the best known are the *Oraisons Funèbres*, but these need to be supplemented by sermons of less restricted application, such as the Panegyrics preached in honour of particular saints. The existence of a modern edition of nearly forty representative sermons is too convenient not to be decisive in determing the selection to be considered here. Throughout his forty years' preaching activity his style changed radically, but he did not so much vary as intensify the basic themes of his message. As one might expect in that century, the theme of Grace frequently occurs, closely linked with that of Reason, but it is in his third main theme, that of Authority, that Bossuet best demonstrates his own characteristic contribution to the questions under discussion.

An early specimen of his views comes in the Panegyric preached in honour of St. Teresa in 1657, before Anne of Austria at Metz. Internal evidence, notably a special exordium addressed directly to the Queen, suggests that Bossuet's sentiments were inspired as much by his exalted audience as by the saint. His main theme is that this world and the next are linked by the common bond of charity. Condemning the falseness of earthly hopes, Bossuet urges his hearers to distinguish this from true Christian hope.

> Considérez en effet, Messieurs, ce que c'est qu'un homme enflé d'espérance. À quels honneurs n'aspire-t-il pas? quels emplois, quelles dignités ne se donne-t-il pas à lui-même? Il nage déjà parmi les délices, et il admire sa grandeur future. Rien ne lui paraît impossible. . . . Mais ô espérance du siècle, source infinie de soins inutiles et de folles prétentions, vieille idole de toutes les cours, dont tout le monde se moque et que tout le monde poursuit, ce n'est pas de toi que je parle. (p. 435)[1]

Here, and in much of his work, a key to his thought is provided by the quotation from St. Augustine: 'Qui non gemuit peregrinus, non gaudeat civis'. The price of eternal felicity must be paid here. In the next part of the sermon he touches on ideas already met in the *Pensées*: 'Combien longues, combien ennuyeuses vous paraissent ces tristes journées que vous passez sans aucun plaisir de

[1] All sermon references are to the 1936 edition of Bossuet, *Oraisons Funèbres et Panégyriques* in *Bibl. de la Pléiade.*

conversations ou de jeu, ou de quelque autre divertissement!' (p. 447)

This he contrasts with Teresa's felicity in the midst of constant mortifications, again using a typically Augustinian phrase: 'Il n'est rien de plus opposé que de vivre selon la nature et de vivre selon la grâce.' (p. 448)

He concludes his sermon by relating the apparently remote facts of saintly life to the actual situation of his noble audience:

Prosternez-vous humblement aux pieds de ce Dieu crucifié; dites-lui, honteux et confus: Puisque vous ne m'avez point jugé digne de me faire part de votre croix, permettez du moins, ô Sauveur, que j'emprunte celle des autres, et que je la puisse porter avec eux. (p. 451)

This general exordium is followed by one addressed to the Queen Mother (an alternative version, not delivered, exists, addressed to the King himself). Wishing the King victory and prosperity, Bossuet goes on:

Mais parmi tant de prospérités, nous ne croyons pas être criminels, si nous lui souhaitons aussi des douleurs. J'entends, Madame, ces douleurs si saintes, qui saisissent les cœurs chrétiens à la vue des afflictions, et leur font sentir les misères des pauvres membres du Fils de Dieu; . . . et pour récompense de ces douleurs que la charité vous inspirera, puissiez-vous jamais n'en ressentir d'autres, et après une longue vie recevoir enfin de la main de Dieu une couronne plus glorieuse que celle qui environne votre front auguste. (ibid.)

This early sermon already contains many of Bossuet's main ideas, though not yet expressed with all the vigour and clarity that were to come later. It shows the extreme difficulty of the task before him. On the one hand he preached, and sincerely believed, an Augustinian *contemptus mundi*, on the other he had to apply this doctrine to those for whom worldly concerns were an occupational disease, and combine a eulogy of mortification with loyal hopes that no material ills would afflict his hearers. St. Vincent de Paul, who had taught him in his early years, had long ago established the tradition of aristocratic charity, honourably practised by the highest in the land (and skilfully exploited by Retz), but useful and admirable as generous almsgiving may be, it barely affected the living standards of those who gave. To forsake all and follow the way of the Cross was given to very few, and such cases as that of Rancé (whose conversion dated from the same year as this sermon) must always remain exceptional in any society. How then can the full spiritual price be paid by those whose rank normally protects them from earthly suffering? Bossuet's answer is that sharing the suffering of others, compassion is all that can be demanded: 'ces pieuses inquiétudes qui travaillent votre Majesté en faveur des misérables'. There may be no better answer, but Bossuet does not perhaps express it in the best way. 'Récompense' is a strong word to describe the relationship between 'ces douleurs' at the sight of others' suffering and freedom from personal suffering here, to be followed by a crown of glory hereafter. It looks almost as though this world and the next are as much linked by feudal privilege as by charity.

Bossuet had no time for fanatics, and the common sense he brought to the religious problems of his age is a principal source of his reputation. In his *Oraison Funèbre* (1663) of Nicolas Cornet, his own teacher and famous as Syndic of the Faculty of Theology during the affair of the Five Propostions, Bossuet lays much stress on moderation, in terms reminiscent of Molière:

> L'ennemi de notre salut se sert également des uns et des autres, employant la facilité de ceux-là pour rendre le vice aimable, et la sévérité de ceux-ci pour rendre la vertu odieuse . . . Aveugles enfants d'Adam, que le désir de savoir a precipités dans un abîme d'ignorance, ne trouverez-vous jamais la médiocrité, où la justice, où la vérité, où la droite raison a posé son trône?
>
> . . . Vous voyez donc, Chrétiens, que pour trouver la règle des mœurs, il faut tenir le milieu entre les deux extrémités. (p. 55)

He becomes positively Johnsonian in his rejection of 'les chicanes raffinées, les subtilités en vaines distinctions' (actually a quotation from Augustine), which had for all that been a matter of life and death for Port Royal. His hearers are exhorted to follow the example of unswerving rectitude offered by Cornet, with his 'respect envers notre monarque, soumission à l'Eglise, amour immense envers son prochain.' (p. 67)

This praise of moderation and obedience closely corresponds with the qualities for which Bossuet showed most regard during his own public life. It is significant that he stresses Cornet's normally pacific nature, but commends his firm handling of the Jansenist dispute. Bossuet too was implacable, and could be vindictive, when roused to anger, as his saddening quarrel with Fénelon shows, and, like many people who are prepared to give unquestioning obedience, demanded it of others.

His sermon (1670) on the death of Henriette-Anne of England makes very much the same points. He begins by explaining why attention should not be fixed exclusively on the vanity of this earthly life, and proposes a more balanced view:

> Il ne faut pas permettre à l'homme de se mépriser tout entier, de peur que, croyant avec les impies que notre vie n'est qu'un jeu où règne le hasard, il ne marche sans règle et sans conduite au gré de ses aveugles désirs . . . Que ce tombeau nous convainque de notre néant pourvu que cet autel, où l'on offre tous les jours pour nous une victime d'un si grand prix, nous apprenne en même temps notre dignité. (p. 98)

The antithesis *néant-dignité* inevitably recalls *misère-grandeur*, and, after drawing the obvious lessons from the contrast between the high estate to which the Princess had been born and the fate which had overtaken her family, Bossuet takes up another Augustinian theme: 'Entrons dans une profonde considération des conduites de Dieu sur elle, et adorons en cette princesse le mystère de la prédestination et de la grâce.' (p. 112)

A moment later he explicitly refers to 'le fidèle interprète du mystère de la grâce, je veux dire le grand Augustin.' His illustrations of how God accomplished His purpose in this case are striking. Speaking of the Protestant faith into which the Princess was born, he says: 'Pour la donner à l'Église, il a fallu renverser tout un grand royaume . . . Mais si les lois de l'État s'opposent à son salut éternel, Dieu ébranlera tout l'État pour l'affranchir de ces lois. Il met les âmes à ce prix; il remue le ciel et la terre pour enfanter ses élus.' (ibid.)

This seems more than just a rather naïve finalism, justified perhaps by the requirements of the genre; it is palpably implausible. For one thing, conversion is no guarantee of salvation, for another there is no theological or other reason why a single person should be saved at the cost of abandoning millions of fellow-countrymen to heresy and civil war, and presumably perdition. It is impossible to escape the implications of privilege, and the elect for whom kingdoms are overthrown look suspiciously like those whom God has already called to earthly dignity. It is particularly ironic that the death of the man sometimes honoured as Charles the Martyr should be regarded as no more than one of the events predetermined to ensure the conversion and salvation of his daughter, but not himself. It is natural that Bossuet should speak with assurance about the saints, whom canonization officially declares to be numbered with the elect, but a coronet is not a halo, and in his *Oraisons funèbres* he seems to be taking too much for granted.

If any saint might be expected to provide a counterweight to these aristocratic tendencies it is surely St. Francis of Assissi. Bossuet's first panegyric dates from 1652, the year of his ordination. This time the aspect of worldliness condemned is intellectual and the theme is that of God's fool, 'stultus fiat ut sit sapiens':

> . . . la raison humaine, toujours téméraire et présomptueuse, ayant entrevu quelque petit jour dans les ouvrages de la nature, s'est imaginée découvrir quelque grande et merveilleuse lumière; au lieu d'adorer son Créateur elle s'est admirée elle-même . . . Ainsi . . . l'homme s'est persuadé que tout l'ordre du monde devait aller selon ses maximes . . . il a voulu que la Divinité se réglât selon ses idées. (p. 261)

As a version of *la superbe des philosophes* this seems peculiarly applicable to Cartesianism. Continuing the assault, Bossuet refers to poverty, but points out: 'Ce partage des biens . . . ayant été autorisé par la loi divine, vous êtes les maîtres et les propriétaires de la portion qui vous est échue. (p. 270) The sanctity of property is a necessary condition of responsible stewardship and for almsgiving, but Francis preferred to renounce all possessions.

According to this sermon, the three great worldly attractions, on which Francis turned his back are wealth, pleasure and 'gloire'. Curiously enough, while expatiating at length on the first two, when Bossuet comes to the last he chooses a single example; the fact that the saint refused priestly orders on the grounds of his own unworthiness. Barely three sentences are devoted to this evidently delicate topic before Bossuet passes on to the general conclusion: 'Radix omnium malorum est cupiditas'. The point of the sermon is that Francis only attained truth by espousing what was folly in the eyes of the world, whose values he rejected.

St. Catherine (of Alexandria) affords another opportunity for consideration of man's intellectual pretentions. Once again St. Augustine is quoted in the opening sentences; this time it is the *libido sciendi* that Bossuet is attacking.

> C'est elle (la science) qui s'est élevée contre la science de Dieu: c'est elle qui, promettant de nous éclaircir, nous aveugle plutôt par l'orgueil; c'est elle qui nous fait adorer nos propres pensées sous le nom auguste de la vérité; qui, sous prétexte de nourrir l'esprit, étouffe les bonnes affections, et enfin, qui fait succéder à la recherche du bien véritable, une curiosité vague et infinie, source inépuisable d'erreurs et d'égarements très pernicieux. (p. 502)

He makes the point that for the Christian knowledge for its own sake is valueless unless it be translated into action, and that the only source of true knowledge is faith. On these points St. Catherine sets a shining example. Bossuet adds a reflection about her sex which deserves quoting *in extenso*:

> Les dames modestes et chrétiennes voudront bien entendre en ce lieu les vérités de leur sexe. Leur plus grand malheur, Chrétiens, c'est qu'ordinairement le désir de plaire est leur passion dominante; et comme pour le malheur des hommes elles n'y réussissent que trop facilement, il ne faut pas s'étonner si leur vanité est souvent extrême, étant nourrie et fortifiée par une complaisance presque universelle . . . C'est la raison principale pour laquelle, si je ne me trompe, on les exclut des sciences; parce que, quand elles pourraient les acquérir, elles auraient trop de peine à les porter; de sorte que si on leur défend cette application, ce n'est pas tant, à mon avis, dans la crainte d'engager leur esprit à une entreprise trop haute, que dans celle d'exposer leur humilité à une épreuve trop dangereuse. (p. 512)

Throughout this sermon the attack on philosophers and scientists is maintained, and it is made clear that their crime is that of attempted independence. As for the *Femmes Savantes*, long before Molière, Bossuet had put them most ungallantly in their place.

In general, *l'art de plaire* is one of his favourite targets from now on.

By 1685 Bossuet's views on reason and its pretentions had not changed nor had he become more lenient on the subject of *l'art de plaire*. In the *Oraison Funèbre* of Anne de Gonzague he describes the pious beginnings of the princess, abruptly disturbed by successive bereavements: 'Mais ce ne fut pas là sa plus grande plaie. Maîtresse de ses désirs, elle vit le monde, elle en fut vue; bientôt elle sentit qu'elle plaisait, et vous savez le poison subtil qui entre dans un jeune cœur avec ces pensées.' (p. 158)

Perhaps some of his hearers thought of Célimène, an equally merry widow.

Marriage, then widowhood, found her alternating between faith and incredulity. Bossuet violently attacks the *libertins* whose influence she felt:

> Il (Dieu) a mis dans cette Église une autorité seule capable d'abaisser l'orgueil et de relever la simplicité . . . C'est contre cette autorité que les libertins se révoltent avec un air de mépris . . .
>
> Leur raison qu'ils prennent pour guide, ne présente à leur esprit que des conjectures et des embarras. Les absurdités, où ils tombent en niant la religion deviennent plus insoutenables que les vérités dont la hauteur les étonne; et pour ne vouloir pas croire des mystères incompréhensibles, ils suivent l'une après l'autre d'incompréhensibles erreurs. Qu'est-ce donc, après tout, Messieurs, qu'est-ce que leur malheureuse incrédulité, sinon une erreur sans fin . . . un orgueil qui ne peut souffrir son remède, c'est-à-dire que ne peut souffrir une autorité légitime? . . . *Ce superbe . . . se fait lui-même son Dieu.* [my italics.] (p. 166)

This quotation contains much of Bossuet's thought on the here related subjects of reason and authority. In his sermon on St. Catherine, twenty-five years before, he had spoken of 'les philosophes . . . protecteurs de l'erreur', and here his indignation is even more marked. The Princess's final and dramatic conversion provides him with a text to celebrate the defeat of reason and pride, the victory of faith and obedience. Marked out by birth for special favours, wealthy enough to dispense the most generous alms, the Princess had gone far along the road to impiety when a sudden flash of divine love restored her to faith. In St. Augustine's words (once again) Bossuet describes her desperate situation: 'Il restait la souveraine misère, et la souveraine miséricorde . . . Il restait ce secret regard d'une Providence miséricordieuse, qui la voulait rappeler des extrémités de la terre.' (ibid.) Defiance, grace, submission, mark the human steps along the path designated by God for His elect.

From the six sermons so far mentioned a recognizable pattern can be traced. Victorious virgin or worldly widow, professional theologian or fool of God, royal convert or mystic nun, each is used to exemplify certain lessons concerning both this world and the next. Providence will never fail, God calls his elect past every barrier of human devising; wealth is a blessing, but only when shared with the needy; the works of reason, philosophy and science encourage man's natural vanity and keep him from God; above all, the Catholic Church, in its authority exercised through human ministers, offers an infallible, and indeed unique, guide to the fulfilment of the divine purpose. The constant references to St. Augustine (it is a pity that no sermon devoted to him has survived) emphasize the great Augustinian current of the seventeenth century, and often bring Bossuet closer to Port Royal than he may have realized. It is here that the affinity with men of such different background as Pascal and La Rochefoucauld can be recognized and understood. In his own life, indeed, he had to face accusations of Jansenism, and such comments as 'l'ordure des casuistes' lent substance to the charge.[1] On the last point to be considered Bossuet stands out by virtue of his official position from the other writers who superficially resemble him. A man enjoying authority and addressing the highest in the land will naturally adopt a tone different from that of private persons, however exalted their lineage. An early, and successful, sermon preached in Metz in 1653 describes the life and work of his fellow Burgundian, St. Bernard, for whom he had a special cult, and it is a pity that Bossuet did not come back to the same subject thirty years later, when he occupied a position not unlike that of Bernard five centuries before. This sermon speaks of the saint's authority, whether with Popes or kings, warriors or heresiarchs,

[1] See whole letter to Rancé, in *Œuvres,* Paris, 1875 vol. xxvi, p. 302.

and attributes it, no doubt correctly, to the fact that he was 'et libre et modeste, également ferme et respectueux'. This follows a less convincing passage, comparing Bernard with 'les réformateurs de ces derniers siècles. Si leur arrogance trop visible leur eût permis de traiter les choses avec une pareille modération, ils auraient blâmé les mauvaises mœurs sans rompre la communion, et réprimé les vices sans violer l'autorité légitime.' (p. 311)

St. Bernard's campaign against Suger of St. Denis, his heavily paternal advice to the Cistercian Pope Eugenius II, his vehement onslaughts on Abélard, even his polemics with Cluny do not leave one with quite this impression of moderation, but then Bossuet himself would doubtless have denied that he overstepped the bounds of moderation in his controversies with those whom an earlier age would have burned before they could answer back. Everything turns once again on the last two words. Long before Bossuet had come within sight of the power that later years brought him he was lamenting the laxity of the post-Tridentine Church:

> Ainsi vivaient nos pères, dans le temps où la piété fleurissait dans l'Église de Dieu. Pensons-nous que les flammes d'enfer aient perdu depuis ce temps-là leurs intolérables ardeurs, à cause que notre froideur a contraint l'Église de relâcher l'ancienne rigueur de sa discipline, à cause que la vigueur ecclésiastique est énervée? (p. 312)

It was left to Bossuet's lifelong friend, Rancé, to restore some of the old spirit, and it is peculiarly fitting that the reformer of La Trappe should have fulfilled in St. Bernard's own order the most austere programme of the century.

This preoccupation with discipline and authority is constant and lasting (it would be instructive to take a count of the number of times the two words appear in Bossuet's work). Two or three years later, in 1654, St. Charles Borromeo inspires similar remarks:

> Voilà son autorité: voilà sa puissance. C'est ainsi qu'il combat pour la discipline ecclésiastique dans l'espoir du martyre. . . . Ah! qui me donnera ce bien que ce grand cardinal revienne encore un coup pour établir la pénitence, qui n'est pas seulement abattue, mais qui est entièrement perdue et anéantie? Nous sommes dans un temps où l'Église est arrivée au dernier relâchement. Le nombre des chretiens croît, mais sa discipline se relâche. (p. 684)

In the Panegyric on St. Francis of Paula, preached at about the same time, there is an extended development of another idea, which later sermons show to be intimately bound up with Bossuet's views on discipline. Starting as so often from a text of St. Augustine, Bossuet goes on:

> He! Fidèles, qu'est-il nécessaire d'employer ici beaucoup de paroles pour vous faire voir que c'est *l'amour-propre* qui fait toutes nos actions! . . . Étant la racine de toutes nos passions, il fait couler dans toutes les branches ses vaines, mais douces complaisances; si bien que l'homme les branches ses vaines, mais douces complaisances; si bien que l'homme, s'arrêtant en soi-même, ne peut plus s'élever à son Créateur . . . Ainsi nous attribuons à nous-mêmes les droits qui n'appartiennent qu'à Dieu; nous nous faisons notre fin dernière. [my italics] (p. 336)

This analysis in terms already met elsewhere is linked a little later with one of Bossuet's favourite themes:

> Comme c'est de la cour que dépendent toutes les affaires, et que c'est aussi là qu'elles aboutissent, l'ennemi du genre humain y jette tous ses appâts, y étale toute sa pompe. Là est l'empire de l'intérêt, là est le théâtre des passions; là elles se montrent les plus violentes, là elles sont les plus déguisées. (p. 348)

There is, however, a difference between this and later sermons. In his final exhortation Bossuet uses words which the influence of Court life were soon to modify:

> Notre temps de délices viendra; c'est ici le temps d'épreuve et de pénitence. Les impies ont leur temps dans le siècle, parce que leur félicité ne peut pas être éternelle; le nôtre est différé après cette vie, afin qu'il puisse s'étendre dans les siècles des siècles. (p. 359)

For a very much modified presentation of this last exhortation one may look at the sermon preached in honour of St. (then only Blessed) François de Sales, in 1660. Praising the *Introduction à la Vie Dévote*, Bossuet makes a less radical distinction between this world and the next:

> C'est une erreur intolérable . . . qu'on ne peut être dévot dans le monde . . . Si [les hommes] ne suivent pas la vertu, qu'ils n'en accusent que leur lâcheté, et non leurs emplois, ni le monde, ni les attraits de la Cour, ni les occupations de la vie civile. (p. 528)

The difference between the two Italian Francis, of Assisi and Paula, and their namesake of Geneva represents a basically opposite approach to the religious life, though both views fall well within the permitted limits of orthodox theory and practice. It is with St. François de Sales that Bossuet henceforth aligns himself at least in public.

By 1665 he is in the full vigour of his career. A sermon on St. Benedict (the second) provides the link between the previously unrelated themes of amour-propre and discipline. Quoting the same text from Augustine as in the sermon on St. Francis of Paula, ('Primum incidit in seipsum') Bossuet draws a rather different lesson:

> . . . notre esprit, détaché de Dieu, demeura premièrement arrêté en lui-même par la complaisance à ses volontés, et l'amour de sa liberté déréglée. En effet, cet amour de la liberté est la source du premier crime . . . Tel est le péché du premier homme . . . qui . . . a imprimé, au fond de nos cœurs, une liberté indomptée et un amour d'indépendance. (p. 609)

This diagnosis is at once followed by a remedy: 'C'est à quoi s'est opposé le grand saint Benoît, lorsqu'il vous [his monastic audience] a obligés si exactement à la loi d'obéissance . . . Dompter par la discipline cette liberté indomptable . . .' Obedience is described: 'C'est la guide des mœurs, le rempart de l'humilité, l'appui de la persévérance, la vie de l'esprit, et la mort assurée de l'amour-propre.' (p. 612)

This is much nearer Bossuet's true way of thinking than so much earlier talk about mortification though, of course, 'discipline' carries both meanings. He was, one may be sure, sincere in his condemnations of worldly attachments, but his own career and the quality of his hearers alike must have borne upon him with increasing force that there was a certain unreality in so much praise accorded to a way of life far removed from that to which he himself was committed. Penitence remained desirable in itself, but if amour-propre were really the root of all sins—and Bossuet found many to agree with him there—and obedience really were its antidote—and who familiar with monastic life would have doubted it?—it was a virtue which had the outstanding quality of being no less applicable to the public than to the private sector.

As one might expect from the subject, the sermon on St. Thomas of Canterbury (1668) brings into sharp focus the problem of relations between Church and state. Though not yet a Bishop himself (his nomination to Condom came the following year) Bossuet speaks with the same authority as if he had for years been living with this particular conflict. Thomas is styled (with what one may suspect as dubious historical justification) 'premier martyr de la discipline'. (p. 629) As in the sermons on SS. Bernard and Charles the authority of the Church is much in evidence: 'le sang de ce nouveau martyr de la discipline a affermi l'autorité ecclésiastique'. (p. 630) As for the relations with princes:

> Elle [L'Église] ne craint point de leur dire que, parmi leurs plus grandes libéralités, ils reçoivent plus qu'ils ne donnent; et enfin, pour nous expliquer nettement, qu'il y a plus de justice que de grâce dans les privilèges qu'ils lui accordent . . . L'Église . . . leur a fait un trône dans les consciences, en présence et sous les yeux de Dieu même: elle a fait un des articles de sa foi de la sûreté de leurs personnes sacrées, et une partie de sa religion de l'obéissance qui leur est due. Elle va étouffer dans le fond des cœurs, non seulement les premières pensées de la rébellion, mais encore les moindres murmures; et pour ôter tout prétexte de soulèvement contre les puissances légitimes, elle a enseigné constamment . . . qu'il en faut tout souffrir, jusqu'a l'injustice, par laquelle s'exerce secrètement la justice même de Dieu. (p. 633)

With the fate of Charles I and the Fronde so recently in mind, this clear statement of the Church's position is hardly surprising. It is pleasant to find the behaviour of this particular English king arousing Bossuet to patriotic sentiments:

> Rendons ici témoignage à l'incomparable piété de nos monarques très chrétiens. Comme ils ont vu que Jésus-Christ ne règne pas si son Église n'est autorisée, leur propre autorité ne leur a pas été plus chère que l'autorité de l'Église. (p. 636)

The king immediately in view is Louis VII, who here receives warmer commendation than Louis XI in the sermon on St. Francis of Paula, and whose piety was recognized and applauded still louder in Bossuet's own royal master. Like St. Thomas, Bossuet 'S'il a toujours songé qu'il était évêque, il n'a jamais oublié qu'il était sujet.' (p. 639)

The *Oraisons funèbres* of Henriette-Marie and her daughter, Henriette-Anne, preached in 1669 and 1670, show that Bossuet's train of thought was indeed inspired more by events of his own lifetime than by those of the twelfth century. These two sermons, dealing as they do with recent English history, read like a continuation of that devoted to Becket.

Taking up the idea of the last phrase quoted, Bossuet speaks of the Anglican bishops:

> Qu'est-ce que l'épiscopat, quand il se sépare de l'Église qui est son tout, aussi bien que du Saint-Siège qui est son centre, pour s'attacher, contre sa nature, à la royauté comme à son chef? Ces deux puissances d'un ordre si différent ne s'unissent pas, mais s'embarrassent mutuellement, quand on les confond ensemble. (p. 83)

There follows a passage of capital importance for revealing not only Bossuet's mentality but also that of the monarch he served:

> Il ne faut point s'étonner s'ils [les Anglais] perdirent le respect de la majesté et des lois, ni s'ils devinrent factieux, rebelles et opiniâtres. On énerve la religion quand on la change, et on lui ôte un certain poids, qui seul est capable de tenir les peuples. Ils ont dans le fond du cœur je ne sais quoi d'inquiet qui s'échappe, si on leur ôte ce frein nécessaire; et on ne leur laisse plus rien à ménager, quand on leur permet de se rendre maîtres de leur religion. (ibid.)

Bossuet's reference to the sixteenth-century Reformers in the sermon on St. Bernard has already been noted. In this sermon he thus describes their motives: 'Chacun s'est fait à soi-même un tribunal où il s'est rendu l'arbitre de sa croyance.' (p. 81) The situation in England derived from: 'un dégoût secret de tout ce qui a de l'autorité, et une démangeaison d'innover sans fin, après qu'on en a vu le premier exemple.' (p. 82)

The full implications of this are stated in a sentence continuing the first passage quoted:

> C'est de là que nous est né ce prétendu règne de Christ . . . qui devait anéantir toute la royauté, et égaler tous les hommes; songe séditieux des indépendants, et leur chimère impie et sacrilège; tant il est vrai que tout se tourne en révoltes et en pensées séditieuses, quand l'autorité de la religion est anéantie! (p. 84)

Of heresy he says: '[Dieu] voulait découvrir, par un grand

exemple, tout ce que peut l'hérésie; combien elle est naturellement indocile et indépendante, combien fatale à la royauté et à toute autorité légitime.' (p. 86)

The repetition of the two last words is a refrain running through all Bossuet's later sermons, and amounts almost to an obsession at the end.

An epilogue to this English theme comes in the sermon on Henriette-Anne:

> nous souhaitons principalement que l'Angleterre, trop libre dans sa croyance, trop licencieuse dans ses sentiments, soit enchaînée comme nous de ces bienheureux liens qui empêchent l'orgueil humain de s'égarer dans ses pensées, en le captivant sous l'autorité du Saint-Esprit et de l'Église. (p. 114)

These texts, taken from sermons preached in successive years, amply demonstrate the evolution of Bossuet's thought. Independence and liberty are the temptations of the Devil, obedience and discipline the way of God, but revealed only in the Catholic Church. The pride and amour-propre of the individual, intellectual and spiritual arrogance, lead, according to this argument, to collective revolt and anarchy. The *autorité légitime* so constantly invoked is a precise and concrete reference to the rule set up on earth by God, who has given authority to temporal rulers, and sanctified their power, on the strict understanding that the supreme rights of the Church remain inviolate. A fuller and clearer statement of these views can be found in the *Politique tirée de l'Ecriture Sainte*, composed for the Dauphin, which defends absolute rule in uncompromising terms, though carefully distinguishing it from arbitrary rule. Some of Bossuet's formulas in this work are so striking that they remain in the mind after the slight modifications imposed by the context have been quite forgotten: 'Ils [les princes] sont des dieux, et participent en quelque façon à l'indépendance divine.'[1] It might be old Horace speaking. One feature of this doctrine of authority is that it is indivisible; civil sedition, religious heresy, state interference with the Church all equally threaten the divinely sanctioned order, and must be

[1] *Œuvres,* Paris 1875, vol. xxii, p. 559 (Livre iv, art. i, prop. ii).

repressed lest they lead to the anarchy of unbridled licence. Cromwell, by combining regicide with an attack on a Church, which though heretical was at least established and episcopal, was guilty in Bossuet's eyes of the ultimate offence against God and man. This nightmare of egalitarianism he associated with the contagion of the previous century, 'je ne sais quoi d'inquiet' and the 'démangeaison d'innover sans fin'. With his remarks on liberty already quoted, this is a plain enough indication of the comment he would make on the present motto of the French Republic. It is particularly interesting to find him bringing in the idea of 'inquiet' in this connexion, for the choice between amour-propre and obedience resolves itself for him into one between *Angst* and security; the security of a voluntary bondage embracing both the spiritual and the temporal orders.

Finally, turning back from England to France, the *Oraison funèbre* of Michel le Tellier (1686), Bossuet's penultimate official sermon, summarizes all that years of official life had made him. Jubilating at the Revocation of the Edict of Nantes, he finds another occasion to 'rendre témoignage à l'incomparable piété de nos monarques très chrétiens'. This 'pieux édit qui donne le dernier coup à l'hérésie' he regards as 'le plus bel usage de l'autorité'. This act, productive of mass, spontaneous conversions, inspires him to cry:

> Touchés de tant de merveilles, épanchons nos cœurs sur la piété de Louis. Poussons jusqu'au ciel nos acclamations, et disons à ce nouveau Constantin, à ce nouveau Théodose, à ce nouveau Marcien, à ce nouveau Charlemagne, ce que les six cent trente Pères dirent autrefois dans le concile de Chalcédoine: 'Vous avez affermi la foi, vous avez exterminé les hérétiques: c'est le digne ouvrage de votre règne, c'en est le propre caractère. Par vous, l'Hérésie n'est plus: Dieu seul a pu faire cette merveille. Roi du ciel, conservez le roi de la terre: c'est le vœu des Églises; c'est le vœu des évêques.' (p. 206)

Those whose countries offered asylum to the skilled and sober Huguenots may find it as hard to forgive the lapse from taste as that from historical accuracy. There is something dangerously analogous to Homenaz in Rabelais's Papimanie here, except that Bossuet's Gallican convictions lead him to speak of 'le roi de la terre' rather than 'celluy Dieu en terre' of his ultramontane opponents. Leaving aside any judgement on the Revocation, foreshadowed already in Richelieu's *Testament politique* and bound to come sooner or later, there should be no illusions about Bossuet's attitude to Louis XIV. Only a patriot would be a Gallican, and only an extreme monarchist the sort of Gallican that Bossuet was. The general rule of obedience to legitimate authority is reinforced by the divine right of kings, and of French kings in particular. If this is not quite a revival of 'gesta Dei per Francos' it is certainly 'gesta Dei per regem', with an explicit reference to Charlemagne to underline the parallel. The *Politique tirée* . . . must be taken seriously, for it offers reasoned justification for such views as those just quoted:

> Ainsi la France . . . peut se glorifier d'avoir la meilleure constitution d'État qui soit possible, et la plus conforme à celle que Dieu même a établie. Ce qui montre tout ensemble, et la sagesse de nos ancêtres, et la protection particulière de Dieu sur ce royaume.[1]

Apart from the justly famous *Oraison funèbre* on Condé, this was Bossuet's last Court sermon, but it by no means marks the end of his active life. His disputes with Protestants, with Fénelon, over Gallicanism and over Jansenism, are of historical importance, but add little that is relevant to the present subject. For amplification of his thought one must go to his private work, to his correspondence and to instruction intended for individuals and only published in 1731, long after his death. Much of what is written there reads like a sad postscript to the years at Court, and inevitably invites comparison with the very different tone of the orator. In the short, but concentrated *Discours sur la vie cachée en Dieu* (1691)[2] Bossuet touches on eternal realities, and shows how brittle is the outer crust of personality:

> Affranchi des jugements humains, on ne compte plus pour véritable que ce que Dieu voit en nous, ce qu'il en sait, ce qu'il en juge . . . On me loue. on me blâme, on me tient pour indifférent, on me méprise, on ne me connaît pas, ou l'on m'oublie: tout cela ne me touche pas:

[1] op cit., p. 528 (livre II, art. 1, prop. xi).

[2] Edited with *Traité de la Concupiscence, Aux Portes de France,* Porrentruy, 1947 Also in *Œuvres* (1875), vol. vii, p. 394. I owe these references to the kindness of Mr. A. Gill.

je n'en suis pas moins ce que je suis: l'homme se veut mêler d'être créateur, il me veut donner un être dans son opinion ou dans celle des autres; mais cet être qu'il me veut donner est un néant. (p. 4)

As so many of the other writers had done, Bossuet looks inward for the principle of truth, but finds instead of self-sufficiency a void. Only that part of him which is seen by the eyes of God *is*, only God's existence saves his own puny *être* from being *néant*.

Such meditations as these emphasize the hollowness of the public figure, and perhaps the struggle to preserve a façade, which in 1691 at any rate Bossuet recognizes as meaningless. A longer discussion of similar themes occurs in the *Traité de la concupiscence*[1] (1694), where the Augustinian echoes are insistent. Often the turn of phrase, or line of argument, recalls Pascal, but with subtle differences characteristic of all Bossuet's work. On amour-propre he is at one with Pascal and La Rochefoucauld:

Quiconque n'aime pas Dieu n'aime que soi-même . . . et demeurant incapable d'être touché des intérêts d'autrui, il est non-seulement rebelle à Dieu, mais encore insociable, injuste, déraisonnable envers les autres; et veut que tout serve non-seulement à ses intérêts, mais encore à ses caprices. (p. 96)

Another striking phrase from the same discussion of amour-propre recalls Pascal's theory of orders, and goes to the heart of the existential problem: 'plus vous mettez ensemble d'êtres crées, plus le néant y paraît.' (p. 101) It follows from this that self-love or worldly attachments lead infallibly to the void of unreality, and can only render man more feeble in the struggle for survival, indeed for very existence. 'Celui qui compte Dieu pour rien, ajoute à son néant naturel celui de son injustice et de son égarement. Ce n'est pas Dieu qu'il dégrade, mais lui-même. Il n'ôte rien à Dieu; mais il s'ôte à lui-même son appui, sa lumière, sa force, et la source de tout son bien.' (p. 103)

This leads Bossuet on to discuss human pride, the cause of the Fall, and its effects on man's life. Here the link between amour-propre, discipline and obedience, seen in the sermons in both a spiritual and a political context, appears very clearly. On the

[1] See footnote 2, p. 190.

subject of liberty Bossuet's emphasis is not quite that of Pascal, and is poles apart from Descartes:

> L'orgueil dont nous parlons consiste dans une certaine fausse force, qui rend l'âme indocile et fière, ennemie de toute contrainte, et qui par un amour exessif de sa liberté la fait aspirer à une espèce d'indépendance: ce qui est cause qu'elle trouve un certain plaisir particulier à désobéir, et que la défense l'irrite. (p. 105)

From Adam to Cromwell the story is the same. Bossuet distinguishes the liberty of the beasts, governed only by their own desires, from that of man, 'créature raisonnable', who 'est libre d'une autre sorte, en se soumettant volontairement à la raison souveraine de Dieu, dont la sienne est émanée.' (p. 107) (cf., 'sur mes passions ma raison souveraine').

Bringing the discussion still closer to the heroic ideals of Corneille, Bossuet concludes this extremely important chapter (xv) on pride by adding to inordinate love of liberty another cause: 'qui est dans l'âme un certain amour de sa propre grandeur, fondée sur une opinion de son excellence propre.' (p. 108) This fatal pride is dynamic, not static, and forces man ever downwards to the bottom. In seeking self-sufficiency within his own reasonable soul man does without God, but then the law of spiritual gravitation degrades him so that his reason becomes the slave of his body, eventually of his basest animal passions: 'l'âme raisonnable tombe de Dieu sur elle-même, et se trouve précipitée à ce qu'il y a de plus bas.' (p. 110) On this analysis, the descent is inevitable, however slow, from rationalist autonomy to brutish servitude, from would-be *ange* to *bête*.

The social effects of pride are vividly depicted. Bossuet ranges widely in the next chapter (xvi), from disputes among peasants over the pew they should occupy in church to intrigues in ecclesiastical elections, from wars of conquest to sectarian rivalry in religion, and sums up: 'Tout cela vient de ce que chacun épris de soi-même, veut tout mettre à ses pieds, et s'établir une damnable supériorité, en dénigrant tout le genre humain.' (p. 116)

This comes very close to Molière's treatment of monomania (cf., Alceste, Dom Juan), and shows the same antipathy for 'gloire' and all it stands for. 'La gloire ordinairement n'est qu'un miroir où l'on fait paraître le faux avec un certain éclat.' (p. 120)

This catalogue of human vanity goes on to include women intent on their beauty, poets and philosophers, and comes to a rather unexpected conclusion, summarized in the chapter heading (xix):

> De la gloire: merveilleuse manière dont Dieu punit l'orgueil, en lui donnant ce qu'il demande.
>
> La gloire est le souverain bien qu'ils [les hommes] se proposent: et vous, Seigneur, comment les punissez-vous? . . . Mais pour montrer combien elle est, non-seulement vaine, mais encore trompeuse et malheureuse, vous la donnez très-souvent à ceux qui la demandent, et vous en faites leur supplice. (p. 129)

Is there perhaps an autobiographical note in that last phrase? At all events, one cannot read such powerful denunciations of human vanity and vainglory without remembering Bossuet's own, albeit unwilling, contribution in so many Court sermons. His long years in what he calls 'l'empire de l'intérêt', his intimate acquaintance with those whom rank or attainment (or beauty) made the highest in the land, to some extent his own identification with the Establishment mentality which his sermons encouraged, are all contributory factors in forming this bleak view of human nature and destiny.

So much stress on obedience, not in the abstract, but to the imperfect human being, whom divine right (and the prudence of a subject) raised above criticism, would have been entirely compatible with a healthy religious teaching if only Louis's faults had been more openly recognized and reproved. For every La Vallière saved there were plenty more waiting to be lost, for every act of absolute justice there were countless acts of arbitrary tyranny. Thus it is not surprising that Bossuet's reflections in old age should be bitter, that he should be so struck by the sheer emptiness of purely human endeavour, for he is partly to blame for what he saw around him. The King and the Dauphin were only too ready to accept that 'les princes sont des dieux', and paid much less attention to the more general lessons of humility which Bossuet freely dispensed. The courtiers understood only too well the benefits of obedience, and when royal favour put butter on their bread it would have seemed pedantic to ask if they had divine blessing. The King's moral example was a welcome excuse for not outshining the sun in virtue. Absolutism was a powerful bulwark against anarchy, heresy and sedition self-evident evils; if the Court preacher condemned independence as the natural source of these evils, the ordinary courtier found it more immediately relevant that he should conform to the patterns laid down and approved from the throne than that he should meditate his dependence on a remoter power beyond the throne. People listen to what they want to hear, and it is hard for an official preacher not to give it to them, unconscious, perhaps, of his own desire for popularity. These very remarkable texts, from works intended for the private spiritual guidance of those already well on the way to truth, deserve to be quoted in themselves, because they so closely reflect sentiments expressed by other authors, and because it would be unfair to Bossuet to conceal the best after exhibiting so much of the worst in him.

Unfortunately they do not redress the balance of Bossuet's contemporary influence, and it may well be that the great contrast between his public and private aspects derives from a fundamental defect of temperament and judgement. Some indications that this is so appear in another late work, his *Maximes et Réflexions sur la Comédie* (1694). This is part of a violent controversy about the theatre, condemned for the usual reasons, notably the immorality of actors in general and actresses in particular and the passions stimulated by all forms of drama. Charity and moderation are not found appropriate when he is denouncing what he regards as a diabolical institution, as we see from his epitaph on Molière:[1]

> La postérité saura peut-être la fin de ce Poète comédien, qui en jouant son *Malade imaginaire* . . . reçut la derniere atteinte de la maladie dont il mourut peu d'heures après, et passa des plaisanteries du théâtre, parmi lesquelles il rendit presque le dernier soupir, au tribunal de celui qui dit: 'Malheur à vous qui riez, car vous pleurerez.'

The specific reason for attacking comedy appears in his final chapter, which first deplores tragedies for arousing strong

[1] *Œuvres* (1875), vol. xxvii, p. 27 (ch. v).

passions, and then considers among other plays: 'Celles dont le dessein est de fair rire, qui pourraient être, ce semble, les moins vicieuses, outre l'indécence de ce caractère dans un chrétien, attirent trop facilement le licencieux.'[1]

Though, as earlier pages have shown, Bossuet often denounces the same evils as Molière, the difference between them is irreconcilable, for Bossuet had absolutely no sense of humour. Obedience is certainly one answer to amour-propre, and may lead to humility, always granted that it is founded on the same respect between men as is naturally commanded in relations with God. Where obedience, moderation and stability are set up as ends in themselves, the 'moi' may find a temporary anchorage, but will never come to port. Bossuet made the mistake of thinking that comedy mocked at truth by making men laugh at serious things; laughter often liberates when tears would bind. A sense of the ridiculous, like that lucidity of which both Retz and Pascal are exponents, is often the safest refuge in a society which demands conformism. It is strange that Bossuet should have come so near to expressing what some modern writers call the absurd without ever sensing the ridiculous. Bossuet was not great enough to model himself on a St. Bernard, who stood up to Pope and King, and would have done better to follow the fool of God, Francis of Assisi. Without reason, inquiry, laughter, the 'moi' will be firm enough on its totalitarian axis, or at La Trappe, but for most men the price is too high. When Francis felt the Devil threaten he used to call on all the gaiety of which he was capable to rout the enemy with joy. It is a pity the eagle of Meaux was not amused.

[1] ibid., p. 76 (ch. xxv).

11: LA BRUYÈRE

LIKE Bossuet, La Bruyère was closely associated with the Condé household, but unlike Bossuet, whom he knew and admired, he was never in a position to assert himself in that or any other milieu. The tribute of the *Oraison funèbre* on *le Grand Condé* is from one great man to another, but in La Bruyère it is the total absence of any sort of greatness which perhaps more than any other factor characterizes his work. Whether dealing with his patrons and employers, or with the *Académie*, or with society in general, La Bruyère shows his constant awareness of a personal mediocrity from which he never tried to escape. For a penetrating and masterly study of Louis XIV and his age we may prefer to turn to Saint-Simon, even Voltaire, but if we want to know what it felt like to be alive in the dawn—and sunset too—of *le roi Soleil*, La Bruyère is the man to tell us.

Totally *engagé* in the system of which he was at once part and critic, La Bruyère came of bourgeois stock as modest as his own achievements. He lacks the lofty, and cynical, condescension which so often exasperates the reader of the *Maximes*; as a sincere but conventional Catholic he neither inspires nor dismays as does Pascal in the *Pensées*; in his range of experience and intention he is probably closer to Molière, without the genius, than to either of the *moralistes* with whom his name is often linked. In their chosen field of observation, the *Caractères* range much more widely than the aristocratic *Maximes*, and even the *Pensées*, whose social context is determined by the status of the type of unbeliever to whom Pascal specifically addressed his apology, though its universal message transcends social limitations. In La Bruyère the canvas is fuller and more representative: from the peasant toiling in the field to Louis shining on his throne all classes make an appearance. Even allowing for a generation's development it is remarkable how often La Bruyère's observations confirm and amplify those of his predecessors. There remains the paradox that the very accuracy and detail of his work from which it derives its documentary value limits its general application, so that in a very real sense the *Maximes*—let alone the *Pensées*—tell us more about civilized man in general than the *Caractères*.[1]

Coming as he does at the end of this century of tension, La Bruyère's testimony is particularly valuable for its references both to the immediate past and to the present; for the future, history speaks for itself. He judges the great men who have gone before, Corneille, Racine, Molière, Bossuet, all either dead or past their prime, as well as Richelieu, Mazarin and many others, and he sees, too, what their legacy has been. The comparison with other *moralistes* may be misleading with regard to the author's method and intentions. It is La Rochefoucauld's aim in the *Maximes* to support his thesis that amour-propre is the mainspring of human actions, just as it is Pascal's purpose in the *Pensées* to show the 'misère de l'homme sans Dieu', followed by the cure. For La Rochefoucauld amour-propre is the centre of his work, for Pascal 'Jésus-Christ est le centre où tout tend'. La Bruyère is rather different; there is no doubt that the centre for him is *le roi Soleil* on his throne; whether he is talking of Paris or the provinces, theatre or church, noble or peasant, everything is ultimately seen *en fonction de Versailles* as it were. The significance of this for the present study is obvious and decisive. As to intention, La Bruyère refers in his Preface to[1] 'ce portrait que j'ai fait de lui [le public] d'après nature, et s'il [le public] se connaît quelques-uns des défauts que je touche, il peut s'en corriger' (p. 61). The somewhat sententious tone of the Preface emphasizes the author's primary aim, a didactic one: 'On ne doit parler, on ne doit écrire que pour l'instruction; et s'il arrive que l'on plaise, il ne faut pas néanmoins s'en repentir, si cela sert à insinuer et à faire recevoir les vérités qui doivent instruire.' (ibid.)

All this is very much like Molière in its insistence on business through pleasure. Didactic as he is, he knows his limits: 'Ce ne sont point, au reste, des maximes que j'aie voulu écrire: elles sont comme des lois dans la morale, et j'avoue que je n'ai ni assez d'autorité ni assez de génie pour faire le législateur.' (p. 64)

[1] All references are to the 1957 edition of La Bruyère, *Œuvres Complètes*, in *Bibl, de la Pléiade*.

While thus disclaiming any ambitions as a moral legislator, La Bruyère was less negative concerning his religious aims. According to the Preface which accompanied the published version of his *Discours prononcé dans l'Académie Française* (1695):

> . . . de seize chapitres qui le [livre des Caractères] composent il y en a quinze qui, s'attachant à découvrir le faux et le ridicule qui se rencontrent dans les objets des passions et des attachements humains, ne tendent qu'à ruiner tous les obstacles qui affaiblissent d'abord, et qui éteignent ensuite dans tous les hommes la connaissance de Dieu; qu'ainsi ils ne sont que des préparations au seizième et dernier chapitre, où l'athéisme est attaqué et peut-être confondu; où les preuves de Dieu . . . sont apportées, où la Providence de Dieu est défendue contre l'insulte et les plaintes des libertins. (p. 485)

This claim that the miniature apology of the chapter 'des Esprits Forts' gives form and meaning to the whole may be meant in good faith, but is simply not true. It is true that the material offered in the *Caractères* is sufficient, when critically organized, to support such religious views by induction from the enumeration of particular instances, but that is not why or how they were originally composed.

The chapter-headings themselves do not afford very much help; as between 'de la Mode' and 'de Quelques Usages', or 'de l'Homme' and 'de la Société' there is no detectably necessary distinction. Though within each section some sort of order can be discerned, many passages could be transposed and the headings changed. One need therefore have less conscience than usual in arranging quotations in an arbitrary but convenient fashion. If some of these quotations sound echoes of earlier writers, this is not surprising; La Bruyère knew the works so far discussed (except that of Retz) and often alludes to them, apart from any unconscious influence he may have undergone. It is convenient to take successively what he has to say about individuals, then private and finally public relationships.

His psychology is familiar, by now almost commonplace for his age:

> Les passions tyrannisent l'homme; et l'ambition suspend en lui les autres passions, et lui donne pour un temps les apparences de toutes les vertus. (Des Biens de Fortune, 50)

Toutes les passions sont menteuses: elles se déguisent autant qu'elles le peuvent aux yeux des autres; elles se cachent à elles-mêmes. Il n'y a point de vice qui n'ait une fausse ressemblance avec quelque vertu, et qu'il ne s'en aide (Du Cœur, 72)

Rien ne coûte moins à la passion que de se mettre au-dessus de la raison; son grand triomphe est de l'emporter sur l'intérêt. (ibid., 77)

The reader who already knows the *Maximes* will find the form and content of these texts less impressive than those of their model; as it is even the expert might be embarrassed at times to decide the problem of attribution.

The conclusion from this is more positive than that found in La Rochefoucauld:

Le motif seul fait le mérite des actions des hommes, et le désintéressement y met la perfection. (Du Mérite Personnel, 41)

Celui-là est bon qui fait du bien aux autres; s'il souffre pour le bien qu'il fait, il est très bon; . . . et s'il en meurt sa vertu ne saurait aller plus loin; elle est héroïque, elle est parfaite. (ibid., 44)

The mechanism and the moral judgement are equally familiar; man is ruled by his passions, and tyrannized by self-interest, so that the reality of virtue is exactly proportionate to the degree of disinterestedness.

In the sphere of personal relationships we know what to expect: 'Il n'y a point dans le cœur d'une jeune personne un si violent amour auquel l'intérêt et l'ambition n'ajoute quelque chose. (Des Femmes, 59)

This however is more misogyny than misanthropy:

Les femmes vont plus loin en amour que la plupart des hommes; mais les hommes l'emportent sur elles en amitié. Les hommes sont cause que les femmes ne s'aiment point. (ibid., 55)

Il y a peu de femmes si parfaites, qu'elles empêchent un mari de se repentir du moins une fois le jour, d'avoir une femme, ou de trouver heureux celui qui n'en a point. (ibid., 78)

Whatever the abiding truth of such remarks, it must be remembered that La Bruyère, like Bossuet, had to fit his experience of women into the pattern of lifelong celibacy, not in itself the most reassuring guarantee of impartiality.

A counterbalance, and perhaps an explanation of these views

is the brief comment: 'Le temps, qui fortifie les amitiés, affaiblit l'amour.' (Du Cœur, 4)

It should already be apparent that for all the superficial similarity between the *Maximes* and the *Caractères* an essential difference derives from La Rochefoucauld's prime object of attacking any idea of *vertu païenne*, and his failure to offer explicitly any positive alternative (whatever may be implicit), as against La Bruyère's more general, and much more positive, intentions. A particularly illuminating text of La Bruyère sets out some of his basic assumptions:

> Il y a une philosophie qui nous élève au-dessus de l'ambition et de la fortune; . . . qui nous exempte de désirer, de demander, de prier, de solliciter, d'importuner; et qui nous sauve même l'émotion et l'excessive joie d'être exaucés. Il y a une autre philosophie qui nous soumet et nous assujettit à toutes ces choses en faveur de nos proches ou de nos amis; c'est la meilleure. (Des Jugements, 69)

The sort of ataraxia represented by the first sentence is not peculiar to Stoicism (which is no doubt the philosophy in question) but very much like the triumph of the will advocated by Descartes, by Corneille and, to some extent, by La Rochefoucauld. This altruism could, notwithstanding La Bruyère's personal Christian beliefs, be an example of *vertu païenne*, at least in the sense in which modern humanists might understand it; what is interesting is the clear rejection of a noble, egocentric philosophy enabling man to win freedom from his passions at the expense of care for others. It is true that the Stoics of antiquity put the brotherhood of man high on their list of articles, but the Stoic ataraxia was the element on which their successors seized. La Bruyère is here closer to Pascal (cf., 'vous serez fidèle, honnête . . . ami sincère, véritable') in seeing human relationships in terms of common joys and sufferings than to La Rochefoucauld, for whom sacrifice followed only after passion had been purged. In that this humanitarian approach is also a recognition of common human needs, as well as an example of Christian charity, La Bruyère heralds the nobler side of eighteenth-century enlightenment.

The emphasis on friendship, for La Bruyère a rule rather than an exception, and the absence of any feeling of superiority, whether due to birth or brilliance, makes the *Caractères* read like the work of Philinte rather than Alceste. As a foundation for public relationships faith in friendship is both positive and solid. There is now more to be considered than the inviolably private integrity of the 'moi'; something must also be shared. Hence the attitude to social conformism can no longer be so ruthless as it was for those who only accepted an external world on sufferance:

> 'Il faut faire comme les autres': maxime suspecte, qui signifie presque toujours; 'il faut mal faire', dès qu'on l'étend au delà de ces choses purement extérieures, qui n'ont point de suite, qui dépendent de l'usage, de la mode ou des bienséances. (Des Jugements, 10)

This caution regarding conformism is explained by what La Bruyère has to say about the contemporary cult of 'honnêteté', by now hardly more than lifemanship:

> L'honnête homme tient le milieu entre l'habile homme et l'homme de bien, quoique dans une distance inégale de ces deux extrêmes.
>
> La distance qu'il y a de l'honnête homme à l'habile homme s'affaiblit de jour à autre, et est sur le point de disparaître.
>
> L'habile homme est celui qui cache ses passions, qui entend ses intérêts, qui y sacrifie beaucoup de choses, qui a su acquérir du bien ou en conserver. L'honnête homme est celui qui ne vole pas sur les grands chemins, et qui ne tue personne, dont les vices enfin ne sont pas scandaleux.
>
> On connaît assez qu'un homme de bien est honnête homme, mais il est plaisant d'imaginer que tout honnête homme n'est pas homme de bien.
>
> L'homme de bien est celui qui n'est ni un saint ni un dévot [faux dévot], et qui s'est borné à n'avoir que de la vertu. (ibid. 55)

What makes this observation of special interest is the idea of evolution it conveys ('de jour à autre . . . sur le point . . .'), and the implied suggestion that it has not always been so. This we know to be the case, and it is one of La Bruyère's merits to have recognized and expressed the distinction so well.

Another remark on a similar subject repeats Philinte's views once more: 'Il me semble que l'esprit de politesse est une certaine attention à faire que par nos paroles et par nos manières les autres soient contents de nous et d'eux-mêmes.' (De la Société, 32)

The last word shows a realistic and penetrating awareness of human nature in society, and is exactly what Alceste refused to recognize. Here, as elsewhere, La Bruyère analyses a phenomenon without attempting to fit it into a moral context, unless by implication. There are moments when he recalls the Johnsonian robustness of Bossuet, and makes things look easier than perhaps they really are. Thus on *ennui* his explanation is less concerned with the universal human predicament than with the particular situation of the idle rich: 'L'ennui est entré dans le monde par la paresse, elle a beaucoup de part dans la recherche que font les hommes des plaisirs, du jeu, de la société; celui qui aime le travail a assez de soi-même. (De l'Homme, 101)

On the metaphysical plane this is no answer to the usual results of idleness, voluntary or enforced, but it squares with the brief glimpses of the laborious peasantry which distinguish La Bruyère from most of the other writers discussed. A hard day's work which leaves no time for *ennui* nor leisure for *Angst* is at least socially useful, even if it is metaphysically irrelevant. Occupational therapy effectively takes the place of Pascal's *Pari*.

On the score of religion itself, La Bruyère has a good deal to say, not only in the chapter 'des Esprits Forts', but also in those 'des Femmes', 'de la Chaire', and 'de la Mode'. He is particularly aware of the problem of *faux dévots*, and does not, as Pascal seems to do, invest going through the motions with any special virtue. Indeed conformism in religious practice is treated in just the same way as social conformism: 'Un (faux) dévot est celui qui sous un roi athée serait athée.' (De la Mode, 21)

The long portrait of Onuphre, first cousin to Tartuffe, shows La Bruyère's gifts to the full, but in this case his subtlety is excessive. Distinguishing the conduct of his Onuphre from that of Tartuffe in a number of similar circumstances, La Bruyère writes: 'Il ne dit point "ma haire et ma discipline"; au contraire: il passerait pour ce qu'il est, pour un hypocrite, et il veut passer pour ce qu'il n'est pas, pour un homme dévot.' (ibid., 24)

In the event Onuphre is described in terms so indistinguishable from the true 'dévot' of La Bruyère's day that the portrait of the latter was prudently omitted from later editions.

On the spiritual consequences of what one might call *religion à la mode* La Bruyère is equally scathing:

> Qu'est-ce qu'une femme que l'on dirige? Est-ce une femme plus complaisante pour son mari . . . plus ardente et plus sincère pour ses amis; qui soit moins esclave de son humeur, moins attachée à ses intérêts . . . ; qui soit plus exempte d'amour de soi-même et d'éloignement pour les autres; qui soit plus libre de tous attachements humains? 'Non, dites-vous, ce n'est rien de toutes ces choses.' J'insiste, et je vous demande: 'Qu'est-ce qu'une femme que l'on dirige? Je vous entends, c'est une femme qui a un directeur. (Des Femmes, 36)
>
> La dévotion vient à quelques uns, et surtout aux femmes, comme une passion, ou comme le faible d'un certain âge, ou comme une mode qu'il faut suivre. (ibid., 43)

On one of the social phenomena of his day he is forthright: 'Le discours chrétien est devenu un spectacle; . . . c'est une sorte d'amusement entre mille autres, c'est un jeu où il y a de l'émulation et des parieurs.' (De la Chaire, 1)

The shades of religious sentiment and behaviour here depicted merge insensibly into those of ordinary churchgoing and piety, and in many ways this picture is more damaging to the cause of true religion than the more obvious attacks on abuses by Molière, Pascal or La Rochefoucauld. Flagrant hypocrisy, lax theology, excessive rigorism, the *engouement* of elderly ladies are all in their different ways obstacles to the genuine seeker after spiritual truth, but when all these have been discounted, there remains the basic fact that in a society nominally Christian and Catholic most people go through the motions of worship for motives both social and spiritual. Depending on the pressure of conformism in any given society, so the element of personal conscience and conviction will become progressively weaker in determining the manner of the individual's religious practice. Since it is of the essence of Catholicism that membership of the Church implies both corporate faith and corporate acts of worship, it becomes fatally easy to infer the quality of the former from that perceived in the latter. For many outside the Church, then more than now, the motions seemed empty of meaning, because they formed part of the social routine of those whose lives did not otherwise show any very clear impact of Christian values. Now that only a minority of the community regularly attends Church their motives can be more easily isolated than was the case in the seventeenth century.

The full implications of the foregoing quotations about religion, and indeed of all the tendencies discussed throughout this and all the preceding chapters, is seen in a famous text describing the chapel at Versailles during a service:

> Ces peuples [français] d'ailleurs ont leur Dieu et leur roi: les grands de la nation s'assemblent tous les jours, à une certaine heure, dans un temple qu'ils nomment église; il y a au fond de ce temple un autel consacré à leur Dieu, où un prêtre célèbre des mystères qu'ils appellent saints, sacrés et redoutables; les grands forment un vaste cercle au pied de cet autel, et paraissent debout, le dos tourné directement aux prêtres et aux saints mystères, et les faces élevées vers leur roi, que l'on voit à genoux sur une tribune, et à qui ils semblent avoir tout l'esprit et tout le cœur appliqué. On ne laisse pas de voir dans cet usage une espèce de subordination; car ce peuple paraît adorer le prince, et le prince adorer Dieu. (De la Cour, 74)

To the Frenchman who had recently had to choose between royal and papal claims in the Gallican dispute, whose spiritual pastors and masters owed their places ultimately to royal approval, who, if a courtier, was obliged to attend Church parade, this picture was a true image of the times. The *roi Soleil* from whom all blessings flowed was not God as Caesar had been God, nor was he Vicar of Christ on earth, but for all practical purposes he was the channel through whom all temporal mercies were directed. If the comparative attractions of present well-being and eternal salvation were not always very clear to Louis's subjects, it must be remembered that the divine right of St. Louis's successors, eloquently proclaimed by such eminent churchmen as Bossuet, tended to blur the dividing line between royal favour and justice and that divine favour and justice of which it was supposedly an instrument and copy.

The last words of the *Caractères* show just how far the author himself accepted the attitude of these courtiers at prayer:

> Une certaine inégalité dans les conditions, qui entretient l'ordre et la subordination, est l'ouvrage de Dieu, ou suppose une loi divine: une trop grande disproportion, et telle qu'elle se remarque parmi

les hommes, est leur ouvrage, ou la loi des plus forts. Les extrémités sont vicieuses et partent de l'homme: toute compensation est juste, et vient de Dieu. (Des Esprits Forts, 49)

In thus expressing his belief in moderation and at the same time in a social hierarchy founded on reasonable inequalities, La Bruyère speaks for the bourgeoisie. Here again he is close to Molière in his reverence for moderation, but nearer to Bossuet in his recognition of authority as the basis of society. 'Si toute religion est une crainte respectueuse de la Divinité, que penser de ceux qui osent la blesser dans sa plus vive image, qui est le Prince?' (ibid., 28)

In these words La Bruyère joins the courtiers in recognizing the unique position of the prince, even if he avoids their visible absurdity by stating his views in abstract terms rather than concrete posture. In these words too he shows how the problem of the 'moi désaxé' had been solved, at least for the time being.

Conformism is strongly, and frequently, condemned in the *Caractères*, either in principle ('faire comme les autres') or in detail (questions of fashion, behaviour and so on), and no class or group is more vigorously criticized than the courtiers. Yet, if La Bruyère's reasoning is followed to its logical conclusion, the uniquely privileged position of the King, with his divine backing, should ensure that what he ordains or merely approves is right. While the King cannot be expected to know in detail everything that happens at his court, there is no doubt that the obligatory residence at Versailles and the strict programme of court ceremonial imposed on those around him was due to no one else. The consequential patterns of behaviour must be attributed to the royal will, and illustrate voluntary obedience to supreme authority rather than passive conformity to social pressures. However much La Bruyère may have deplored particular aspects of this situation, it is one whose cause and principle he applauded. The 'moi' undoubtedly had an axis, solid and stable, in Louis XIV and theoretically in his new idea of kingship; the ripples of royal influence, weakening, but ever widening, as they spread farther out from Versailles, provided a motive force for culture and society. Absolutism and centralization were united in Louis with a dynastic, religious and, above all, personal prestige conspicuously lacking in Richelieu, let alone Mazarin, whatever power they had enjoyed. The subject of such a master might be no less a bondman, he could at least preserve the illusion of self-respect in such divinely sanctioned servitude.

There is one last point which distinguishes La Bruyère from most of the other writers discussed, except perhaps Molière, and which is of some importance for the perspective of the following century. One of the most famous of all the *Caractères* is that describing the peasant:

> L'on voit certains animaux farouches . . . répandus par la campagne . . . en effet ils sont des hommes; ils se retirent la nuit dans des tanières où ils vivent de pain noir, d'eau et de racines; ils épargnent aux autres hommes la peine de semer, de labourer et de recueillir pour vivre, et méritent ainsi de ne pas manquer de ce pain qu'ils ont semé. (De l'Homme, 128)

This shows a spirit of compassion, and the stirrings of social conscience, but very clearly assumes a barrier between the author and those he is describing. It is well to keep this in mind when considering the other famous text, of which the last sentence is too often quoted alone: 'Faut-il opter? Je ne balance pas: je veux être peuple.'

The actual context gives this apparently defiant choice a different significance:

> Si je compare ensemble les deux conditions des hommes les plus opposés, je veux dire les grands avec le peuple, ce dernier me paraît content du nécessaire, et les autres sont inquiets et pauvres avec le superflu. Un homme du peuple ne saurait faire aucun mal; un grand ne veut faire aucun bien, et est capable de grands maux. L'un ne se forme et ne s'exerce que dans les choses qui sont utiles; l'autre y joint les pernicieuses. Là se montrent ingénument la grossièreté et la franchise; ici se cache une sève maligne et corrompue sous l'écorce de la politesse. Le peuple n'a guères d'esprit, et les grands n'ont point d'âme: celui-là a un bon fonds, et n'a point de dehors; ceux-ci n'ont que des dehors et qu'une simple superficie. Faut-il opter? Je ne balance pas: je veux être peuple. (Des Grands, 25)

These remarks prompt several reflections: La Bruyère was not, and never could have been, one of the *grands* whom he is here attacking, so that the apparent choice at the end is in fact a simple statement of self-satisfaction, inspired by a sour-grapes reaction. Then, when one considers the 'peuple' of the passage it is clear that there is no existing class or group to whom the qualities enumerated would specifically apply, and that the downtrodden peasants of the other passage have nothing to do with the frank and natural 'peuple' of this one. What La Bruyère is really choosing is the qualities themselves, and in so doing constituting a moral group under the appearance of a social one. Another way of presenting his opinion is to say that he condemns those qualities most conspicuously associated with the *grands*; he prefers therefore to belong to some other class (*non-grands*), and endows this class with the requisite qualities as well as the name of pure convenience 'peuple'.

In another passage La Bruyère gives among definitions of 'peuple': 'Il y a le peuple qui est opposé aux grands: c'est la populace et la multitude; il y a le peuple qui est opposé aux sages, aux habiles et aux vertueux: ce sont les grands comme les petits.' (Des Grands, 53)

His choice is clearly for *populace et multitude*, but if pressed further he would have to add words indicating that the majority of which he wished to be a member was not a statistical majority of the population, but simply a majority of those with whom he normally came in contact, leaving the depressed peasantry and the very poor city-dwellers in a minority. The crowd, not the rabble, is La Bruyère's choice.

We have come a long way from the supermen of Descartes and Corneille, from the aristocratic heroes of Retz and La Rochefoucauld, from the chosen few of Pascal and Bossuet. Molière provides the common-sense and family feeling of the bourgeoisie, but it is not until we come to La Bruyère that we meet the now so familiar doctrine of 'the people can't be wrong'. Before—and again after—the noble savage the ordinary, decent instincts of common folk constitute a literary motif of growing importance. Today mass media have known how to make the most of it. Far as he is from socialist, egalitarian, even democratic sentiment, in La Bruyère can be found the first timid stirrings of articulate mass-psychology. Supported all round by its equals in mediocrity, firmly controlled from above by a king ideally combining national, spiritual and personal authority, the 'moi' is no longer 'désaxé', still less *maître de moi, comme de l'univers*; it is a tram, rather than a space-ship. Happily men like Bayle, Fontenelle, and, in his own way, Fénelon had opened up an alternative route.

CONCLUSION

THE selection of authors studied above is arranged in a sequence that is chronological and only to that extent intended to be causal. Without Montaigne before him Descartes would have been something else, without Descartes Pascal's message would have been differently expressed, and so on. At the same time these outstanding men, chosen in the first instance for their sheer distinction, are guides along the road of human development in the seventeenth century, and stand in a recognizable relationship one to another. The claim that, 'Cogito ergo sum' becomes 'l'état c'est moi'—not to speak of 'après nous le déluge'—is only unacceptable out of context, which is how most formulas end their half-life of usefulness. Basically it is true that the spirit that led Descartes to seek the warmth and seclusion of his German winter quarters turned out to be something of a *malin génie* for those who tried to follow him, and many of them came no nearer to the 'lumière naturelle de la raison' than the universal Sun of Versailles. This, like most other judgements, is a question of emphasis. It would surely not be hard to find a numerical majority of Frenchmen of more or less educated class whose inner lives continued almost without a flicker of change throughout the generations from Richelieu's assumption of power to the death of Louis XIV, from Descartes's schooldays with the Jesuits at La Flèche to Voltaire's with the Jesuits at Louis le Grand. Material preoccupations must then, as now, have conditioned the thought of even the best educated. But one is not dealing with numerical majorities, and the process here traced in history is far from spent. The circle of the privileged, the seventeenth-century Establishment, with its periphery of salons, academic and religious houses, was a tiny minority in the total population of France, wielding an overwhelming preponderance of power and influence. If one asks whether Mme de Sévigné, or La Fontaine, or Fontenelle (to take three names not so far mentioned) were influenced by Descartes, or Retz, or

Corneille, the answer is so self-evident as to make the question seem almost absurd. The same would be true of almost any name figuring, however humbly, in the pages of the century's history, literary, religious, political. This is a minority phenomenon, but the very fact of its limited dispersal makes for cohesion and durability.

It may help to retrace the steps already sketched out. Descartes, born just too late to know the horrors of civil war, was brought up in its immediate aftermath by men who had no illusions as to what was at stake. To these men, a real *corps d'élite*, he owed a formal education which could not have been bettered anywhere in Europe. It is to the very excellence of this education, and his own successful academic record, that he ascribes his early discontent; if the promises made for such a training left him only with doubt and error, where could certainty be found? Seeking it in himself, and convinced of his divine mission for reasons which we cannot properly assess, he established his first principles and his method. Of the method, the least one can say is that it worked, as the development of coordinate geometry testifies; of the first principles one must say that they altered the method of philosophical inquiry for generations, but also that they led (ironically enough through Descartes's disregard of his own warning against 'prévention et précipitation') to such quaint ideas as his theory of the circulation and the functions of the pineal gland. The central argument, and that on which all the rest depends, may be formulated thus: 'Dubito ergo Deus est'. Everything is there; the first person, the Cartesian 'moi', comes first, supreme and sole arbiter of all things; the comfortable Pyrrhonism of Montaigne, the passive doubt of one who knows he cannot know for certain, becomes here the desperate act of will, the active doubt of Descartes resisting the blandishments of the *malin génie* whom he himself had conjured up; finally, the intellectual step from this primary consciousness of self in an act of will, God exists. For what? God exists not to guarantee my existence, nor my will, nor the truth of clear and distinct ideas, to all of which His discovery is a subsequent step, but to guarantee the continuity of time, and thus my memory, then my previously suspect sense-perception, through which alone I have knowledge of other things (including my own body) and other people (including, but only by analogy, their souls). Since the very method precluded the formulation of a definitive moral code, and since the exigencies of daily life demand an ethic, however provisional, for the free exercise of philosophical speculations, the *Morale Provisoire* of the *Discours* occupies a far more prominent position than it strictly deserves.

The resultant pattern is thus of a 'moi', a will guided by reason, balanced on the one hand by a God whose principal attribute is veracity, on the other by a moral code compounded of moderate Stoicism and social conformism. The order of priority is clear, so are the conditions of validity; in their different ways God (as the materialists showed) and the ethics are equally provisional. Nor must one forget the declared aim of all this; to become 'maîtres et possesseurs de la nature', perfecting reason to that end. If the reward is costly, so are the stakes.

In Corneille, aiming at entertainment rather than formal instruction, the broad lines are not so very different, although the working is naturally less detailed. The will is again the kernel of the 'moi', reason guides it in its battle against unwanted passions (not all are unwanted, for instance pride and vengeance) and, except in *Polyeucte*, no guarantee is necessary *sub specie aeternitatis*, because pagan gods are false, though the additional emphasis consequently thrown into the scale of social conformism more than redresses the balance. In Corneille the hero is working for himself, not for mankind, so that he need not worry over bequeathing to posterity the mastery of nature. Instead he aims to be 'maître de moi'. Descartes was hoping to found 'la plus haute morale' at the end of his inquiry, Corneille dispensed with absolute moral standards altogether, replacing them by social pressures and dramatic predicaments. Heroism, generosity, virtue (in a Roman sense) play a major part in Corneille's tragedy, but such qualities owe nothing to truly moral concepts. It is the will, by Corneille's definition, or monomania by another, that rules his characters. Reason—of a sort—shows them the path to follow; will removes the obstacles of weakness, in the event usually the claims of other people to be considered as persons; 'gloire' once defined is a self-justifying pursuit, and in the last analysis encourages a solipsist view of the world. Compassion, love, humility, human solidarity are a few of the qualities for which Cornelian 'gloire' leaves little room, and it is just these qualities one seeks in vain in Cartesianism. The cry is for greatness and success, at whatever price—even, indeed especially, if it costs a glorious death in splendid isolation.

With Retz the last vestiges of morality have gone. 'Gloire' for him is the reward for lifemanship conferred by a discerning public. Not individuals alone, but the Paris mob, the French people are to be the pawns in his prodigious game. Archbishops, even coadjutors, should not publish their libidinous adventures, but since chastity is not a necessary part of an *honnête homme*'s qualifications, he must perforce conduct his amours in private. It helps to be brave, since the hurly-burly of civil war can too easily put one's valour to public test, and this Retz successfully achieved (albeit at some risk). Loyalty to sovereign, party or friends, on the other hand, is an expendable commodity when treachery can so easily be made to pass for address. Birth and position are advantages to be exploited, not responsibilities to be shouldered. Theological skill and judicious almsgiving assort well with the *persona* expected of a rising prelate, so these are exercises to be performed, techniques to be acquired. It is a salutary thing that Retz wrote what he did when he did, otherwise men might have been tempted (and we with them) to take Corneille's heroes at their face value, believing that such examples, if followed, could only have made the world a better and a nobler place. The moral insulation of the tragic stage allows such conduct to be seen in the abstract; Retz's account shows in as concrete a form as one could wish exactly what happens when real people try to act as they have seen others act on the stage.

It cannot be too strongly emphasized that Descartes's methodical omission of ethical rules, Corneille's dramatic disregard of morality and Retz's historical contempt for any standards save those of expediency are three different but complementary aspects of the same attitude. What mattered was self-fulfilment, the exploitation of everyone and everything else for the benefit of one's own will and reason. In the only play of Corneille's where God is called upon to supply the motive force, he does virtually what Descartes's God does for him; he sanctifies with his name and authority powers which have already been arrogated and exercised. It is not stretching the comparison too far to recall at this point Retz's exploitation of a liturgical function to assert himself over his enemies Condé and La Rochefoucauld, who knelt to receive the Archbishop's benediction, when an hour or so earlier or later either might have run through the man without the mitre.

La Rochefoucauld, whether kneeling before Retz or menacing him with sudden death as he sticks fast in the doors, shared the history of this same generation, and thus far acted Cornelian heroics in real life. Death robbed Descartes of the chance to draw up a balance-sheet, Corneille broke silence after the Fronde to write for fifteen years more, but hardly changed his outlook, Retz found a belated, and perhaps suspect, religious vocation in later life, but La Rochefoucauld, whose escape from death had been almost miraculous, came back to Paris to finish his life in a quite new role. Now enjoying enough leisure to read, he became a leading figure in the salons, found a doctrine to his taste at Port Royal and spent his declining years criticizing his own society from the standpoint of one who now knows better. Retz's critique is above all on tactical, not moral, grounds; an action is wrong if it fails. La Rochefoucauld analyses the life he sees around him and reduces it to the basic motives of amour-propre, *intérêt* and conflicting passions. It is open to question whether he had in fact emancipated himself from the toils he so accurately describes. One can at least appreciate the brazen impudence of Retz, not to speak of his coruscating wit, but the anonymous actors on La Rochefoucauld's stage are shabby and shameful without even the gift of self-mockery to redeem them. Negative criticism could hardly go further than the *Maximes*, and the *Mémoires* (of La Rochefoucauld) only serve to point the sad lesson. It takes a great man to be a solipsist—or else a very stupid one—and in La Rochefoucauld's portraits greatness is a quality as rare as good-

815346 P2 S.I.S.

ness. After the Fronde, in which his part was at least as important, and rather more noble, than Retz's, he lived on in a world too frightened by naked manifestations of will to stray far from the precepts of social conformism. Because of their political disgrace, neither he nor Retz belonged to the world of Versailles, but they wrote about a society for which there could be no other end.

With Pascal all these tendencies, of before and after the Fronde, are reflected in one way or another. His personal acquaintance with Descartes, and his deep disquiet over the metaphysical as well as the scientific implications of Cartesianism are major factors affecting his work. The connexion with Port Royal, though never amounting to formal training, did none the less strike a still young man (who for reasons of health had been educated privately) in a manner comparable with the Jesuit upbringing of Descartes and Corneille. As an earlier chapter has tried to show, the *Provinciales* have implications going far beyond contemporary party-strife or the technicalities of moral theology. In the codification of sin and the invention of extenuating circumstances, especially the latter, Pascal saw a threat to the whole spiritual content of religious practice, an attempt, largely successful, to reduce it to the level of the lifemanship, which had already degraded secular concepts of honour and virtue. Finally in the *Pensées* he takes up the not very obviously Christian thesis of La Rochefoucauld concerning *vertu païenne*. Bringing all his arguments to bear on the question of man's proper centre, himself or Christ, he offers a solution which is based from first to last on the psychological needs of his age, whatever faults it may have on other scores. Many harsh things have been said about Pascal, from Voltaire to Mr. Turnell:

> In the seventeenth century the emphasis shifts from intelligence to sensibility, from the collective to the personal experience. One of the main authors of the change was Pascal. . . . He is the source of the contagious religious unrest which has caused such havoc among eminent men of letters in the twentieth century. I do not think that it is an exaggeration to describe him as the poisoned source.[1]

[1] M. Turnell, *The Art of French Fiction*, p. 360.

If this study has done nothing else, it may be hoped that it has at least put Pascal in a truer historical perspective. One may dislike his fanaticism, distrust his Jansenism, regret his conversion from science to piety, but it is going a little far to make Pascal 'the poisoned source' when his century had already produced the *Cogito*, the devils of Loudun, and was soon to produce Mme Guyon. This is not the place to suggest where the real poisoned source might profitably be sought, but in Pascal's defence—not that he needs it—it must be said that he is reacting in the most explicit terms against what he considered a blasphemously frivolous Pelagianism on the one hand and an arrogant solipsism on the other, both man-centred to the utmost degree.

That Pascal created and wanted to create unrest is not in dispute. It was for this reason that his friends at Port Royal treated the unfinished *Pensées* with such caution. After the Fronde, the quarrel over the Five Propositions and the death of Mazarin, Louis wanted only to rule unchallenged, and unrest formed no part of his programme. If the burning problems of the individual's rights and responsibilities are no longer the centre of discussion it is because a working solution has been imposed. Authority, in a word, had to be accepted. Racine's characters know what risks they are taking, and pay the price. The passions win, the passions destroy, and no Rodrigue, or Horace, or Cinna is left to trouble the body politic. Perhaps *Bérénice* alone recalls the earlier formulas. Anarchy can be represented on the stage, but its condign punishment must not be left in doubt when the curtain falls.

With Molière 'tout rentre dans l'ordre'. Not that all is sweetness and light in Molière's plays, for he asks more questions than he answers. The great lesson of Molière's plays is that problems can and must be solved *ici-bas*, whatever metaphysical hangover may await us *là-haut*. Within the limits of everyday life virtue can be practised, mental aberrations corrected or neutralized. If this means leading a life of unheroic compromise, sometimes of conscious insincerity or mild sensuality, we must remember that the age of Titans is past, the ordinary man has come into his own. For all Descartes's protestations of fellowship with the average reader, it is not to him or his generation that we must turn to find 'l'homme moyen sensuel' who is coming to resemble ever more closely the *honnête homme*. The bourgeois values of stability, based on wealth and prosperity, of moderation, of conformism are the mental complement of Louis's rule at Versailles, which had transformed nobles into courtiers, ceremonial menials dependent on daily changes of the royal favour.

Bossuet's early abortive attempts to bring Louis to a juster appreciation of his personal obligations only made him more assiduous in supporting royal authority in later years and laying down strict standards of morality for all subjects, even the most illustrious. Molière, on the wrong side of the social footlights, saw the moral climate of his age as a proper subject for comedy; Bossuet, from the height of his pulpit, as a theme for commination to include the impious comedian. Considering the stations in which they had been called to serve their royal master it is hard to see how either could have acted differently. From now on order is the watchword. In politics, in religion, in art, in social habits, the party-line is drawn with more or less finality, though it would be foolish to exaggerate either the restrictions or the gross flattery to which this gave rise. That most cherished of all freedoms, freedom from choice, is generously bestowed upon his subjects by a king sincerely convinced that he has their interests at heart. All Bossuet could do was to offer a mutual security pact, and his personal Gallican sympathies gave him a fairly free hand for doing this. For the rest, when he inveighs against spiritual wickedness in high places, against the depravity of the court or the presumption of reason, his battle is already lost. Bishoprics, like the other hierarchical plums, civil, military, artistic, were at Louis's disposal. Bossuet's function as court preacher and hammer of the heretics illustrates that necessity for daily compromise which, in other contexts, he so violently condemned in Molière.

Last comes La Bruyère. The story might have ended with Saint-Simon, but then he is really an eighteenth-century figure and stands too far away from central issues to have known them truly from the inside, as did all the others here discussed. A bourgeois like Molière, a courtier like Bossuet, a lay apologist of Christianity like Pascal, La Bruyère represents in the mediocrity of his personal character and in the excellence of his style the typical end-product of his age. He shares with Molière one positive and novel contribution to this study of the 'moi', that of finally cutting his losses, renouncing the socially bankrupt standards of a literally bankrupt aristocracy and opting for what he rather vaguely terms 'peuple'. His instinct was right; the closed circle, for all its infusions of wealthy plebeian blood, was too small for the events it had to face, and a class problem was not far off on the horizon. La Bruyère knew what it was he was contracting out of; he had no desire to remain an underling of a class he both feared and despised, but his intellectual training as well as his economic needs kept him in his place. The metaphysics of solipsism mattered very little for his generation. The world was too much with them, but the new problem of socially displaced persons was coming into prominence. Montesquieu, Diderot, Voltaire, Rousseau had other things to worry about than solipsism. Exteriorizing a conflict has obvious therapeutic value, and when the death of Louis left only the empty sham of Versailles, there were enough economic and political consequences to keep men busy until 1789. It is to La Bruyère's credit that he seems dimly to have foreseen this, and if he did not actually point the way forward, to this extent he set his back on the past.

'From *poêle* to *palais*' might thus be another of those slick and lapidary formulas which on inspection prove to offend more against taste than reason. This study has tried to show by taking some of the best-known writers of the seventeenth century, in their texts, that a clear line of evolution reaches from Descartes (or Montaigne) through to La Bruyère (or Voltaire). The heroic age of Descartes and the Three Musketeers failed to survive the Fronde. The new heroes are Turenne, Vauban, Colbert, great servants of the Crown now. In place of the egocentric confidence of the first period comes feverish concern for normative behaviour, for support from above and from all around. The casualties of the Cartesian offensive were not restored to life, and the time-lag between the rejection of old, outworn ideas about God, man and the world, and the adoption of new ones, which could be seen, at least approximately, to work, is part of the crisis described. The centre of this crisis remains where Descartes set it: the 'moi'. His destructive methods provided the clear site for building, but as each successive structure appeared, some new (or old) stress brought it down again, exposing time after time the unprotected 'moi' at the foundation, which can clearly not be dispensed with, but which was never meant to bear such weight. It has been left to later ages to show that Descartes's dualism of mind and matter (the ghost in the machine), far from consolidating the position of our immortal souls, or thinking minds, or what you will, has simply been the prelude to unexpected and now multiple cracks within the mind itself. Descartes was a particularly lucid and articulate thinker, but he was only codifying (rather as Boileau did) a loose climate of opinion already in existence. It is as silly to put the blame on Descartes for what happened as on Boileau for Classical mistakes. Historically, though, there is no question which way the milestones point; from Descartes's stove, through the Fronde to the later salons, and then Versailles, and then 1789 . . .

Because men felt, and maybe feel, lost without an axis, there is no reason to claim that they have a right, or even a natural propensity, to be other than 'désaxé', and the brief halt at Versailles will probably be the only part of this process that some readers will regret. Whatever its contemporary relevance, the historical lesson is surely of value to literary studies. This book has attempted no more than to put long familiar phenomena in a sharper focus. This has inevitably involved the exclusion of peripheral subjects, and to complete the process of evaluation each reader must chose his own field of vision. 'La diversité de nos opinions ne vient pas de ce que les uns sont plus raisonnables que les autres, mais seulement de ce que nous conduisons nos pensées par diverses voies, et ne considérons pas les mêmes choses.' [1]

[1] Descartes, *Discours*, p. 92.

INDEX

The Index does not include authors and works to which chapters have been devoted, since references to them are so frequent as to make a list of no use. For convenience, however, plays of Corneille and Molière quoted or discussed are indexed in chronological order under their respective authors. Italicised page references indicate chapters or major sections of chapters devoted to the subject of the entry.